Power, Politics, and the Playground

T0372862

Presented as a series of case studies, this book offers the reader an insider's account of the power dynamics in Australian education and how the application of that power influences education policymaking.

The authors, Adrian Piccoli and Don Carter, have been in the room when some of the biggest decisions in Australian education have been made. This book traverses various theories of power and authority to explore the selected experiences of the authors who come from opposing sides of the political spectrum (a former National Party minister for education and a former teacher, union member and left-leaning academic) to share a behind-the-scenes story of education in Australia not readily available to the public. The chapters capture their personal experiences in senior education leadership roles, where they made key decisions on diverse topics such as how to allocate multibillion-dollar education budgets, the split of school funding between education sectors, contentious curriculum decisions and other policy and political objectives. Drawing on organisational theory, international relations and education, a variety of resources such as hard and soft power, credibility, persuasion and notions of capital are used to make sense of their experiences in education. Through this, the authors explain who has the biggest influence over those decisions and why these complex power dynamics, when not used properly, can mean that the best interests of students are not always at the heart of the decision-making process.

Written for teachers, school leaders and other education professionals, this book presents a rare insight into power and authority in the Australian education system.

Don Carter is an associate professor at the University of Technology Sydney and has worked in a range of positions including teaching English (government and nongovernment schools), head of department, ESL consultant, inspector of schools and teacher education academic. He has published widely on education issues including literacy, curriculum history and teacher workload.

Adrian Piccoli was the New South Wales minister for education (2011–2017) and a member of the NSW Legislative Assembly for 19 years. As the former director of University of New South Wales's Gonski Institute for Education, Adrian led a team of researchers to address inequality in Australian education and improve access to high-quality education for school students. In 2017, Adrian was made a fellow of the Australian Council of Educational Leaders.

Power, Politics, and the Playground

Perspectives on Power and Authority in Education

Don Carter and Adrian Piccoli

Routledge
Taylor & Francis Group

LONDON AND NEW YORK

Designed cover image: © Getty Images

First published 2024
by Routledge
4 Park Square, Milton Park, Abingdon, Oxon OX14 4RN

and by Routledge
605 Third Avenue, New York, NY 10158

Routledge is an imprint of the Taylor & Francis Group, an informa business

© 2024 Don Carter and Adrian Piccoli

British Library Cataloguing-in-Publication Data
A catalogue record for this book is available from the British Library

ISBN: 9781032320298 (hbk)
ISBN: 9781032320281 (pbk)
ISBN: 9781003312451 (ebk)

DOI: 10.4324/9781003312451

Typeset in Galliard Pro
by Apex CoVantage, LLC

Contents

Preface

Don Carter and Adrian Piccoli

In many ways, this book and our partnership came as something of a surprise. We come from different ends of the political spectrum with Adrian a former New South Wales (NSW) education minister in a Liberal/Nationals[1] coalition government and Don a longtime union member, former schoolteacher and education academic who has always voted for the Australian Labor Party.[2] While these differences might have discouraged a joint project, we found that we share many views about education, including a strong commitment to the provision of quality education for all children.

Associate Professor Dr Don Carter is an education academic at the University of Technology Sydney. His work centres on teacher education, particularly for those students who will graduate as secondary English teachers and primary schoolteachers. Over the years, Don has worked in a range of educational roles. He began his career as an English and history teacher, working in several government secondary schools in New South Wales, Australia. He also worked as an English as a Second Language consultant for the NSW Department of Education, before moving into head of department roles in both government and nongovernment secondary schools. His next move was into the education bureaucracy in curriculum development and as a school inspector. This significant role required working with schools in compliance issues and working with stakeholders in the development of syllabuses, particularly English syllabuses, and a range of support materials for schools. Importantly, Don liaised with the national curriculum authority, the Australian Curriculum Assessment and Reporting Authority (ACARA) in the development of Australia's national curriculum. These roles provided Don with many insights into the intricacies and mechanics of how decisions are made and who 'calls the shots'.

Professor Adrian Piccoli spent almost 20 years representing a very large rural and remote electorate in far western NSW. A lawyer by training, Adrian became one of the longest-serving ministers for education in NSW. He is well known for his work on the Gonski school funding reforms, advancing rural and remote education and supporting the increased professionalisation of the teaching profession. The NSW minister for education has the responsibility to operate one of the largest public education systems in the world and the responsibility to regulate all schools in NSW including the Catholic education system and independent schools. In the modern era, where ministers change portfolios regularly, Adrian served in the one portfolio for six years. This longevity allowed him to gain unique political expertise on what power means in education decision-making at the highest levels and who exercises it. From negotiating intergovernmental funding agreements to what is in and what is out of the curriculum, how much teachers get paid and closing schools, Adrian has seen it all. He has the lived experience of exercising influence over those decisions. Knowing how those decisions are made and what influences and who influences those decisions is crucial if we truly seek better decisions that lead to better outcomes for children in schools.

Notes

1 The Liberal/National coalition is an alliance of centre-right political parties forming one of the two major groupings in Australian federal politics.
2 The Australian Labor Party (ALP) is the other major group in Australian federal politics.

Acknowledgements

The authors would like to thank Dr Jennifer Carter and Associate Professor John Buchanan for their feedback, proofreading and support throughout the compilation of this book.

Introduction

Don Carter and Adrian Piccoli

This book represents a 'first' in education. No other book focuses on the experiences of a former government education minister whose role was to manage one of the biggest education systems in the world and an academic whose previous role was to manage a major part of the curriculum in that same system.

This book is about power, authority and decision-making in education. We have deliberately written this book because of the unique nature of education. Education decision-making at all levels – from classrooms to principals' offices, the executives running school systems, the minister of the day – relies largely on human-to-human relationships of trust and understanding. That means the creation and use of power in education is different to other areas of public policy, politics and business.

Our stories provide unique insights into how decisions at the highest levels of education are made and the kinds of power that are needed to make those decisions. We have written this book because we are both often asked how and why certain decisions in education – both good and bad – are made.

There is also a general interest in knowing what happens behind the closed-door world of politics and policymaking. There is interest in how politics, political parties and government bureaucracies work. There is also a genuine interest in knowing where the ideological, policy and funding fights happen and how these battles lead to decision-making in education.

This is not a book about theories of power or leadership. Instead, it takes the experiences of two people in key roles, how they understood the power they had, how they developed that power and authority and then how they used it to make decisions. Those experiences are then deconstructed in the analytical contemplations. This kind of case study followed by an academic analysis of the actual real-life experiences has not been documented previously.

In compiling this book, we suspect that the average citizen is uninterested in the nuances of the term 'power' and its relationship to and conflation with other key terms such as 'authority' and 'legitimacy'. We assume that public interest is more centred on the outcomes of power and decision-making, and

DOI: 10.4324/9781003312451-1

we believe that the general public should better understand some of the inner workings of government that influence education policy and its operations.

Thus, we hope that through a heightened public understanding of these issues and workings, a curiosity to explore the differences between 'power', 'authority' and 'legitimisation' will emerge and be applied to current events and issues. For, as the great English philosopher Francis Bacon once remarked, "[K]nowledge is power."

How this book began

In May 2017, Don and a colleague from the University of Technology Sydney met with Adrian in his parliamentary office in Sydney to discuss a proposed project focusing on school-based education in rural New South Wales. In the weeks before this meeting, Don had made a number of appearances in the media criticising NAPLAN, the Australia-wide literacy and numeracy tests. He had also been critical of changes made to the tests where students would be required to achieve a band eight standard in the year 9 NAPLAN reading, writing and maths to guarantee eligibility for the NSW matriculation credential, the higher school certificate, HSC. Adrian had been the architect of these changes as well as the HSC 'blueprint' released the year before. Don had also been publicly critical of that initiative, not because he did not believe in the importance of working with students to achieve high standards; he felt that the focus of the initiative was too narrowly focused on workplace skills rather than developing a broader range of skills and knowledge for students. Needless to say, Adrian and Don had an animated discussion on both issues.

However, they kept in touch and, over the next few years, met on a semi-regular basis to discuss education issues. And what became clear very quickly was that we both agreed on most issues about education, despite our political differences. Over the years, we had maintained both diaries and notes about our experiences in our roles, and it was these notes that became invaluable for this book. The decision to write this book was made in October 2021, where we were discussing several issues related to education. Adrian had already begun to compile his experiences as education minister in writing and, given that he was about to spend 12 months in Italy with his family, felt the time was right to document more of his experiences. For Don, the opportunity to document his experiences in education in a jointly written book was attractive.

About the book

In this book, we seek to understand how power, authority and legitimacy are manifested in the social phenomena described by each of us in our respective chapters. By doing this, we act as gatherers of information and as interpreters of that information. When Stake (1995) argues that there are "multiple perspectives or views of the case that need to be represented, but there is no way to establish, beyond contention, the best view" (p. 108), we would agree. What we have observed over the years and the conclusions we have drawn in this book are provisional and tentative in that our conclusions might be different from those drawn by the reader or by other people described in the recounts. Our conclusions might also provoke further research by others into the manifestations of power, authority and legitimacy in education, at a local level. We hope the book sparks conversation, reflection and continued work to provide quality education for all Australian children.

But having said this, we need to declare the following important points which we believe act as signposts that both appropriately limit and enable our study. Therefore, we are aware of the following:

1 Our perspectives on education have been constructed according to our own experiences and the people and organisations with whom we have interacted.
2 This book is the sum of our own subjectivities – that is, our personal beliefs, attitudes, biases and ideologies that underpin our selection and interpretation of the events in the book. The fact that we selected the specific incidents included in this book is an act of selectivity in itself based on our beliefs of what is of 'value' to the reader. Of course, it could be the case that one reader dismisses our recounts as unimportant while another reader considers them worthy of inclusion, or somewhere in between.
3 In the analysis of our experiences, we chose not to adopt one specific theoretical framework to interpret our experiences because we do not seek to present ourselves as adherents of any one theorist or approach to power and authority. To announce that we seek to promote a specific approach would only serve to limit the scope and nature of our observations and ultimately limit the scope and depth of our conclusions. In preparing this book, we found certain frameworks valuable, in that the ideas were informative and assisted in revealing important features of our experiences.

While the points above serve to outline the limitations of this book, we did not feel they were sufficient to 'silence' us and preclude the compilation of this book. The inclusion of an analysis of each recount chapter is worthwhile because it constitutes a "process of generating critical consciousness within researchers and practitioners" (McIlveen, 2008, p. 6) and offers the opportunity to create "new understandings and actions (and) transformation" (p. 6). This emphasises the importance of acknowledging the presence of the individual who, in the specific context, is providing the account of events. One common criticism of qualitative research has been that the researcher is 'invisible' in the research (Clifford & Marcus, 1986), as though they are somehow objectively detached from the research, omniscient and 'untouched' by the research being undertaken. For us, we were certainly visible to the other participants in the events we outline in this book. We were fully participating and "highly visible . . . with (our) own feelings and experiences incorporated . . . and considered as vital data for understanding the social world observed" (Anderson, 2006, p. 384).

How this book is structured

We have chosen a structure that we hope will be accessible for the reader and provide insights into our experiences by drawing on established theories of power and authority. The structure of the book involves the 'pairing' of sets of chapters. Both of us present a chapter which recounts specific events or sets of events of other people, organisations and associations involved in education. These recounts are mainly descriptive, with some evaluative comments occasionally integrated into the narrative.

However, each recount is 'paired' or accompanied by another chapter which analyses the descriptive recount. We have labelled each accompanying chapter of analysis as "Analytical contemplation" for two reasons. First, the term 'analytical contemplation' has currency in research practices that attend to the 'presence' of the researcher (Alansari, 2018; Davis & Breede, 2015; Kirsch & Royster, 2010); and second, it allows us to reflect on our own ideological positions and by acknowledging our own "embodied experiences" (Kirsch & Royster, 2010, p. 659). In the analytical contemplations, we explore the relationship between what we experienced and theoretical frameworks related to the study of power and authority and, in doing so, open spaces for discussion of our findings and insights that we hope will contribute to the body of research currently available on power in education.

And finally, one of the conclusions we hope the reader of this book will arrive at is that as two educationists writing about our experiences, we show ourselves to not only be passionate advocates of quality education for all, regardless of background and circumstance, but that we have also shown ourselves to be two "people grappling with issues relevant to membership and participation in fluid rather than static social worlds" (Anderson, 2006, p. 384).

Chapter 1

Case study as a research methodology

Don Carter

Case study, as a qualitative research methodology, is an intensive study about a person or a group of people and is usually intended to answer the question "[W]hat is going on?" (Jacobsen, 2002, p. 1). Moreover, the case study approach to qualitative research provides a "unique example of real people in real situations" (Cohen et al., 2011, p. 253). With these two points in mind, we selected case study as the most appropriate and manageable research methodology for this book. In addition, we felt that an important feature of case studies is acknowledgement of the researcher's subjectivities, where the "narrative visibility of the researcher's self" (Anderson, 2006, p. 378) is apparent. We considered this approach as appropriate because the case study approach encompasses three distinctive features relevant to our study:

1 *Particularistic* in that it focuses on particular situations, events, programmes or phenomena.
2 *Descriptive* because it offers rich, thick descriptions of the phenomena under study.
3 *Heuristic* in that it illuminates the reader's understanding of the phenomenon under study.

(Merriam, 1998, p. 27)

The book centres on our experiences and perceptions of the situations in which we found ourselves, and as such, our own subjectivities were at the core of the book – our personal reactions and responses to different situations and experiences. Accordingly, the book could not be an objective account of those experiences, in that we were not working in a laboratory setting where the behaviours and attitudes of participants could be controlled and scripted. This means that the ontological basis for our study is relativist, meaning the 'reality' being constructed by us as social beings in the book renders the notion of an 'objective' world as an illusion (Guba & Lincoln, 1994). For all individuals, the way in which we perceive the world and truth is based on our value systems and ideological positions, and as such, there are no 'value-free' positions and,

DOI: 10.4324/9781003312451-2

therefore, no 'value-free' research: we interpret the world from our own individual standpoint. By acknowledging and undertaking a relativist approach in this book, scope is created for how humans understand phenomena and their often-complex responses to phenomena, where meanings are constructed by individuals as they engage with the world they are interpreting (Orlikowski & Baroudi, 1991).

Another important feature of case study pertinent to this book stems from the premise that qualitative research is a relational activity, focusing on the "interrelationships between the researcher and others to inform and change social knowledge" (Davies, 2012, p. 184). While introspection can be a component of qualitative research, we believe the case study approach will avoid the semblance of solipsism and indulgence through its analysis of the social worlds under investigation, promoting "dialogic engagement with others" (Anderson, 2006, p. 385). We are seeking to understand the social worlds of education in which we have participated and to interrogate those worlds via the application of different theoretical perspectives on power and authority. In conveying those experiences, we have sought to avoid "author saturation" (Anderson, 3006, p. 386), by providing an analysis of each recount and, in doing so, contribute to scholarship in studies of power in education.

We also point out that at the time of the experiences we recount in this book, neither of us was conducting formal research as such. However, as noted earlier, both of us had documented the events and interactions we witnessed and had even partially written up these notes for future publication in a journal or in a monograph. The important point here is that by adopting a case study approach, we are provided with the freedom to draw on previous experiences to reconstruct events and interactions and to use the documentation based on those experiences for new audiences. We found that by using a case study approach, we were offered the opportunity to "play in the space between fact and fiction, past and possibility" (Henson, 2017, p. 222) as well as engage in a kind of reflective analysis, which we explain later. The case study approach also allowed us to engage with a process of "self-reference" (Davies, 2012, p. 5). This feature is a crucial component of our book because it is here that our work engages with the production of "critical consciousness" (McIlveen, 2008, p. 6), where we recognise and acknowledge that we have selected the experiences recounted in this book from our own personal perspectives.

Therefore, we argue that this book offers insights into social phenomena as part of the capacity of case studies to "investigate and report the complex dynamic and unfolding interactions of events, human relationships and other factors in a unique instance" (Cohen et al., 2011, p. 253). More than providing an insider's view and attempting to evoke an emotional response from the reader, the application of case study methodology provides an account of social interactions that goes beyond describing 'what is going on' and moves into identifying and applying analytical practices that are directed towards theoretical growth, improvement and extension. When the results of the research and observations are assembled, they constitute a "mediation that is itself a conduit for further mediations, in particular between author and various possible audiences" (Davies, 2012, p. 214). The conclusions are tentative and provisional but offer themselves for further investigation and research.

Chapter 2

Why getting schools right matters

Adrian Piccoli

I first met Alex when he was in kindergarten at a school in southwest Sydney. I had been the NSW minister for education for a few years, and we were visiting his school as part of my regular round of visits talking to principals and teachers. During the visit, I was taken to a classroom where Alex was working away quietly alongside his teacher's aide. The principal had pointed him out to me and explained that he was one of the many great successes of the school. I was introduced to his mum who happened to be there as part of the parent engagement programme the school was running.

So I stood at the back of this class talking to Alex's mum about the challenges Alex faced in his young life and with his schooling and what had changed for Alex. His mum explained that Alex had a number of learning difficulties, including that he was nonverbal when he had started school. Having not spoken a sentence before starting school, Alex had never had the chance to utter the words 'I love you' to his mum. Thanks to his great teachers and the additional funding the school had access to, Alex's school could afford a full-time teacher's aide in the class plus speech therapy services for Alex. All this was happening without taking anything away from the other children in his class who were also powering along in their learning.

Then the magic of education happened. His mum told me the story about when his life and the life of their family changed. Alex's mum was away on a work trip, and while she was away, with the help of his dad, Alex recorded a short video and sent it to her. Sitting in her hotel room, miles from home, she played the video of her son. "Hello, mummy, I love you", he cheerily said, with his bright eyes shining back at her. She broke down in a sea of tears. He was now powering along, and life has changed for Alex. He was now stringing sentences together, expressing a son's love for his mother and catching up to the other kids in his class.

His story is moving and heartwarming, but it was his mother's story that really struck me about the true power of education. Of course, this giant leap was life changing for Alex, and his mum was of course delighted for him. But it was more than that. What education was doing to Alex's life was about more than just Alex. Alex has a brother who hadn't had much attention in the last

DOI: 10.4324/9781003312451-3

few years because so much effort was going in to supporting Alex. His mum now proudly told me that Alex's success in education means his brother can now get the mum and dad attention that every child deserves. Alex's parents now looked to a future where instead of planning on what Alex's welfare dependence needs might be, they are now planning on what sort of job he might get. His parents are now planning a new life of opportunity for not just Alex but his brother and the whole family.

On some days, a personal story just comes along and smacks us between the eyes to wake us all up about why education matters and why it matters so much that we get every decision we make in education right – ministers, principals, teachers and parents. No one gets to choose who their parents are or the circumstances into which they are born – whether it's into a home of wealth and privilege or into the home of a drug-addled teenage single mum or to be born with a disability. Whatever the circumstances at the time of a child's birth, it is not at the choosing of the child.

It is the role of education, especially in a rich, first-world country like Australia, to level the playing field for all children wherever they are born. It is to redress the inherent unfairness of life for the disadvantaged and to not unfairly enhance the fortunes of the advantaged at the expense of the disadvantaged. It is to provide the opportunity for every child to reach their full potential.

It is to make sure all children go to a school that has the resources to satisfy their individual needs. It is to make sure every child gets at least a year's worth of growth for every year of schooling. It is to make sure every teacher standing in front of every classroom in every school, every day, is highly skilled, highly respected and is highly in tune with the learning needs of every student, not just in their class but in their school.

Making sure we let children, teachers and schools know what we expect of them and what we believe they are capable of. To set high expectations and, when they are met, to raise those expectations further. But at the heart of everything we do is ensuring we strive for fairness and equity in education. The idea that every child gets what they need to have an equal opportunity in education has to be at the centre of everything we do with whatever power we have.

Every decision in education must have these as their clear and unequivocal objectives. These core principles are the basis of what people who care deeply about education must demand from decision-makers. While I was minister, I applied these core principles to every decision we made. Is it fair, does it work in schools and are children's best interests at the centre of every decision? These principles don't belong to me. They are universal truisms in education and leadership. If I could ask one thing of educators, that is to insist that these principles be at the heart of every decision they make, whether they are a parent, teacher, principal or the minister. These principles that are helping children like Alex reach their full potential will survive individuals and will drive education in this country to the places it needs to go.

Chapter 3

Some observations on power and authority

Don Carter

During the compilation of this book, our thinking was informed by a number of theorists, some of whom are well known for their contributions to education, while others are acknowledged experts in other domains, including international relations and management theory. We considered that by drawing on the work of theorists beyond education, a wider array of useful interpretive lenses would become available to us. We believe this to be beneficial because it allows us to illuminate aspects of our recounts by using frameworks from other disciplines which are not usually utilised by education researchers. For example, we turn to a theory called a "situational view of authority", which has a long and rich history in management theory, and we also use a principle called the "law of the situation" (Follett, 1940, p. 33) to shed light on our experiences.

One of the areas we draw on is international relations. A significant development in this area occurred in the early 1990s when the American political scientist Joseph Nye (b. 1937) developed the idea of 'soft' and 'hard' power to explain foreign policy strategies of nations and to distinguish between different categories. Soft power relates to achieving goals without the exercise of force or coercion. Such strategies include the promotion of shared values, establishment of institutions to promote these values and cultural initiatives which might see the exchange of higher education students between different countries (Nye, 2021). Hard power, on the other hand, can utilise coercion, inducement, force, payment, bribes and sanctions (Nye, 1990). Both appear in the recounts of our experiences.

Throughout the book, we draw on Pierre Bourdieu's four types of capital – economic capital (financial), social capital (social networks), cultural capital (educational and cultural background) and symbolic capital (an accumulation of the other types of capital) (1990, p. 112). We also use the idea of 'symbolic' power to explain and illuminate aspects of Adrian's recount, while in Don's recount, titled "Schools, power and books", we turn to Max Weber's traditional, charismatic and rational-legal typologies to make sense of the experiences documented in that chapter.

DOI: 10.4324/9781003312451-4

We also found Pardo and Prato's (2019) and Prato's (2000) work on legitimacy to be useful in unpacking our experiences. Both scholars have conducted significant urban anthropological research throughout Europe and the United Kingdom investigating the relationship between social and cultural change and global processes, such as the politics of immigration and transnational power relations. In addition, we found Luhrmann's (1979) work on trust, familiarity, personal trust and trust as opportunity and constraint as examples of power resources to be invaluable. Our hope is that by drawing on the work of these scholars and others from disciplines beyond education, we are providing education researchers and scholars some possible alternative theoretical frameworks and interpretive lenses that might prove useful for their work.

The study of power and authority

So what exactly is power? As Uphoff (1989) aptly asks, is it a 'thing'? An abstract property? A relationship? Something homogenous? A collective of fundamental elements? Or a descriptive term embracing "operative relationships"? (p. 296). At the very least, power is an "imprecise" (p. 296) term; however, it can refer to things that are tangible and concrete and, as such, can be seen as an outcome of the "ability to bring events to pass" (Joullié et al., 2021, p. 3). Indeed, the concept of power is central to our understanding of society, both past and present (Clegg & Haugaard, 2009), with our view of historical events often refracted through the lens of the actions of monarchs, dictators and national leaders.

However, given the vast array of accounts of power, it is more accurate to regard power not as a single entity but a "cluster of concepts" (Clegg & Haugaard, 2009, p. 3) or an "organising idea" (Höpfl, 1999, p. 218). To define the concept of power is problematic because there is no "single essence" (Haugaard & Lentner, 2006, p. 9) but, rather, a number of features which overlap, as in a "large family, which define membership" (p. 9). Each single theory applicable in its local context may not be completely applicable in different contexts (p. 9). And when we throw into the mix terms such as 'force' and 'influence', we have a recipe for confusion through the interchangeability of those terms (Bachrach & Baratz, 1970). This is not altogether surprising because over a long period of time, theorists have pointed to the confused use of the terms while, at the same time, added to this confusion by promoting their own particular definitions. For example, Bachrach and Baratz (1970) apply the same level of generality to the terms 'power', 'force', 'influence' and authority, while Parsons (2010) argues that the use of the term 'authority' should only cover power relationships considered legitimate. The conflation of legitimacy and authority is also found in the work of Lasswell and Kaplan (2014), which identifies power with authority and defines power as "participation in the making of decisions" (p. 75). And these examples of conflations and confusions are only a brief snapshot of the controversies in the field of power studies. In short, a definition is difficult to pin down, in spite of the importance of power in the popular imagination and in academic disciplines.

Over time, power has been one of the key concepts of political theory which sociologists have sought to define, by drawing distinctions between *power* and *authority* and *power* and *force* (Hardy & Clegg, 1999). According to these distinctions, one definition of *power* is the capacity of the holder to "exact compliance or obedience of other individuals to their will" (Bell, 1974, p. 678), while *authority* is anchored in social organisations where recognition of special or greater competence affords an enhanced status and command (p. 678), in a kind of "taken for granted legitimacy" (Gordon, 2009, p. 260). *Force*, on the other hand, is a "compulsion, sometimes physical" (Bell, 1974, p. 678) which may involve the threat of force. An important aspect of power is *legitimacy*, which resides in a principle – for example, consensus between the lawmaker and the governed. According to Gordon (2009), efforts to separate the terms became apparent in studies in the mid-twentieth century.[1] In these studies, power was exercised by actors not formally sanctioned with power, and as such, their actions were deemed as "illegitimate, dysfunctional and . . . irrational" (Gordon, 2009, p. 260).

History, power and authority

The study of power has a long history. Aristotle, in *Politics* (1962), reduces governmental structures to three main types: monarchy, aristocracy and democracy, the characteristics of which in their various forms account for all forms of power (De Jouvenel, 2009, p. 19). He further distinguishes three aspects of power: as a source of change, as a capacity of performing and as a state in virtue of which things are unchangeable by themselves (Metaph, IV (5) 12). Modern thinking about power stems from Nicollò Machiavelli's *The Prince*, published in 1532 (Clegg & Haugaard, 2009). Here, we find the figure of the prince using power as a means rather than a resource, to ensure strategic advantages over others, particularly military advantages. Management of the state is therefore undertaken through manipulation of the "flows and movements of power" (Clegg & Haugaard, 2009, p. 2). In this context, the strong dominate the weak, the distinction between legitimate and illegitimate power is blurred and the measure of success is evidence of "practical success or failure" (p. 2).

An alternate and influential approach to power was promoted by Thomas Hobbes (1588–1679), who argued that power flows from society to the individual, in a kind of "causal effect" of "agency or structure" (Torfing, 2009, p. 109). Hobbes advocated the sovereign, hereditary monarch as the ultimate protection against the terrifying chaos of the world, where ungoverned, self-interested individuals will descend into unbridled and violent struggles for scarce resources, condemning society to an unstable and fearful world.

However, the self-interested individual – in the interests of personal security and safety – is prepared to transfer self-defence to a sovereign power which, in turn, creates social stability through the imposition of "laws, sanctions and punishment" (p. 110). Thus, a civil society is an "artificial construction" (p. 110), where political power is the "cause of the social" (p. 111), made possible by the repressive state.

Hobbes' approach was influenced by the development of the new science of mechanics in the seventeenth century (Torfing, 2009). Here, causality can exist between separate individualised but conterminously related entities, exercising intentionality through unfettered activities. The interactions of such individuals represented a Hobbesian view, where their motivations, needs and inclinations activate causal effects on each other and can be conceptualised as power relations (p. 110). Hobbes and Locke defined power as the ability to make or receive change, with Hobbes adopting the view that power is the source of motion. The study of the concept of power requires various questions such as whether power is an accident or a perfection of substance and whether it is distinct from it. However, the concept of 'power' is not simple and uncomplicated (Avelino, 2021; Clegg & Haugaard, 2009; Lukes, 2005). Any discussion of power must attend to its multidimensionality and at least acknowledge dimensions such as 'power to' and 'power over' (Göhler, 2009), as well as "centred versus diffused, consensual versus conflictual, constraining versus enabling, quantity versus quality, empowerment versus disempowerment and power in relation to knowledge" (Avelino, 2021, p. 425). However, these questions and considerations were further investigated by a range of theorists in the twentieth century.

Twentieth-century thinking about power and authority

The German sociologist and economist Max Weber's work has been influential throughout the twentieth century (Houghton, 2010; Gaventa, 2003; Matheson, 1987). While a comprehensive account of Weber's substantial opus is beyond the scope of this book, we briefly outline his "tripartite typology" (Guzmán, 2015, p. 73) of traditional authority, rational-legal authority and charismatic authority in the analytical contemplation following chapter 4, "Schools, power and books". We found these typologies useful to identify and classify behaviours, processes and incidents we have experienced and witnessed.

Weber continued the rational Hobbesian view of power and developed organisational thinking in his emphasis on the "project of rationalization" (Gordon, 2009, p. 257). This project stemmed from the Enlightenment, which held that European modes of thinking and ways of doing were superior to other groups such as Indigenous people, who were considered savages and for whom the adoption of European social ways and general laws of reason could only be beneficial. Clegg (1989) contends that during the twentieth century, Weber's work was used to establish legitimacy for the process of rationalising less 'rational' forms of life out of existence, thus creating "rationalized obedience" (p. 232). In his interest in the bureaucracy, Weber connected power with the ideas of authority and rule (Sadan, 1997, p. 35), with his work subsequently forming the basis of further investigations into power, including the following:

- 'Power as capacity' (Arendt, 1958; Parsons, 1947, 1963).
- 'Power as entity' (Dahl, 1957; Gouldner, 1971).
- 'Power as strategy' (Foucault's archaeological, genealogical and analyses of the concept of 'care of the self', which were subsequently modified and extended by Haugaard, 1997).
- 'Power as knowledge' (Barnes, 1990; Clegg, 1989; Foucault, 1981; Giddens, 1984; Haugaard, 1997).

However, the theorising of power, authority and legitimacy was not limited to management theory, international relations or anthropology. The last century spawned a series of influential figures, some of whom we acknowledge in this book, such as Pierre Bourdieu, Michael Apple, Michel Foucault, all of whom influenced (to varying degrees) thinking about education, social class and power.[2] We draw on the work of these theorists in particular throughout this book plus the work of several others.

Of course, we recognise that there are many more who have made significant contributions to the study of power that the scope of this book (and space) precludes us from. Scholars such as Stephen J. Ball, Maxine Greene, Hannah Arendt, bell hooks, Antonio Gramsci, Basil Bernstein, Jacques Rancière, Ivan Illich, Jürgen Habermas and Henry Giroux are just a few who have proven influential over the years, and we acknowledge their contributions without having drawn on their work for this book.

In the following chapter, Adrian recounts some of his experiences in Parliament, with his Liberal and Nationals parliamentary colleagues and the Department of Education. As explained earlier, each chapter which recounts our experiences is followed by an analysis, titled "Analytical contemplation", reflecting our intention to present information that is not available in the 'standard' book about education and, in doing so, reveal the underlying discourses related to power in education.

Notes

1 See Thompson, 1961; Dubin, 1957; Bennis, 1959; Mechanic, 1962; Crozier, 1964; French and Raven, 1969; Hickson et al., 1971; Pettigrew, 1973; Pfeffer & Salancik, 1959.
2 This is an understatement. These theorists traversed a range of disciplines and social sciences.

Chapter 4

The role of Parliament and politics in education

Adrian Piccoli

Power is the resource essential to produce creative outcomes. Whether it is the hard power of Parliament or the soft power of persuasion, either way, nothing can be achieved without it: it must be created, consolidated, used strategically, conserved, not wasted, and constantly renewed.

– Adrian Piccoli

Power is the currency of politics – hard to gain but easily and quickly lost

Being sworn in as the New South Wales minister for education after the 2011 NSW state election was a proud moment for my family and me. The ceremony itself was appropriately formal and solemn, but the smiles of my colleagues who were also being sworn in captured the joy of that election victory. We had been swept into office with a majority of 69 seats. The new premier, Barry O'Farrell, appointed me as the new education minister after having spent two years as the shadow minister for education.

Upon taking up the position, however, I noticed a strange phenomenon – it seemed everyone wanted to keep the powers that came with the office a secret from me. Having been appointed as the minister responsible for the NSW Department of Education, with almost 100,000 staff, a $12 billion budget[1] and one of the largest and most influential organisations in the country, no one really filled me in on what powers I had. On day one, in any other job, the boss or the senior partner or a senior manager would come in and tell you what you could or could not do. In any other job, there would be a position description at least. As a minister, none of that happened.

It is a crazy system and a big reason why changes in government or changes in ministers cause such long periods of public policy inertia. I suspect that the bureaucracy does not really want to tell a minister, and their predecessor is not likely to tell them either, especially if they are from a different political party. The responsibility, as opposed to the power, of a minister is a different matter and, in many ways, is an even more closely guarded secret.

DOI: 10.4324/9781003312451-5

The hard legal power granted to ministers by virtue of being a member of Parliament (MP) and being part of the executive arm of the government is significant. What ministers need to and can do with that power is not so obvious.

The power of elected members of Parliament

Being elected to public office confers significant authority. Through the process of an election, voters have authorised their representative to vote in Parliament on their behalf. This authority is different to power. MPs have limited power. They do not employ their staff – this is done by Parliament, and they have only a small administration budget. There is little scope for them to direct anyone to do anything. However, MPs have significant authority, and this resides primarily in the fact that they are able to vote on legislation and command media attention that is eagerly reported by various news outlets. The very fact that voters have elected an MP means they have given their trust to that local representative and therefore granted that person significant authority to speak on their behalf and to vote in Parliament on their behalf. An MP is invested with authority by the voters in an election.

However, voters in a liberal democracy cannot force MPs to do anything or force them to vote a particular way. An MP has absolute authority to say anything, within the law, and vote in any way, completely independent of what their constituents might think. If an issue arose in Parliament and a poll was conducted in an electorate and the results showed the majority wanted the MP to vote no, they are in no way compelled to vote no.

Of course, political considerations would come into play here as well. That is, constituents have other ways of influencing their elected MPs through protests, media campaigns and direct lobbying and through the support of alternative candidates – witness the rise of the teals[2] in Australian politics. Most MPs do their best to follow the views of their community, but they are also elected to lead, and sometimes that requires them to vote a different way to what their constituents might want and to make the case for their decision to their constituents. And every three or four years, their constituents have the chance to let them know if they got it right or not.

No MP is immune from community pressure, as I discovered in 2013, when legislation was introduced into the NSW Parliament on expanding the use of stem cells in medical research. Not surprisingly, some religious leaders did not support the new laws. The pressure was on. The archbishop of Sydney, the late cardinal George Pell said at the time that any Catholic who voted for the new law should not be entitled to communion.

> Cardinal Pell angered many Catholic politicians this week when he warned that if they voted in favour of the legislation they would face consequences in their life in the church.
> (SMH, 7 June 2007. Pell hopes NSW will keep stem cell ban.)

Of course, constituents or lobby groups are entitled to their opinion, and in a case like stem cell research, their opposition reflected the long-held and publicly known beliefs of their religion. When these 'moral' issues arise in parliaments, the central issue is the degree of political influence that the lobbyists are able to exert on politicians. In an electorate like mine[3] in rural western NSW, quite conservative and with a large Christian population, I had no doubt that the majority of the electorate did not support the new laws. But as an elected MP, I am not compelled to follow the views of my electorate. And, as a Catholic, I saw the stem cell debate differently than simply a black-and-white decision based on what the church teaches. By that stage, I had already indicated publicly that I would support the new laws.

As debate intensified, things became increasingly personal. One constituent phoned me to tell me what a terrible person I was and that I would go to hell if I voted in favour of the new laws. He proceeded to tell me what the Bible says about the sanctity of life and that stem cells derived from human embryos was a sin. He could not have been more black and white about his views. My response to him was that I envied the fact that he saw life in such a simplistic, black-and-white way, when for me and, in my view, most people, the big moral issues in life are complex, multidimensional and exist in various shades of grey.

My position was that the use of stem cells to cure disease was definitely in the grey. And I understood the sanctity of life argument – what happens to the unused embryos. But this issue was also personal to me too. I have friends with sick children whose health would benefit from such treatment, and there is no way I could look them in the eye and say, "No, I am going to deny you the chance to have your daughter's Type 1 diabetes cured." There was also no way I could look at Mike Neville, the mayor of Griffith at the time, who had been a paraplegic since the age of 18 after a football injury, and say to him, "No, sorry, I'm going to deny the chance that stem cell therapies might allow you to walk again one day."

If certain constituents of mine disagreed with my decisions and how I voted on specific issues, of course, they had an opportunity to remove me from office by voting me out at the next election. That is the way democracy works in the Westminster system, and every elected representative is judged by their community at every election. It constitutes an extensive performance review. If voters do not like what you have done during your term, then you are out. At the following election in 2015, I am not aware of any Christian MP who lost a vote because they voted for the stem cell legislation.

While this is a form of limited power, elected MPs are free to vote or say whatever they like.

The hard power of government: the power to create laws

Exercising power and influence through the parliamentary process by the passing of laws is an essential responsibility of governments. Every legislative change as well as key policy and funding decisions made by the government must be approved by the cabinet[4] or one of the cabinet subcommittees. The cabinet is essentially the governing board of the government. It comprises all the ministers in the government, each with the responsibility to lead their respective government departments and is chaired by the premier or prime minister.[5] Ministers prepare cabinet minutes, a document specifying the issue as well as providing recommendations for actions that need to be taken by the cabinet. These minutes might propose changes to legislation or regulations or new policy decisions for the government. Ministers receive the minutes several days ahead of the meeting, so it is always fair to presume that ministers had read the documents. During those meetings, ministers present their minutes with a short introduction, and then the issues are debated.

In my time as a minister, I never witnessed a vote in the cabinet. However, what I did witness was the power of the premier to usually carry the day on contentious cabinet minutes. If a minute had the backing of the premier, then it would usually pass. That is an example of the soft power of the leader. If a minister was not across the detail, then that was usually exposed, with sometimes embarrassing consequences.

To change laws, a new bill, or draft legislation, is introduced into Parliament after going through the cabinet process. Most bills pass Parliament with almost unanimous support and therefore do not need a formal vote.

In some cases, however, the true hard power of 'numbers' has to be used, when bills are disputed by MPs. This is the hard power of the Westminster system of government. Whoever can muster more than 50 per cent of the vote in Parliament can have laws passed without requiring consideration from the rest of Parliament. This does happen but not nearly as often as the public would believe. Most of the debates in Parliament involve very calm and boring speeches by members from all sides of politics, putting their position on Hansard, the parliamentary record, and then the 'vote' is taken and decided 'on the voices' – that is, by MPs saying 'yah' or 'nay', without a vote.

The hard power of ministers: the power to create policy

In the Westminster system of government, the political party (or coalition of parties) that can command a majority in the House of Representatives is the party that forms the government of the day. The leader of that party, elected by the MPs, who are members of that party, is the prime minister in the Australian Commonwealth Parliament or premier in state parliaments.[6]

The prime minister or premier then has the power to appoint ministers and to dismiss them with or without reasons. In that sense, some of a minister's power and authority to act independently is compromised because it is not an elected position but rather an appointed position. The effect of being an appointed position is that personalities and factions come into play when appointments are made and when ministers are dismissed. It can be for poor performance, but it can be for very personal or political reasons despite a strong performance. Many a minister has been dismissed because a political leader needed a scapegoat rather than based on performance.

What ministers have the power to do is clear cut. Technically, ministers can make any decision they want, with respect to the department for which they have responsibility, provided it accords with the law. A minister cannot, for example, breach an industrial award or commit a crime, of course, but, with respect to the budget of the department and operational decisions, they have the power to dictate whatever they like to the government department for which they are responsible. In reality, ministers do not do that. They take advice from their departments and from other sources and make decisions they see as in the best interests of the public and the government.

What ministers are responsible to do, or should do, is a harder question. This question dictates how ministers use their power to deliver on their responsibilities.

In education, the responsibility must be to improve the educational and wellbeing outcomes of students. But there are other considerations that can cut across that general responsibility. Is there a responsibility to attract enrolments towards a particular education sector at the expense of others? Even the question of 'improvement' and how to achieve it is hotly contested. One minister might pursue a neoliberal, free-market approach[7] to education to achieve that 'improvement', whereas others might pursue a command-and-control approach, where every decision is centralised.

These approaches are often guided by the ideological preconceptions of political parties. Some may argue that they have a 'mandate' from voters at the last election because the government had made various education promises, even though the election was not determined by education policies. In my case, all ministers were issued a letter from the then-premier, Barry O'Farrell, outlining the premier's expectations. This letter included two important items that were key performance indicators for all ministers in the government. One was that ministers must deliver on election promises, and the other was the expectation that ministers and department secretaries would manage their departments within the allocated budget.

Delivering on election promises is a clear objective. Promises were made, and governments must find the funding and perhaps change laws to reflect those promises. But that is only the beginning. Once a minister is appointed, they must start thinking about how they deliver on their responsibilities – in the case of education, to improve student academic and wellbeing outcomes. This thinking is guided by the department, but it takes time for a minister to work out their responsibilities and how they intend to deliver on them.

Ministers often have to work it out for themselves, usually by exercising power in one way or the other and slowly learning the extent of their powers. But power is a tricky thing. An education minister has the power granted under the Acts of Parliament over which they have authority, but in reality, those powers are rarely used. In my six years as a minister, we introduced and passed only six bills. These were all amendments to existing legislation.

The reality is that education in Australia is not regulated by many Acts of Parliament. The most significant power is the soft power to influence, persuade, cajole and threaten and, occasionally, the power to expose.

Where education ministers fit into the political power ecosystem

Every new minister wants a couple of things.

First, they want to perform well in their role at a political level. That is, they want to stay in their role as minister for as long as they can and be seen to be performing well. Sometimes, that is because they have a personal or professional interest in their portfolio or, not uncommonly, because the portfolio is a stepping stone to something larger and more powerful or their area of particular interest. Power means more than the ability to direct someone or an organisation to do something. While decision-making and the ability to direct people and resources is the hard power of politics, access to, and the ability to, influence decision-makers is a significant power in and of itself.

A lot is spoken about factions in politics. Often, factional 'players' are not even MPs, yet they wield significant power over decision-makers in Parliament. This power derives from the fact that in a democracy, to get into a position of power requires supporters inside and outside Parliament as well as money. Those who can provide that support, be it to garner votes for a preselection or someone who can gather the required votes, in the parliamentary party to help elect the leader of a party or be appointed a minister can wield significant influence over those decision-makers. Donors and other supporters also tend to get access to decision-makers from where they can influence decisions.

While access to power is important, so are the size and reach of a minister's portfolio. The larger the portfolio budget, the more power comes with that role. Premier or prime minister is, of course, the pinnacle role, then treasurer and then finance minister. These three ministers oversee what are called the central agencies, and they have a lot of influence over what happens across education and every other government department because they are the budget ministers.

These three ministers in NSW are key members of the expenditure review committee (ERC). ERC is the most powerful subcommittee of the cabinet. It usually comprises the premier, treasurer (chair), finance minister plus one or two other senior ministers. They set the budgets for every agency, they monitor how agencies are going with their spending and they approve any spending outside what has already been approved in the annual budget. It is also where ministers and their departments are grilled about their budgets – whether they are operating within their budget, and if not, why not.

Not surprisingly, ERC is where the very big arguments happen within the government. Every minister goes into ERC wanting more money in their budget, and they must compete for that money with every other minister who has different priorities. It is often a question of whether the government builds new schools or new hospitals or new roads or employs more child protection workers. These are real issues, and they can be very hotly debated behind these closed doors.

In 2011, as minister for education, I was required, as all ministers in the NSW government at the time were, to find what were called 'savings' or 'efficiency dividends'. The reality was that the government was looking for cuts to the costs of running the Department of Education. In the case of education, the ERC required the education department to find $1.7 billion in savings over four years. That sounds like a significant amount of money, and it is. But when compared to the budget for the Department of Education over those four years of $50 billion, it puts that number into perspective. What we were really being asked to do was to slow the growth in spending for the department. So instead of spending growing at 5 per cent a year, it would reduce that growth to 3 per cent a year. That still meant job cuts and merging administrative functions amongst other measures.

The prospect of finding those savings was not an easy task but a task that central agencies want to be involved in and 'help' departments like education find those 'savings'. While we appreciated any help we could get, it was sometimes quite challenging to have people with no understanding of how schools worked suggesting where we could cut costs.

On one memorable occasion, a treasury official noticed in the endless spreadsheets that are needed to manage such a large government department that there were many people employed as 'administrative support' in NSW public schools. To this official, the obvious answer was that because they were administrative staff and not teachers, we could, therefore, cut these positions to make the savings.

This proposal would mean the NSW education department would have to cut the number of administrative staff in schools by one-third. I had to very calmly explain that they were proposing to cut one-third of the people who work on the reception at schools, who do the bookkeeping, who answer parents' inquiries when children call in sick or when they come in to pay for school excursions. Many of these staff are women. Cutting one-third of the administrative staff would be a disaster for schools and a public relations disaster for the government and at the ballot box. The idea was quickly dropped.

After the central agencies come the large spending portfolios of education, health, police, transport and so forth. Education and health have sizeable budgets, but they also have broad reach across the community and across electorates. There are multiple schools in every electorate and, in most cases, one hospital or health care facility in every electorate, plus everyone goes to the doctor or interacts with a hospital at some stage. MPs understand this and are very aware and sensitive as to how these portfolios are being managed by ministers. If MPs are getting pats on the back, then the minister looks good. If they are getting complaints and there are negative stories in the media, then there might be trouble with the premier. Ministers want to be seen as effective members of the government, performing well in the media, in public opinion, within the party and especially amongst their colleagues in Parliament.

If ministers are fielding calls from unhappy constituents about the decisions and actions of the minister, then that minister may find themselves in some party-political trouble and may lose their job next time the government changes ministers – in a cabinet reshuffle.

The second outcome most ministers want is to make a positive impact on their community through their portfolio. They want to do a good job. There is massive personal satisfaction in this for anyone. Making a positive impact is not about managing the portfolio and keeping negative stories out of the media and running the department under budget but, rather, changing people's lives for the better through improving and reforming the way the government works.

Achieving the second outcome is much harder than the first.

What's the point of power if it lacks purpose?

In 2008, at the height of the global financial crisis, the then–Commonwealth Labor government introduced the building the education revolution (BER). It was a $16 billion financial stimulus to the Australian economy through multimillion-dollar projects in every school in the country. As with any major government spend like this, especially when done quickly, the errors, overspends and wasted money soon became apparent, and the media went wild.

In some cases, multimillion-dollar buildings were built in schools only a year or so before they closed (Bilbul Public School in my own electorate is an example – I was the minister who closed it), and building costs were often significantly higher than they should have been. I was the opposition spokesman for education in NSW at the time, and we were highly critical of both the Commonwealth Labor government and the state Labor government in NSW,[8] who were doing the actual construction. At the same time, the federal opposition leader, Tony Abbott, was also highly critical of the rollout of the programme as were many local schools because they were not seeing value for money in the projects at their school. Some schools complained that the projects they actually needed were being ignored and instead were given buildings they did not need – in some cases, a new hall was built next to an existing hall.

In 2011, when I became minister for education, the programme was almost finished, and most of the money had been spent. There had been a great deal of media attention with a lot of criticism levelled at both the Commonwealth and NSW government on the way the funds had been spent, so I was keen to know how much money was still left because I did not want to make the same mistakes. I knew there was some money left over, so I asked the department for detail on how much was left over and what NSW could do with it. We had a maintenance and minor capital works backlog in our schools of more than $200 million, so I wanted to spend the money on those projects.

The department provided me with advice that there was $100 million left over. I was advised that the rules of the contract between the Commonwealth who provided the money and the state of NSW who did the work specified that any excess money could only be spent on items that were directly attached to buildings built using BER money. This would mean that NSW could only spend the leftover money on rainwater tanks or solar panels. This was crazy. There was no way I was going to spend $100 million on rainwater tanks. We would be laughed out of office after the merry hell we had kicked up because of what we had perceived had been such wasteful spending by the previous government. But my department and my staff were insistent that the rules were the rules and I was told, "No, Minister", you cannot change them.

What can a minister do in this situation? There is a rule under the Ministerial Code of Conduct (a breach of which will see you referred to the Independent Commission Against Corruption) that says ministers cannot direct their departments to "provide advice with which the agency does not agree".

Section 5 of the NSW Independent Commission Against Corruption Amendment (Ministerial Code of Conduct) Regulation 2014 under the Independent Commission Against Corruption Act 1988 states:

s.5 Lawful directions to the public service;

(1) *A Minister must not knowingly issue any direction or make any request that would require a public service agency or any other person to act contrary to the law.*
(2) *A Minister who seeks advice from a public service agency that is subject to the Minister's direction must not direct that agency to provide advice with which the agency does not agree.*
(3) *For the avoidance of doubt, this section does not prevent Ministers discussing or disagreeing with the advice of a public service agency, making a decision contrary to agency advice or directing an agency to implement the Minister's decision (whether or not the agency agrees with it). Nor does this section prevent an agency changing its advice if its own view changes, including following discussions with the Minister.*

Fair enough. To give such a direction could lead unscrupulous ministers to make corrupt decisions by telling their departments what advice they want and then defend that decision by hiding behind the fact that they had been given that 'advice' from their department. However, the rule still allows a minister to ignore the advice they are given (subsection 3) and make a different decision to the advice that had been provided. A minister has the power to do this, but of course, they would want good reasons to reject the advice. If the minister ends up being wrong, you can be assured someone will wave that initial advice under their nose one day.

Provided it is not illegal activity, ministers can make decisions contrary to the advice they are given. So, in the case of the leftover BER money, I said, "No! I'm not taking the advice." I made it clear I would seek to have the rules changed. That is the power to reject advice and to make decisions using ministerial power.

Then the question becomes how to use your political power to not just reject advice but to change policy? It was not enough to simply reject the advice. We still had $100 million to spend wisely, I hoped. Together with my office, we developed a policy and political strategy to have these rules changed. I asked the NSW Department of Education for a list of $100 million worth of priority minor works, like fixing toilet blocks and fixing leaking roofs. I also asked that the federal electorate of each affected school be listed next to each project. I wanted to show the Commonwealth that a sensible policy change like this also had positive political outcomes for them as well. That is, there would be positive and popular announcements that MPs could make in their electorates.

Later that month, I sat down at a Bondi Café with the then–federal Labor minister for education, Peter Garret,[9] before we were both due to visit a school together. Peter is a great guy and very committed to students and committed to doing the right thing. I always enjoyed working with him. I showed him the list and explained to him the rationale for making the changes I was proposing.

To be honest, my backup plan was to show him how easily we could embarrass, or to use the political term 'wedge', the Commonwealth if they did not agree to our request. These were projects to fix toilet blocks, replace roofs, paint classrooms. I suggested it was either this list or thousands of rainwater tanks. "Which would look better on the TV news?" I asked. I was making the not too subtle point that if the Commonwealth failed to agree to these changes, I would blame them publicly for wasting $100 million on rainwater tanks. There would be many schools willing to show the media the maintenance jobs that needed to be done at their schools. Peter did not need to be wedged because he wanted the best for students, and he could immediately see the value in what I was saying.

He could also see the sense of the proposal at both a policy and political level. Peter's government faced a looming election, and these projects would go down well in various electorates. Peter let me know that the decision to change the BER rules was not within his area of legislative responsibility. Changing the BER rules could only be done by the Commonwealth assistant treasurer, who at the time was the Hon Bill Shorten.[10]

Peter made the necessary introductions. Two weeks later, I took the list to Bill Shorten in Canberra. He took one look at it and could immediately see the sense in what was being proposed. Bill said, "Of course, we must do this, but can I propose a change to the way the list has been prepared. I have been the Parliamentary Secretary for Disabilities and Children's Services and I have seen a lot of these schools that need a lot of maintenance work done. Could the NSW Department come up with a similar list of minor capital works projects in special schools?" In NSW, special schools are called SSPs or schools for specific purposes. Of course, this was a brilliant idea, so I said yes straightaway. I went away and had the list redone. Bill went away and got the rules changed, which was not an easy process through the bureaucracy, but he persisted and got it done.

There we were a National Party state education minister and a Labor Party Commonwealth minister. Together, by rejecting advice and using our combined power, we totally rebuilt 19 special schools right across NSW. This ended up being the single biggest capital investment in children with disabilities in the history of NSW. Together, we cleared the way for this rule to be changed. But there was an edge to this story of bipartisan political cooperation. It was clear that if this rule had not been changed by the Commonwealth government, I would have given them political hell. The TV news would have had images of leaking school roofs while we were being forced to buy 100,000 rainwater tanks. It taught me a valuable lesson about how and when to use the soft power I had as a minister. Find the right partners and stakeholders who share your values, use all the leverage you have (media, politics, sound moral and ethical argument), clearly communicate the benefits of the decision even to opponents and make it clear that it is never wrong to do the right thing!

I could have let this issue go. It was not the biggest issue we were dealing with at the time. But what is the point of power if it does not have a purpose? This was not about buildings; it was about people. At the official opening of the Wilson Park SSP in Lismore, one of the schools Bill and I rebuilt with the leftover BER money, one of the fathers took me aside and with tears in his eyes thanked me profusely. He said, "Schools like Wilson Park are beautiful and happy places for children, but they are filled with parents with broken hearts." The best answer I could give him was "Please don't thank me. It's not my money, it's yours." His tears were for the love of his children and an appreciation for what this new school meant for the future of his child.

I have never been humbler in the presence of a parent nor prouder to have used my power to replace a good idea with an even better one.

Notes

1 In 2021, the NSW Department of Education was responsible for 823,000 students, 2,220 public schools and 94,067 teachers and staff (NSW Education in numbers for 2021).
2 In the 2022 federal election in Australia, 'teal independents', won seven seats in what had previously been considered safe Liberal Party seats on an agenda of

environmentalism and other issues including support for a Commonwealth anti-corruption body.

3 Adrian represented the electoral district of Murray in the NSW Legislative Assembly from 2015 to 2017 and the district of Murrumbidgee from 1999 to 2015.

4 For more information about the cabinet and the cabinet process, go to aph.gov.au/About_Parliament/House_of_Representatives/Powers_practice_and_procedure/Practice7/HTML/Chapter2/Cabinet

5 The Commonwealth and some state governments operate their cabinet system a little differently, with senior ministers forming the inner cabinet while the more junior ministers are not in the cabinet and are in what is called the 'outer cabinet'.

6 There are some variations to this, including how the Australian Labor Party elects their leader if there is a contested leadership ballot.

7 For an account of the neoliberal approach to education and health of the federal government led by John Howard from 1996 to 2007, see Redden, G. (2017). John Howard's Investor State: Neoliberalism and the Rise of Inequality in Australia. *Critical Sociology.* 45(4–5), 713–772.

8 parliament.nsw.gov.au/Hansard/Pages/HansardResult.aspx#/docid/HANSARD-1323879322-40389/link/9

9 Peter Garrett is a former federal Labor politician. In the 2007 election, Garrett was appointed minister for the environment, heritage and the arts. Following the 2010 election, he was made minister for school education, early childhood and youth.

10 Bill Shorten is a federal Labor politician who was appointed Assistant Treasurer in 2010 and then as Minister for Financial Services and Superannuation and Minister for Workplace Relations was Minister for Education until the Labor Party's defeat at the 2013 election.

Analytical contemplation

The role of Parliament and politics in education

Don Carter

As noted earlier, this book is intended to be more than a series of stories about our experiences in education. A book of storytelling might have been fun and enjoyable to compile but perhaps of limited value for the reader. Thus, we have structured the following chapters to first provide the recounts of incidents we have experienced – and then to follow up each recount with a chapter analysis written by Don on how power and authority are manifested in the recounts. Each chapter analysis is called an "analytical contemplation" and covers the important aspects of the recounts to shed light on aspects of power in education. Therefore, in this analytical contemplation, the following key points are discussed:

- Hard power and education – curriculum and funding as examples.
- Authority – situational and possessive authority as power resources to explain the accrual and application of power.
- Legitimacy – as derived from authority and sanctioned by the public.
- Trust and familiarity – building trust through familiarity as power resources.

Hard power and the state

Earlier in this book, I noted several important points about power. 'Power' is a problematic and contested notion that subsumes authority and force as an 'umbrella' term (Uphoff, 1989). Power largely constitutes the ability to affect the behaviour of others to achieve one's goals often through threats, payment and attraction (Nye, 2021, p. 196). Power is often conflated with 'legitimacy' and 'authority' and is used differently by different theorists (Locke, 1990). I recognised that the notion of power is too complex and multifaceted in its origins and effects to reduce to one dimension (Barnett & Duvall, 2005). In addition, I observed how theories of power have proliferated over the last part of the twentieth century, with many theorists building on the seminal work of Max Weber. In the previous chapter, Adrian uses the terms 'hard power', 'legitimacy' and 'authority' to convey his experiences in education. These terms are part of a 'power lexicology' and, as such, are important terms

DOI: 10.4324/9781003312451-6

to interrogate and define as best we can because they provide insights into how power was manifested in these experiences.

As noted earlier in this book, the exercise of power often requires the use of the types of coercion witnessed in authoritarian regimes by dictators and despots (Pardo, 2000). When coercion is used, we call this specific use of power 'hard power', a term which is used and explored extensively in several domains, including managerial theory, political theory and international relations. In the latter domain, hard power is associated with a traditional understanding of power, where nation-states exist within potentially anarchic contexts (i.e., potential threats from regional neighbours) and are sometimes compelled to use hard power to establish and maintain order, usually through the use of force. Basically, hard power refers to coercion, regulation and governance – all of which combine to establish the capacity to influence another entity in ways that entity would not have done otherwise (Wilson, 2008). In international relations, hard power sees the imposition of sanctions, military intervention and 'coercive' diplomacy (p. 114), and throughout history, hard power has been considered as being dependent on a nation-state's population size, territory, natural resources and its military capacities (Giddens, 2015).

However, when we use the term 'state', we need to recognise that this term in its own right is complex, as are the state's attendant powers. Jessop (2009) describes these powers as "hypercomplex and changeable phenomena" (p. 367) and explains that no single theory or theoretical framework can fully uncover and untangle the extent of their structural features and subtleties (p. 367). That being the case, and for the purposes of this book, I have adopted a definition of the state that is workable and manageable: that the state constitutes a set of core institutions, including public administration, political executive, legislature, army, police, judiciary, media, trade unions and religion (p. 368), with its features including the size of its territory and resources, population and state mechanisms for the retention of social stability (p. 369). The state holds the resources necessary for the maintenance of a functional society through its capacity to formulate and implement policy (Zwitter & Hazenberg, 2020) and sometimes uses these resources to oppress unrest and opposition, as we have witnessed in nondemocratic countries for many decades. The state also legislates and regulates across numerous domains, including health, education, media, property, family and education (Apple, 2012), and oscillates between the application of hard power, legitimisation and soft power (which is discussed in the following chapter).

Generally speaking, the state is organised by traditional "hierarchical command-and-control structures" (Apple, 2012, p. 4), relying on "authoritative institutions" (p. 4) to justify policies and ensure public compliance. The state has the capacity to intervene via the funding of scientific research, create and, to a certain degree, control commercial markets, deploy military forces and create positions in the public service (p. 49). The French Marxist philosopher Louis Althusser (1918–1990) argued that the state encompasses two fields of influence – "Repressive State Apparatuses" (RSA) and "Ideological State Apparatuses" (ISA) (1971), with the former including police, prisons and the army, and the latter including the church, families, social media and the mainstream media and schools (1971, p. 146). Or to put it in a rather dramatic way, the state mediates and governs individuals, organisations and behaviours and owns a "wide arsenal of tools of power and violence" (Kestere et al., 2015, p. 7).

While Althusser's (1971) nomenclature of 'repressive state apparatuses' might appear more applicable to dictatorships and nondemocratic states, perhaps we can see examples that are closer to home than we might have expected. Take, for example, the COVID-19 lockdowns in Melbourne, Australia, a few years ago which saw six lockdowns equalling 262 days, or nearly nine months' duration, between March 2020 and October 2021 (Kelly, 2021),[1] with the threat of hefty fines for noncompliance. Pandemic lockdowns were also enforced by police in Sydney, where residents in the western suburbs were directed to stay indoors and threatened with heavy financial penalties. That impost contrasted with policing in Sydney's more affluent eastern suburbs, where local residents were permitted to access local beaches, shopping precincts and other facilities[2]. However, by 2022, more than 33,000[3] Sydney residents had been fined for breaches of the lockdown laws (News.com, 22 November 2022) in a display of the hard power of the state. Perhaps Althusser's 'repressive state apparatuses' label is appropriate after all.

Hard power and education

The hard power of the state is also apparent in the realm of education. Here, the state has the capacity to create an education system that imposes and promotes particular ideologies, values and knowledge (Apple, 2012; Biesta, 2013). This is reflected in the creation of a school curriculum, which necessitates decisions about the content to include and exclude, how student performance will be measured (and, subsequently, rewarded or punished), how education programmes and research will be funded – all of which potentially influence and manipulate the behaviours and attitudes of not only the students in the education system but the wider community as well (Depaepe & Hulstaert, 2015). The development of a school curriculum is neither easy nor simple, with competing interests often at loggerheads. To resolve or at least subdue the demands of these interests and to maintain legitimacy, the state must be able to accommodate and integrate the various and often-competing interests of stakeholder groups and individuals. This necessitates continuous processes of "compromise, conflict, and active struggle" (Apple, 2012, p. 27) to ensure the durability of the state as a functioning and ongoing entity of power and to win the "active consensus over whom they rule" (Mouffe, 1979, p. 182). In addition, the state utilises hard power at the "intersection of politically coercive and symbolic power" (Jessop, 2009, p. 369). And this type of hard power is evident when we investigate funding for education and schools.

In the previous chapter, Adrian points out that ministers of the state who have responsibility for budgets, particularly large budgets, exercise hard power. Education budgets are generally high across developed nations; for example, in the United Kingdom, £116 billion[4] was spent on education in 2021 and 2022, second only to the health budget. And in the United States, $174.97 billion[5] was spent in the 2023 financial year. The large budgets and related costs are due to education's close association with creating and strengthening human capital and the economic robustness of the state and individual citizens – a "traditional hard power resource" (Raimzhanova, 2015, p. 17). In fact, we can see examples of how education ministers have used education funding as hard power in Australia.

One example occurred in 2008 with the federal Labor government of Kevin Rudd as prime minister and Julia Gillard as education minister. In this incident, Gillard threatened to withhold education funds from the states and territories. The issue at the centre of this dispute was the government's plans to implement school league tables as part of its overarching strategy, titled the 'Education Revolution'. The government's impetus for the leagues tables was based on New York reforms, led by Joel Klein, the chancellor and former a school superintendent, which claimed to have improved student learning outcomes (these claims were later alleged as misleading)[6]. Gillard eventually prevailed with the My School website, launched to "support national transparency and accountability of Australia's school education system through publication of nationally consistent school-level data" (ACARA, n.d.); the reform remains controversial to this day.

Another more recent example of hard power at the national Australian level occurred in 2018, when the then–coalition federal education minister Dan Tehan threatened to withhold funding for nongovernment schools unless the states agreed to a funding deal proposed by the federal government (*The Guardian*, 27 September 2018). At the heart of the issue was Tehan's threat that the states would need to make up for a funding shortfall should they not agree to the deal. This threat followed the government's school funding package, which promised $4.6 billion[7] for Catholic and independent schools but nothing for public schools (*The Guardian*, 21 September 2018). The use of hard power in education is not limited to threats related to funding but using education funding as a threat is a potent weapon, especially given Australia's history of 'funding wars' in education (for more on school funding, see Greenwell & Bonnor, *Waiting For Gonski: how Australia failed its schools*).

But possessing power and holding onto power is not merely a case of funding and threats; it requires authority, legitimacy and trust (Arendt, 1972; Weber, 1978). When a leader or government loses power, it is because they have lost authority and legitimacy, and sometimes this is because they have lost the trust of the public. But how do we define 'authority' and 'legitimacy'? And why are these important? In the next section, I explore the notion of authority and relate it to Adrian's recount in the previous chapter.

Authority and power

If 'power' is an umbrella term and is used in different ways by different theorists, often subsuming other terms, how do we define 'authority'? Traditionally, authority has been acknowledged as pivotal to organisations and essential for people to fulfil their work roles (Crozier, 1964; Follett, 1940; Weber, 1978). Usually, an individual's authority has been considered as originating from their position in a hierarchy (Aghion & Tirole, 1997; Fayol, 1949). In addition, authority has been linked to people's expertise (Barley, 1996; Bendix, 1956) or acceptance of a communication as authoritative (Barnard, 1938; Simon, 1997). Weber argues that authority entails the holder occupying a special role or position that enables them to issue commands and orders and to back them up with rewards or sanctions (Weber, 1978) and is often referred to as "legitimate power" (Uphoff, 1989, p. 296). Authority, defined in this way, manifests as "compliance relationships" (p. 301) – the "probability that a command with a specific content will be obeyed by a given group of persons, despite resistance, regardless of the basis on which the probability rests" (p. 301). Authority generally requires a special position or role, with the capacity to deliver rewards and sanctions (p. 301). In Adrian's recount in the previous chapter, two different types of authority are apparent – 'situational authority' and 'possessive authority'.

Situational authority

In Adrian's recount, we can see the use of a specific type of authority called "situational view of authority" (Bencherki et al., 2019, p. 6). This perspective on authority has a rich history in management theory (see Barnard, 1938; Follett, 1940; Simon, 1997) and is anchored in a principle called the "law of the situation" (Follett, 1940, p. 33). This 'law' disallows the issuing of commands or instructions to another party, preferring instead to establish agreement between the involved parties in deference to "what the situation dictates" (p. 6). This particular kind of authority sees participants "alter their relationships within each situation as they respond to it" (Bencherki et al., 2019, p. 7), constituting a "situational accomplishment" (p. 7). In Adrian's account of his work with the federal minister for education, Peter Garrett, he outlines how both education ministers put aside the fact that they were from opposite sides of politics with a host of accompanying ideological differences. Both were motivated to do what they considered to be the 'right thing' for Australian schoolchildren by implementing a substantial list of school building and maintenance jobs instead of spending the large sum of money on hundreds of rainwater tanks. As Adrian recounted, he and Garrett enlisted the support of the Labor Party's Bill Shorten, then the Commonwealth assistant treasurer, who then steered a series of legislative changes to ensure that the funds went to school improvement and maintenance programmes, with each accepting the merits of the other's ideas.

This type of authority – 'situational authority' – is a potent entity because it "belongs to a group . . . empowered by a certain number of people" (Arendt, 1972, p. 44). The alliance between three government ministers – one at state level and the other two at the federal level – creates a significant and irresistible force because they altered normative attitudes and behaviours to respond to this specific situation to create a "situational accomplishment" (Bencherki et al., 2019, p. 7). However, I also note in Adrian's previous chapter his determination to achieve this outcome and his willingness to "embarrass" or politically "wedge" the Commonwealth government had Garrett and his federal colleagues refused his plan. As we are all aware, this line of thinking (and action) is common in politics and is a form of coercion (some might say 'blackmail'), and while Adrian's recount had a positive outcome, it points to another phenomenon, the different types of 'influence' – power, coercion, force, persuasion, manipulation, inducement (Stinebrickner, 2015).

Possessive authority

As noted earlier, authority is a contested term, and no one definition is accepted as conclusive for all theorists. Adrian's interaction with fellow politicians Garrett and Shorten took the shape of 'situational authority'; his experiences also reflect another kind of authority – 'possessive authority' (Tello-Rozas et al., 2015). This type of authority constructs authority as something some people 'have' or 'own'. For example, someone who 'has' authority and power might mean that they possess resources which are used to exercise power; for example, they 'own' property, labour and capital.

This idea is not new – the English philosopher Thomas Hobbes (1588–1679) advocated that a sovereign, hereditary monarch who 'owns' resources is able to provide the ultimate protection against the terrifying chaos of the world, where ungoverned, self-interested individuals potentially condemn society to an unstable and fearful future. In other words, the monarch 'possesses' or 'owns' power and authority. Various theorists have investigated the notion of authority, with Giddens (1984) arguing that authority derives from the "capability of harnessing the activities of human beings" (p. 258), while Haugaard (1997) contends that possessing "authoritative resources" (p. 111) enables the authoritative (and powerful) figure to "influence the life chances of others and/or patterns of structural reproduction" (p. 111).

To possess economic and legal resources also enables the "right to decide" (Aghion & Tirole, 1997, p. 2) how and where those resources are to be allocated within an "explicit or implicit contract" (p. 2). The possession and wielding of natural and technological resources (Mitchell, 2013) also empowers the state (or an organisation or individual) with authority, enabling that actor the opportunity to impose rules, regulations and prohibitions or to deregulate and liberate. This is apparent in Adrian's interaction with the federal Labor government with regard to funding.

Adrian's account highlights the centrality of a possessive authority perspective in education. As minister, he enjoyed the capacity to administer or redirect funding – or, at least, identify the mechanisms to achieve this redirection. By virtue of the fact that he occupied the position of minister, this provided him with access to other ministers and, in this case, federal ministers (Garret and Shorten). Possessive authority also includes the "rights of office" (Höpfl, 1999, p. 223) – a concept originating from the Roman *officium*, indicating a role that is "specialized in character" (p. 223) and allocated to specific individuals with an accompanying right to act according to the statutes of the given office. We can trace the origins of the word 'authority' to Latin. Here, 'authority' finds its origin in the Latin word 'auctoritas', which has its beginnings in the meaning of "to begin something, to set something in motion, to originate, to cause, to establish, to found, to make something grow" (p. 219). To be an 'auctor' is one whose "influence, advice, counsel, command" causes events to happen because an auctor acts as the "contriver, instigator, counsellor, adviser, promoter" (pp. 219–220). Adrian's role as minister embraces this tradition of status and influence, and his actions portray him as an actual 'auctor', with the ability to "set things in motion" and to "initiate and inspire respect" (p. 222).

Legitimacy

The concept of legitimacy is linked to authority in that persons who are subject to another person's state-sanctioned authority must be convinced or persuaded that it is appropriate and proper that they obey the person of authority (Weber, 1978) – one who possesses "ample force or (by) control" (Uphoff, p. 303) of available information, resources and social status. Legitimacy depends on an "utterance or performance" (Höpfl, 1999, p. 230) that convinces others that an "institution, practice, custom, conduct or office is right" (p. 230). While Weber and Uphoff's definitions both have a military-like flavour to them, Pardo and Prato (2019) argue that legitimacy is based on ruling by consent instead of hard power or coercion. And when we consider Adrian's recounts in the previous chapter, we can see authority and legitimacy at work regarding his position as minister and his relationship with the education bureaucracy. Here, he occupies a position that is bestowed with the capacity to issue instructions and directions.

According to the Organisation for Economic Co-operation and Development (OECD), legitimacy is based on four sources (2010). The first source relates to inputs and processes, the agreed rules and procedures; the second is outputs and/or performance, linked to the quality and effectiveness of public goods and services. The third is the shared beliefs of the political community and the influences of tradition, religion and 'charismatic' leaders; while the fourth is international legitimacy, which is the recognised sovereignty and legitimacy of the state and its international relationships (OECD, 2010, p. 9). What is important here is that these different sources interact, and no individual or state can rely on one single source only to successfully administer political agendas (Pardo & Prato, 2019).

Therefore, a politically astute individual or a state requiring the approval of its citizens needs to seek legitimacy from "people's shared beliefs and traditions" (OECD, 2010, p. 10). In Australia, educational equity is situated within the issue of rates of school funding. Over the past 25 years, national statements about the aims of education have targeted equity with numerous bipartisan government statements on education highlighting the importance of fairness and equity in education (see the Ministerial Council on Education, Employment, Training and Youth Affairs, 1989, 1999, 2008; and the Education Council's Alice Springs Mparntwe, 2019 Declarations). Looking further back in time, we see that in 1963, "state aid" became a hot political issue with the then–Liberal prime minister, Robert Menzies, who had offered a "token amount" (West, 1983, p. 414) of funding for science laboratories in public schools, eventually mobilising the lobbying group "Defence of Government Schools" (DOGS) in 1965 (p. 414). The controversy deepened in the 1970s under the conservative government of Malcolm Fraser (p. 415) and continues in the present day. Fairness and equity continue to loom large in the mind of the public and are sites of "popular and political consternation" (Lee & Stacey, 2023, p. 1). In a recent study of the nearly 2,000 participants' perceptions of fairness in Australian education, most participants considered the current system of funding as "unfair or very unfair" (p. 1).

As education ministers, Adrian and Garrett were aware of school funding as controversial. Both knew that to use a large sum of public money for water tanks – or something potentially controversial – would not only be detrimental for the public standing and their respective governments, such a move would also attract significant criticism from the public, damaging the trust both Adrian and Garrett had developed.

Adrian discusses the role of an MP, highlighting the fact that the MP represents the electors of that particular electorate. Whereas Weber (1978) presented the issue of political representation as an exercise of authority 'over the people' in a kind of 'master/servant' arrangement, in most Western democracies, elected officials are more the 'agents' of the electors and act in agreement with the will of the people, thus strengthening the democratic system Pardo & Prato (2019). The OECD (2010) provides a clear pathway to explain legitimacy and, in doing so, sheds light on Adrian's recount.

As a minister in the NSW state government, Adrian was obliged, like all ministers, to observe due process and relevant legislation, particularly legislation related to the expenditure of funding. However, the state and its ministers are able to establish and maintain legitimacy through four sources of legitimacy (OECD, 2010), which enable broad agreement across the political and social spectrum about the processes and procedures for decision-making. The first source is "Input or process legitimacy" (OECD, 2010, p. 23), where the legitimacy of the state is anchored in constitutionally agreed rules, through which it undertakes "binding decisions and organises people's participation" (p. 23). However, sitting alongside and intimately connected to power, authority and legitimacy is a quality that is often overlooked – trust. In the next section, we explore this quality and explain why it is important in Adrian's recounts.

Trust and familiarity

While we can discuss power, authority, legitimacy and responsibility, there is another quality that resides within and around human interactions and relationships – trust. In the previous chapter, Adrian begins with an observation about information being withheld from him when he commenced his role as education minister. As Adrian noted, he was curious and a little perplexed about this – after all, one might quite reasonably expect that commencing work in a high-profile public position, one of significant fiscal and policy responsibility, would automatically entail immediate and comprehensive briefings on the responsibilities, processes and protocols bound up in the position. At first glance, this situation is reminiscent of the aphorism "knowledge is power", attributed to the English philosopher Sir Francis Bacon (1561–1626), where those with power (the bureaucrats) are reluctant to surrender power to the newcomer (Adrian). This is probably a simplistic response, and we can only speculate as to why key information was initially kept from Adrian. However, this episode is worthy of further exploration and points to a key component in the possession and exercise of power – the nature and role of trust.

Trust is a basic premise and integral part of daily life, and because its 'inner workings' may escape notice, it is worth briefly exploring some ideas about trust. First, to trust in someone or to trust something is, in reality, to attach yourself to an unknown future. However, when we place our trust in someone, we (generally) feel a degree of certainty that their history and past actions will reward us in the future because they will adhere to that observable (and in our eyes) acceptable past. We are able to do this because we have built up knowledge and expectations of that person, and we expect that they will not disappoint us. In this type of scenario, we are dealing with a distinction between 'future present' (the future that will become the present) from the 'present future' (the future as seen in the present) (Morgner & King, 2022, p. xii). Unanticipated events can disrupt the 'present future', meaning that decisions need to be made to restore (as much as possible) the originally anticipated future. In particular – and to shed light on Adrian's experience with the education bureaucracy – we need to examine trust and familiarity, personal trust and trust as opportunity and constraint, and the work of the German sociologist and philosopher Niklas Luhmann (1927–1998) is useful to draw upon at this point.

We tend to trust the accustomed, the regular, the familiar and what becomes expected. Trust and familiarity are key components and are 'paired' so that familiarity becomes a precondition for trust (and distrust) (Luhrmann, 1979, p. 19). Familiarity allows us to entertain reliable and stable expectations of what might happen and to construct a future which is favourable – one that is based on "history as a reliable background" (p. 20). In the often-frantic activities of day-to-day life and the complexities of the workplace and all its activity, familiarity as the basis of trust allows us to visualise and determine a stable future – one in which unwelcome surprises and upsets are diminished. Familiarity and trust form a "new mutually stabilizing relationship" (p. 20), which allows 'history' to be more than the "remembrance of things experienced" (p. 20), where the 'shutting out' of the unfamiliar and unwanted was a matter, of course. Familiarity and trust now provide a "predetermined structure" (p. 20) for specific social and workplace interactions and the planning for future activities, strategies and initiatives.

When considering Adrian's recount regarding the education bureaucracy, we are able to view this through the lens of trust and familiarity; the bureaucracy was unfamiliar with Adrian as a minister – his expectations, work processes and motivations. Public service personnel may well have been familiar with Adrian's policy statements while in opposition and familiar with his public positions on education issues; however, his occupation of a ministerial position with all the resources available to a minister may well have engendered a cautious approach from the department. What Adrian embarked upon, was a programme of meeting with members of the bureaucracy (and not just senior managers), which enabled him to identify key issues and key personnel and glean insights into the motivations and priorities of others. It was also the opportunity for the bureaucrats to get to know him – to see what priorities he believed were important to pursue – the stakeholders he considered as crucial.

Conclusion

Through these many and varied interactions over the early period of his tenure as minister, Adrian was able to present himself as a "social identity which builds itself up through interaction and which corresponds to its ie. [his] environment" (Luhrmann, 1979, p. 62). Accordingly, Adrian was able to bank trust because he interacted with others and built the expectations of others in doing so. In other words, as people became familiar with him and his views and ways of doing things, he established expectations in their minds, which he was able to satisfy. As Luhmann argues, "[T]he path to trust is by way of entering into the expectations of others in a general way" (p. 62). Adrian was able to do this successfully and for an extended period of time.

Developing trust as an individual within a group or workplace setting is different from an elected official and their relationship with the voting public. Adrian also mentions the trust that is extended by the voters through the election of an individual to office. This trust is based on the policy pronounce-ments of the candidate in the lead-up to an election and subsequent actions (or inaction). The statements of the elected MP establishes trust, upon which constituents judge the performance of the MP.

This same principle applies regarding Adrian and the public. Over a period of time, an MP 'reveals' themselves to the voting public through their announce-ments, interactions with the public at meetings and, informally, how they vote in Parliament and policy decisions. Adrian's "self-presentation" (Luhrmann, 1979, p. 61) establishes a 'public self' and a set of expectations from the pub-lic, upon which voters establish the criteria through which they decide on an MP's electability and trustworthiness.

Familiarity and trust, however, is only one dimension of how trust works. The role of personal trust is also a key concept in explaining how human beings work together and avoid chaos – that state of 'un-being' where it is impossible to predict and generalise. We can define trust as the "generalized expectation that the other will handle his (*sic*) freedom, his disturbing potential for diverse action, in keeping with his personality" (Luhrmann, 1979, p. 39) – the per-sonality one chooses to reveal. When a person chooses to reveal themselves by selecting specific and consistent actions, they are, in fact, inviting others to judge their trustworthiness. Every action of the individual and every interac-tion with others is an invitation to evaluate that person's trustworthiness. And the opportunities for action increase in proportion to the increase in trust – "trust in one's own self-presentation and in other people's interpretation of it" (p. 40).

Large organisations, where the extent of official responsibility exceeds the individual's capacity to enact the various roles and responsibilities, see the manifestation of "very significant relationships of personal trust between supe-riors and underlings" (Luhrmann, 1979, p. 63) and between "parliamentar-ians and the higher civil service" (p. 63). This situation, which involves an overloading of responsibility for the 'superior', results in the conferring of trust to the subordinates, who, in turn, accept the trust and its attendant conditions and restrictions. Luhmann argues that this arrangement must not be disrupted or undermined through deception; otherwise, the subordinate deceiver will find the ongoing "discrepancy between appearance and reality exceptionally tiring" (p. 63) and ultimately unrewarding and untrustworthy.

The substantial role of education minister requires this transference of trust to those working with Adrian. The advisers become trusted and part of the 'inner workings' of the minister's office, contributing to the varied and com-plex issues that confront the minister, from funding allocations to curriculum and policy shifts and the maintenance of positive and working relationships across the education sector. The background to these issues is the "problem of complexity" (Luhrmann, 1979, p. 63), and in conferring trust, the minister (Adrian) "unburdens himself of complexity which he cannot sustain" (p. 63). The person who might abuse that trust must thus accept the burden of that complexity and accept the responsibility of managing and manipulating the information that is conveyed to the minister; otherwise that person will find themselves "collapsing under the pressure of complexity" (p. 63).

Notes

1 https://www.reuters.com/world/asia-pacific/melbourne-ease-worlds-longest-covid-19-lockdowns-vaccinations-rise-2021-10-17/
2 https://www.reuters.com/world/asia-pacific/we-are-not-virus-two-tier-delta-lockdowns-divide-sydney-2021-08-10/
3 https://www.news.com.au/finance/money/costs/legitimacy-of-covid19-fines-challenged-in-new-south-wales-supreme-court/news-story/cb6685f9fe508a17b6461aa27adf1bf5
4 The Institute for Fiscal Studies (2022), https://ifs.org.uk/microsite/education-spending#
5 The calculations are in Australian dollars.
6 The Independent Education Union (Australia) published several stories disputing Klein's claims of improving education outcomes for New York children. New York Local Takes Klein to Task - Independent Education Union of Australia (ieu.org.au). *The Washington Post* (2012) described Klein's autobiographical details of his "impoverished" childhood as "misleading".
7 Australian dollars.

Chapter 5

Schools, power and books

Don Carter

Book power and controversy

When I was a head teacher of English at a country high school, I was teaching a year 8 class a novel set in rural NSW. The main character was a boy about 12 years of age, and when a Buddhist monk comes to live in the town, the two become friends. The story tracks their friendship and the prejudices from some of the townsfolk, and overall, I thought it was a positive and rather inspirational novel – until I received a complaint from the parent of one of my students. I invited the parent to a face-to-face meeting where I could listen to her concerns. The student's mother explained to me that, as a Christian, she did not want her children being exposed to any religion other than Christianity. I was taken aback and explained that the novel was full of positive messages: friendship, compassion and acceptance. She remained unmoved. I then explained to her that our options were limited. Her son could stay in class and study the novel with his peers, or I could sit him outside the classroom and study another novel. The mother said she would consider the options. I never heard from her again, and her son stayed in the class and studied the novel like his peers.

I must admit that I had not expected an objection about this book. I understand the concerns parents might have with books that deal with sex, violence, abuse, suicide and other dark issues, and generally, schools are careful in their text selections and tend to avoid such themes. I understand objections to children being exposed to these types of themes, but this parent's objection to her son being exposed to another religion (Buddhism) reinforced how powerful books can be in different ways and to different people. My experience of books has always been positive from childhood onwards. Although at times I have been shocked or disturbed[1] by the contents of some books, they have been the pathway to imaginative worlds and journeys of exploration.

And it was quite a few years later that I found myself objecting to an issue involving books. But my objections were not based on the content of a book but on a decision by the NSW Curriculum Authority about what types of texts

DOI: 10.4324/9781003312451-7

should be studied by students in their English matriculation examinations. And I made my objections public.

Book power and the media

The first time I was interviewed by radio shock jock Alan Jones was in 2017. I spent a sleepless night in anticipation of the 6:00 a.m. phone call from his producer to begin the interview. The topic of the interview was the literary texts school students were required to read in English in their final year of study. This topic had been covered in the news over the preceding days, largely due to the efforts of a colleague from another Sydney metropolitan university[2] and me, both of whom had hit the radio airwaves and published opinion pieces in the media. The issue that had angered us was a change to what students had to read in their final year of schooling. Basically, the change was that the study of a novel or poetry in their English examination (the higher school certificate) was to become optional. To me, as an English teacher and as a former English inspector at the NSW Board of Studies, this was an outrage, a betrayal of a long and rich history of English curriculum in NSW.

This decision had been made by the curriculum authority, the New South Wales Education Standards Authority (NESA – my former employer), as a result of consultation for new senior syllabuses that were due for release later that year. In my view, it was staggering that many English teachers themselves were in favour of this move, who argued that there were too many texts to be studied in the final year of schooling who argued that there were too many texts to be studied in the final year of schooling.[3] I was angry about this proposal and wrote a scornful opinion piece for Sydney's tabloid newspaper, *The Daily Telegraph*. In this piece, I mocked the move by NESA by claiming that soon, students would be able to graduate from high school with a Bachelor of Facebook.

The wider media picked up on this column, and I was invited by numerous radio stations to discuss the issue. One memorable moment that occurred in an interview with a Newcastle radio station was when the host paused and asked, "So, soon you'll be able to leave school without having read a book in your last year . . .?" When I answered that this was correct, there was a pause before he replied, "Extraordinary." Yes, it was extraordinary, and this is why Alan Jones had picked up on it, and being a former English teacher and an advocate for the study of literature, he wanted to interview me.

So the phone rang at 6:00 a.m., and I steeled myself for the questions that would follow. I waited to be introduced by Jones . . . and waited. With the phone to my ear, I could hear Jones talking to his audience. He told a few jokes. He then told another joke or two and played what seemed to be an interminable number of advertisements. Finally, he introduced me. The interview went well. He strongly supported my stance and, in fact, did most of the talking, recounting school stories (his own and as a teacher) and talked about the importance of literature in his childhood. I warmed to the task and talked about the historical importance of literature in school curriculum and its worth for the development of the individual. We agreed with each other on this topic,[4] and for me, it was a rather exhilarating experience, though I was glad he and I were allies on this issue rather than adversaries.

Following this interview and the article in *The Daily Telegraph*, NESA reversed its decision and reinstalled the study of a novel for the HSC as mandatory.[5] I would like to think that the intervention of my university colleagues and my efforts were central to the reversal of this decision. I would also like to think that NESA realised that the decision to cut the study of a novel and poetry from the final English examination was short-sighted and a betrayal of curriculum history. I suspect we will never know.

This brief recount is a prelude to a discussion of who determines what books are studied in schools and the processes involved in selecting the books. And if you have ever wondered about how texts are selected, then I can fill you in based on personal, close-up experience.

Power and book selection

From 2005 to mid-2012, I was an inspector (of English) at the NSW Board of Studies. This role had several duties attached to it. First, I was responsible for the development and maintenance of the English curriculum in NSW for kindergarten children to students in their final (year 12) year of study. I also led inspections of nongovernment schools around the state, verifying their compliance in a range of areas, including governance, buildings and maintenance, finances, child protection and curriculum. One of the high-stakes duties was to oversee the selection of texts for the higher school certificate English courses. This list of texts was at the front of every English teacher's mind because it dictated what was taught in the final year of English and allowed teachers the opportunity to teach some of their favourite texts. This last point is important because many English teachers entered the profession to pass on their love of literature and specific books.

Decisions about what texts to include and what to exclude in a text list are not undertaken by one person sitting in a city office or a small group of bureaucrats. Decisions are made by a representative committee comprising a range of stakeholders, including professional associations, academics, teachers' unions, parent and community groups and representatives from the three education sectors: the Department of Education, the nongovernment schools' sector and the Catholic Education Office. While this might sound an ideal arrangement, I can assure you that it is not an easy process, and the text selection process is replete with examples of influence being exerted through persuasion, manipulation and even coercion.

The last year of schooling is high stakes for many students in NSW because the vast majority of students undertake a series of examinations for their school leaving credential, the higher school certificate (HSC). While there is choice for students in the subjects they study, English is a compulsory subject, meaning that most students must study a certain number of books specified by the NSW Curriculum Authority,[6] for their English examination. This list is not so much a 'book list'; it is more accurately called a 'text list' because its contents now include film, websites and multimedia texts. This is because the definition of 'text' broadened to include a wider range of compositions beyond what we traditionally recognise as a 'book' since a series of reforms to the senior years of schooling was implemented following what is known as the 'McGaw Reforms', initiated in 1996 by Professor Barry McGaw.[7]

Across all Australian states and territories, in the text list for year 12, you will inevitably spot one or more of Shakespeare's plays, and in NSW, up to half a dozen, in fact. This is because it would be 'political suicide' for a government or curriculum authority such as NESA not to include Shakespeare, widely regarded as the greatest writer in the English language. For an education minister to sign off on a list that does not include Shakespeare would be unwise to say the least. But Shakespeare is not the only author who must be included. If you were to look through the text lists over the past 50 years, you will see names such as Jane Austen, Emily Dickinson, Elizabeth Gaskell,[8] Charles Dickens, William Wordsworth, Samuel Taylor Coleridge, John Donne and William Blake.

The second reason is that, for many people, the inclusions on a text list – and the exclusions – are the gauge by which the worth and robustness of the entire English curriculum is judged. Even though I would expect that the average citizen does not engage with the English syllabus in detail, the text list is easily accessed and a quick way to check to see if the books that are considered as canonical are included. And it has been the case that the inclusion of certain titles has attracted media controversy.

Compiling the list is not a straightforward exercise. The representative group members spend many meetings discussing, selecting and eliminating titles. This means that members are avid readers, are passionate about books and the importance of books and reading and have strong views on what specific books should be included and why. Inevitably, there are disputes.

The power of textual disputes

One dispute I remember clearly involved the decision whether to include a work by Patrick White or to avoid White in favour of a more contemporary author. My view was that because White is a Nobel Prize–winning author and iconic in Australian literature, he should be included. I also argued that *The Tree of Man* should be the selected text, more so than *The Vivisector* or *Voss*. I should add that I read *The Tree of Man* at school as part of my year 11 studies, and it made a huge impact on me. My belief was that students in their final year should have the opportunity to study this major Australian literary figure.

A number of my colleagues disputed this, arguing that White's style of writing and subject matter would not engage young people who are interacting with digital technologies in a fast-paced world. These colleagues preferred to countenance the inclusion of a graphic novel such as *The Sandman* (Neil Gaiman).

My point of view was slightly different from that of my colleagues, in that the function of the text list was manifold: it provided teachers and students with a range of choices across print media, multimedia and digital texts. Additionally, and importantly in my mind, the list stood as an 'artefact' of its time. This meant that it constituted what we – as a representative committee, curriculum authority and society – value in textual studies. To me, this was important. I wanted a list that in the future when curriculum historians examined the list, they would think we had struck an appropriate balance across authors, contemporary and canonical texts and types of texts. And at the political level, the list was ultimately a government document because it was produced by a government agency. The discussion went back and forth until the colleagues who had been arguing against the inclusion of White relented. They understood my arguments, and while they may have thought that I was adopting an overly conservative position, I believed I was right.

Another dispute arose between two committee members who had a history of animosity. I could tell they did not like being in the same room as each other, let alone having to spend a series of meetings at the same table, discussing the titles of books. At one meeting, during a discussion concerning the choice of films, the disdain for each other spilled over, with some pointed and sharp words exchanged across the table. The group discussion stopped. The committee members gaped at what had just been said. Something about competence. A retort about the other's competence. A snarl. A responding snarl. Silence. This interruption had the potential to derail the meeting and the process. While both committee members felt (and displayed) their animosity freely and without embarrassment or hesitation, I needed both on the committee and, due to their expertise, needed them to be able to work together. They did not have to be friends – just muster enough tolerance to get through the task.

After the initial shock, the other committee members resumed the conversation. I stood up and walked around to the other side of the large meeting table to one of the committee members who had been involved in the tense exchange and quietly suggested that we get some water and have a chat. I was somewhat relieved that this request was accepted, and we moved to another part of the office, where I let her make a number of statements about the other committee member (that I am very glad that she had not made public in front of the committee). I filled a jug of water, and we sat for approximately 20 minutes while I listened and explained to her that we needed her (and her antagonist) for the text selection process. Both antagonists possessed the knowledge and skills required for the text selection, and in addition, I did not want her to resign and spark a controversy in the committee that would make its way out of the building into the networks of English teachers. We sat, I listened, she talked. I reassured, she calmed down. Eventually, we returned to the meeting while everyone pretended that nothing had happened. Later that day, I did the same with the other committee member. She had calmed down by then, and we were able to return to the meeting with the agreement that both would do their best for the selection process.

Power, politics and Australian literature

In 2008, the NSW education minister, John Della Bosca, decided that it would be a good idea to highlight the place of Australian literature in the NSW English curriculum. And to do this, the Board of Studies would consult with the community on the theme of 'strengthening the study of Australian literature'. I was bemused by this theme, and while I did not disagree with such an emphasis, there were already about a third of the 120 texts listed for study on the HSC list that were Australian. However, that was the request from the minister, and plans were developed to compile teacher responses from around the state. Over a series of 12 meetings in metropolitan and regional centres, my team and I met with teachers. Most of the meetings were quiet, and like me, the attendees were bemused at what appeared to be – in the words of one teacher – "a waste of time because there are plenty of Australian texts on the list".

The media picked up on the campaign, and I was interviewed on several radio stations across NSW. The task was quite simple:

[W]e have around a third of the HSC text list as Australian, including writers such as Tara June Winch, Gail Jones, Judith Wright, Patrick White but we are always looking for ways to make the list stronger and we are keen to hear what teachers have to say.

One of the radio interviews I did was with Adam Spencer on Sydney's ABC 702. At the time, I was in the Riverina region of NSW, undertaking a number of school inspections, and the interview was set for just after the 6:00 a.m. news the next day (Why do I always seem to score the early interviews? I asked myself). In preparation, one of the media officers phoned me on the day before the interview to plan how we would approach the questions we expected me to be asked. In these types of planning meetings, it is generally strategic to have three main points to emphasise in the interview and to do so at every opportunity. My three points were that just over one-third the HSC text list[9] is Australian texts; significant Australian authors such as Gwen Harwood, Henry Lawson and Tim Winton are listed; and that the list constitutes a 'robust' list of quality Australian literature.

On the morning of the interview, and after a restless night's sleep, I rose early and went over my notes and the list. I steadied myself as the phone in the room rang and the motel's receptionist announced that the ABC was on the line. Adam Spencer's producer introduced himself and let me know that I would be on air in a couple of minutes after the news. I waited as calmly as I could, and when I heard Adam on the line introducing me, I knew we had begun the interview. The questions indicated to me that he was not going to attempt a 'gotcha' question and that he was genuinely interested in what texts were currently on the list, what percentage were Australian and what was behind Della Bosca's directive.[10] I explained that the rough formula for selection was to ensure about one-third of the list came from Australian authors, with attention to the distribution of male and female authors as well as the representation of Indigenous, international and multicultural texts and authors.

My media colleagues had advised me not to repeat and question lead-ins that might be negative, such as "Some people have a negative view of the text list and say there aren't enough Aussie texts on the list", followed by my response, "There's no reason to have a negative view because . . ." and so on. Every chance I had, I would lead my answer with the names of Australian authors who appear on the list: "Banjo Paterson, Katherine Thomson, Rosemary Dobson and Raimond Gaita are just a few of the Australian authors". The interview went smoothly, and I even enjoyed it, though I did issue a sigh of relief when it was over. Not long afterwards, I received numerous phone calls from colleagues congratulating me; it seemed that more people listened to Adam Spencer than I had realised.

The power of bad press

In 2013, the *Sydney Morning Herald* was running a column called The Heckler, where readers could submit a piece about any topic that made their blood boil. In September that year, a satirical piece was published in which the author described the English syllabus as a "temple to deconstructionism"[11] in which its designers have managed to take the "passionate, poetic and inspirational and make its study pallid, plodding and soulless". The critique went on to assert that the English syllabus is "not devoted to truth, which is the only thing literature is good for". This raises many philosophical and esoteric questions about the role of literature and the nature and, in fact, existence of 'truth'. However, this book is about power in education, so we will leave these weighty topics for others to ponder.

The study of literature in schools is potentially controversial. Former Liberal Party Australian prime minister John Howard regularly issued condemnatory statements about the study of English, including the 'dumbing down' of English by "rubbish" postmodern literature.[12] Similarly, in 2006,[13] Howard described the syllabus as "incomprehensible sludge" and claimed the study of English was being "dumbed down" by postmodernism, announcing that it was "falling victim to postmodernism and political correctness".

Conservative commentators are very much in tune with what is on the text list and can manufacture bad press. Take, for example, Kevin Donnelly's *How Political Correctness Is Destroying Education and your child's future* (2019), which argues that the teaching of poetry "is central to education" (p. 153) and advocates the teaching of William Blake, Gerard Manley Hopkins, John Keats and other deceased white male poets in preference to female poets and those from diverse backgrounds.[14] His 2010 polemic in the conservative *Quadrant Online* periodical criticises the Australian curriculum and its promotion of the idea that textual study should recognise the contributions and value of texts from other cultures, stating, "[O]ne can envisage the situation where students experience ten years of school without any encounter with such seminal authors as Shakespeare, Swift, Dickens, Austen, Orwell, Lawson or Malouf."[15] In this particularly vitriolic piece, he labels the Australian curriculum's statements about the inclusion of Indigenous and Asian texts as "politically correct clap-trap" and unsubtly suggests that the curriculum has been driven by the "Balmain basket-weavers and Carlton latte set" of the Australian Labor Party.

School curricula, text selection and the inclusion of social issues in the school curriculum underline the fact that schools have "long been sites of political conflict because of their capacity for socialisation and social reproduction" (Collins, 2009, p. 33). And it appears that political conflict is more likely when conservative education commentators believe they have detected so-called left-wing or 'woke' sentiments in the school curriculum.

Notes

1 I was 15 years of age when I first read Norman Mailer's *The Naked and the Dead*, and although I enjoyed it, I found some of the contents disturbing. In 2016, I read another of Mailer's, *The Castle in the Forest*. I loved what I considered as the book's monstrous imagination, although it was another disturbing work.

2 A number of academics and English teachers were deeply concerned about this development.

3 In my view, the number of texts was not the problem: it was the complexity of the requirement of studying the texts through different theoretical 'lenses' such as 'Belonging' or 'Journeys'.

4 I agreed with Jones' position on this issue. On most other issues, I do not believe he and I would have agreed.

5 Disappointingly, the study of poetry remained optional. Students (or their teachers) had the choice between the study of poetry or film. I am sure we are able to predict the favoured choice of students and teachers.

6 The only HSC English course that does not prescribe texts is *English Studies* – teachers of this course choose the texts for study. I led the team that wrote this course, and the underlying principle was to develop a course that appealed to students for whom English was not their passion.

7 The summary of reforms led by McGaw can be accessed here: https://scpp.esrc.unimelb.edu.au/objects/reports/NSW-2005-ShapingtheirFuture1997.pdf

8 This imbalance is long-standing and controversial and reflects the ongoing debates about the 'literary canon' where (dead) white males dominate the list. While

attempts have been made to redress this imbalance, many would argue there is still a long way to go.

9 The HSC text list has approximately 130 texts.

10 The advice we had received in the office about this initiative was that the premier (Morris Iemma) had instructed government ministers to each come up with a 'good news story' for their respective portfolios. The Australian literature was Della Bosca's contribution.

11 *English syllabus an incomprehensible farce* (Fleming), *Sydney Morning Herald*, 23 September 2013, English syllabus an incomprehensible farce (smh.com.au). Deconstructionism is a theory of criticism (literature or film) that seeks to reveal deep-seated contradictions in a work by delving below its surface meaning.

12 *Academic denies the dumbing down of the English syllabus*, 1 January 2003: Academic denies the dumbing down of the English syllabus – CSU News. According to Farhan (2019), postmodernism "marked a radical shift in emphasis from Modernism and it became a visible happening in Literature, Art, Philosophy and Architecture. One of the things that characterize postmodernism is the breaking down of ground between high culture and low culture. Postmodernism is oriented towards the democratization of collective consciousness and also postmodernism signifies the triumph of individuality."

13 Gratton and Rood (2006), PM attacks 'dumb' English (theage.com.au).

14 While I do not disagree with Donnelly's argument regarding the importance of poetry, I argue that what we regard as a text has broadened in the past 40 years or so due to poststructuralist and postmodern influences on education and English teaching in particular.

15 Donnelly (2010), The Ideology of the National English Curriculum – *Quadrant Online*.

Analytical contemplation

Schools, power and books

Don Carter

In the previous chapter "Schools, power and books", I describe several scenarios where power and authority are being exercised in some way or another. In this analytical contemplation, the following key points are discussed:

- The power of books in relation to media controversies, text selection and the place of Australian literature in schools.
- Weber's tripartite power typology and schools.
- Curriculum and literature as mechanisms for cultural transmission.

Books can be controversial. From John Della Bosca's authority as an elected government minister to disputes in a book selection committee or the recount of a complaint from a parent about a novel promoting friendship and compassion, each scenario involves a complex network of social interactions and relationships shaped by context, self-identities, self-importance and regulatory practices.

This analytical contemplation analyses aspects of 'power and books'. To do this, I have undertaken a slightly more expansive approach by first exploring briefly the role of schools, followed by a discussion of some aspects of power directly related to schools – an area of research that has yielded valuable insights. I then use Max Weber's "tripartite theory of power" (Muller & Young, 2019, p. 7) as an interpretive lens to identify several key points about power and schools, followed by a brief discussion about the role of curriculum and literature in school-based education. I have approached the analytical contemplation in this way because the study of books in schools is shaped by wider social, historical and cultural values, as well as the individual contexts of schools, and as such, any analysis should attend to these wider contexts and specific values.

The role of schools

The role of schools in society is directly linked to larger questions about the purposes of education. When we look to the media, stories about schools and education are often limited to a small number of recurrent themes: public

DOI: 10.4324/9781003312451-8

versus private education, single-sex versus co-education schools, school fees, declining standards, teacher and teaching quality, school uniforms, spelling and grammar and the occasional scandal. However, there is very little debate and discussion about the purposes of education (Biesta, 2013; Ozoliņš, 2017; Reid, 2019; Webster, 2017; Winch, 1996; Young, 2013). This is an important point because if we do not engage in such debates, or fail to articulate what we see as the purposes of education, we become distracted about specific issues such as student test performance, and the issue itself becomes a substitute purpose of education. As Reid (2019) argues, "[I]n the absence of clearly articulated purposes, education can be shaped to serve – by design or default – particular interests or ideologies" (p. 168).

The evidence is that people care about education. In a comprehensive research project across several European countries, findings indicate that "citizens care deeply about education and therefore also about education policy reforms" (Busemeyer et al., 2020, p. 309).[1] Investing in education is seen as a necessary and desirable response to changing economic contexts (Bell, 1974; Drucker, 1993) and promotes economic growth (Hanushek & Woessmann, 2012), while the role of education and schools in maintaining social cohesion is also seen as important (Busemeyer, 2015; Solga, 2014). Education and schooling appear to loom large in the public consciousness, and as social institutions, schools reflect (and replicate) the values of the wider community.

The notion that schools reproduce the mores and values of society means that schools and their curricula do not exist independently of society (Apple, 2012; Hunter, 1987; Luke, 1991) and do not sit "outside of ideology, values and politics" (Giroux, 2020, p. 1). Both are socially constructed and constituted as part of wider social, political and historical relations of power, helping to shape students' views of the world and of themselves. The implementation of education policies act as the "apparatus of pastoral surveillance and moral training" (Hunter, 1987, p. 6) and monitor the ethical and moral development of young people. This constitutes the historical and current imperative of education systems.[2]

Schools and power

Schools are sites of power, and their hierarchical structures convey powerful messages to students about status, authority and legitimacy. Since the second half of the twentieth century, much work has been undertaken to identify the types of power and authority inherent within and applied in education systems, schools, and classrooms (Bidwell, 1970; Erickson, 1987; McDermott, 1974; Metz, 2003; Spady, 1974; Pace, 2003; Werthman, 1963). For example, Hurn (1985) argues the period from 1960 to 1980 marked a departure from traditional authority in schools and in society, generally. This shift was largely the result of the social and political upheavals of the 1960s, where all forms of authority were questioned and scrutinised and where demands for equal rights and an end to the Vietnam War were the centre of many protests and campaigns. Hurn also argues that because of these politically charged years, disciplinary procedures in schools were constrained, leading to a more relaxed school atmosphere.

Also significant in this era of education research were Silberman (1970) and Kohl (1967), both of whom promoted teacher authority as being centred on educational matters and professional expertise as the source of legitimacy: that is, the ability to educate young people. This involved granting students a degree of freedom of choice and the right to be informed of the reasons behind directives. Progressive educationalists were strongly influenced by the philosophy of John Dewey (1899, 1916, 1938, 1964), who advocated education based on developing curricula which recognise individual student interests and provide real-life experiences and pedagogical practices that encourage moral and intellectual autonomy as well as joint reflective inquiry. The progressives dismissed traditional authority because it restricted the "intellectual and moral autonomy" of students (Hurn, 1985, p. 45) and occasioned discrimination against students from diverse backgrounds. However, these approaches and analyses were (and continue to be) dependent on the degree of compliance from the students in the care of the school, its staff and the wider community. In the following section, I discuss the relevance of Weber's power typology in relation to how schools are organised and conducted.

Weber and power

Weber's definition of power and authority promotes *intention* as the individual's "will" (Clegg, 2019, p. 73) and *authority* as a "modality of power", where an individual or organisation asserts (or imposes) its will on others using specific resources such as the law and regulation (Weber, 1978, p. 133). Weber identifies three sources of authority, or what can be labelled as legitimation, to activate power: the traditional, the rational-legal and the charismatic. This "tripartite typology" (Guzmán, 2015, p. 73) provides the platform for a deeper understanding of power, authority and legitimacy.

First, traditional authority is intimately linked to the precedents passed down from the past and is closely bound to rules (Langlois, 1998). This type of authority is reminiscent of feudal lords, tribal chiefs and monarchs, anchored in customs and inherited traditions. Traditional authority appeals to stability and order and is impersonal and nonrational (Houghton, 2010). It establishes rule-following behaviour, where "repertoires of routines" (Nelson & Winter, 1982, p. 15) facilitate patterns of habitual behaviour and tacit skill-like knowledge. Traditional authority underpins bureaucracies, where "intellectually analysable rules" (Langlois, 1998) drive compliance and accountability measures as traditional authority's distinct modes of traditional action (Langlois, 1998, p. 318). Actors in bureaucracies often consider their status as "natural and inevitable" (p. 55) – a direct consequence of a shared belief in the authority of the rules that establish the basis of order and stability (and, possibly, inertia) within the specific bureaucratic structure. The traditional order within a bureaucracy also relies on regular activities to perpetuate the work of the bureaucratically governed structure, where the authority to issue commands stems from the coercive, physical or sacerdotal (p. 319).

Weber's second type of authority is the rational-legal, which is founded on laws, rules and power stemming from legitimate positions or office, thus activating the authority found in bureaucracies (Langlois, 1998). This authority is based on order and stability, rationality and logic and cultivates a devotion to rules and habits, particularly from actors who operate within bureaucratic structures and processes (Nelson & Winter, 1982, p. 15). The third type of authority is the charismatic. This is based on a leader's extraordinary personal characteristics that have the capacity to inspire others and has manifested at times in the form of religious leaders, military figures and political leadership (Langlois, 1998). Essentially, it is the opposite of rational bureaucratic authority and traditional authority and entails no hierarchy. The charismatic leader "preaches, creates, or demands new obligations" (Langlois, 1998, p. 8), engendering a "belief in the extraordinary quality of a specific person" (Matheson, 1987, p. 208) alongside a reverence for the "sanctity of . . . persons, groups or norms" (p. 208).

As Weber himself wrote, charismatic leadership is based on an "emotional form of communal relationship" (Weber, 1978, p. 360), where the leader "merely intervenes in general or in individual cases when he [sic] considers the members of his [sic] staff inadequate to a task to which they have been entrusted" (p. 361). Largely devoid of administrative branches of control, formally endorsed rules and legal principles and insights gleaned from precedent, decisions and judgements are based on individual cases and the leader's own personal wisdom or as "divine judgments and revelations" (p. 361). The charismatic organisation is often the antithesis of traditional or bureaucratic authority.[3] Where the latter constitutes forms of everyday routine control of action and is intricately linked to logically detectable rules, charismatic authority is irrational, in the sense of being unconnected to all rules. Traditional authority is an articulation of the precedents from the past and, as such, is also focused on rules. Charismatic authority, however, disavows the past and presents itself as a uniquely revolutionary force (Weber, 1978, pp. 361–362).

Schools and power resources

The authority of schools (and the legitimacy that flows from this authority) is based on Weber's second component of the tripartite typology: "rational-legal authority" (Houghton, 2010, p. 450). As noted earlier, this type of authority stems from the rules and laws and the power that emanates from a "legitimate position or office" (p. 450). Bureaucracies, particularly education bureaucracies, are examples of this type of authority, with their main aim being to provide stability and order. This is achieved through an emphasis on principles and processes based on agreement between actors, rationality and precedent (p. 450). Rational-legal authority affords individuals in higher positions in the bureaucratic hierarchy (or school) the right to issue commands and instructions and the resources to enforce compliance through the application of rewards or punishments.

While it is not uncommon for individual teachers or principals to exhibit aspects of charismatic leadership with their colleagues and students, teachers, in general, use rational-legal authority due to their position as 'leader', though they seldom use this type of authority by itself. This is one reason why I was able to address the parent's concerns about the novel the class was reading – I possessed the rational-legal authority as a head teacher to offer two options to the parent: study the book with the class, or study another text by himself outside. The parent did not challenge the options – she withdrew from the dialogue. Teachers (and school executives) are equipped with this type of authority, though the success and extent of its use vary according to school context, the willingness of students and school community to accept this authority and the willingness of staff to use it.[4]

In addition, teachers use another type of authority called "professional authority" (Blau, 1974; Parsons, 1947). This authority stems from the expertise required to achieve agreed aims and is characterised by teachers who possess a strong command of the subject matter and demonstrate high-order pedagogical skills. Several theorists have argued that this claim to legitimacy is most relevant for teachers because it highlights their capacity to achieve educational goals (Grant, 1988; Pace, 2003). As part of their daily work, teachers interpret and explain the major issues and current dilemmas, as well as representing and upholding the moral authority and order of the school and society. In general, they have access to a range of other resources at their disposal, including the dissemination or withholding of information, credibility and access to others in higher positions in the hierarchy, to name a few (Hardy & Clegg, 1999, p. 755).[5]

Curriculum as power

Power and authority reside not only with certain individuals and within organisations but also within structures and apparatuses. In education, one piece of apparatus is the school curriculum, which has been the focus of several theorists for the past 40 years or so (see Apple, 1997, 2012; Ball, 1990; Bourdieu, 1990; Foucault, 1981). Apple (1997), for example, argues that schooling has been used as a tool for the reproduction of power and control through the influence of the structures and practices of business and industry, which result in the perpetuation of inequality. More affluent parents, for example, who have the power to articulate, have access to material resources and are able to exert influence over the day-to-day activities of the school, which results in the "successful conversions of economic and social capital into cultural capital" (Apple, 2006, pp. 473–474). In Australia, an ongoing debate about school funding is linked to notions of advantage and disadvantage, where advocates of the government-funded public school system argue that funds provided to the private school sector bolster an already wealthy sector (Greenwell & Bonnor, 2022; Reid, 2019; Thompson et al., 2019).

The curriculum schools implement transmits powerful ideas, attitudes and values. No curriculum is value-free or ideologically neutral, and the curriculum implemented in schools is largely shaped by changes in work and across society, national and global economic trends and new technologies; while new uncertainties at local and international levels often provoke changes in thinking about curriculum (Priestley, 2011, p. 21), school curriculum acts as a sample of the knowledge and skills valued by the wider community. In addition, the academic knowledge reproduced in the school curriculum is different to 'everyday' knowledge because both stem from different systems of meanings (Bernstein, 2000). Academic knowledge is categorised through specific subject disciplines, which have distinctive parameters and language, clearly distinguishing themselves from other disciplines.

The power of literature as cultural transmission

In the state of New South Wales, Australia, the first literature syllabus for secondary school students was released in 1911. This syllabus – like all curricula and other individual syllabuses – was a product of its time (Carter, 2012). This syllabus was imbued with the "vestiges and inheritances" (Manuel & Carter, 2017, p. 91) of the era and conceptualised literature as the "sovereign instrument for self-formation" (Manuel & Carter, 2019, p. 228). It promoted the view that literature acts as a "civilising and moralising and nation-building force" and featured a "predominance of British canonical literature" (p. 91). The syllabus was framed as a means through which the values of the British Empire could be strengthened and extended in the colonial outpost of Australia, where the individual student embraces the "private and public responsibilities of adult age" as part of the development of mature "habits of thought and conduct" (1911, p. 1).

The syllabus included a list of (mostly male) English authors, including Chaucer, Shakespeare, Dickens, Holmes, Ruskin, Carlyle, Austen, Eliot, Gaskell, Alcott, Emerson, Addison, Burke, Kingsley, Stevenson, Bacon, Gibbon, Milton, Lamb, Coleridge, Shelley, Byron, Wordsworth, Kipling, Longfellow, Scott, Tennyson, Arnold and Lowell. It was, indeed, "a homage to the male writers of English canonical texts" (Carter, 2016, p. 44). The syllabus reveals the continuing ideological predisposition that only a certain type of literature, representing a particular set of "hegemonic assumptions" (Manuel & Carter, 2019, p. 231), is suitable for what the early twentieth century saw as the "refining and ennobling" (1911, p. 18) function of literary study in English.

Traditionally, the study of English and literature has long been a lightning rod for controversy. As Goodwyn (2001) observes:

> [S]ince its formation, subject English has been the centre of controversy . . . perceived by many as the most important subject in the school curriculum, it has been a barometer for the curricular weather systems surrounding it. . . . English has been more than part of larger changes in education and society: it has been the focus of those changes.
>
> (p. 149)

For many, the 'health' of education resides in the books listed for study in schools, with the book list a readymade indicator of what is happening in schools and society. These texts are also the means by which values and attitudes are transmitted to a younger generation. Are our children being taught wholesome values, or are they being taught by social activists, with 'leftist' leanings? Are they being provided with the opportunity to study the great works of literature? While controversies raised in the media often centre around students' poor grammar and spelling, contentious themes or issues in the books studied at school constitute another flashpoint for controversy. And these controversies are often played out in the arena of (social) media, with conservative commentators advocating a return to a more traditional approach involving formal examinations, direct teacher instruction on spelling and grammar and the inclusion of canonical literary texts in the curriculum.[6]

Whereas a text was once only regarded as a print medium artefact, the term now encompasses not only print but also digital, multimedia, visual and aural forms of communication. This shift in thinking is reflected in text lists from a series of jurisdictions, including Australian states and territories and internationally. In the Australian state of Victoria, the broadening of text types studied in the final year of schooling to include forms such as graphic novels and film (Bacalja & Bliss, 2019) reflects shifts in text lists from other states such as NSW. While the range of types of texts have broadened, all texts convey messages about social issues, the nature of society and the attitudes and behaviours of individuals and groups which are deemed acceptable or unacceptable (or somewhere in between).

The texts selected by committees were guided by policies to "foster values of inclusivity and diversity of culture and for texts that reflect these values in constructive and affirmative senses" (Bacalja & Bliss, 2019, p. 165). When I was working with the representative group that compiled the HSC text list, we were very aware that texts convey values. For example, we recommended that Mark Haddon's *The Curious Incident of the Dog in the Night-time* (Haddon, 2003) be included on the text list because its protagonist had an autism spectrum disorder and the committee believed that (apart from being a well-written book) it would promote the acceptance of 'difference' and diversity among its readers as well as heighten awareness of this condition. Another text that was recommended for study was the Australian SBS television series *Go Back to Where You Came From* (Special Broadcasting Service, 2011–2015), which followed six Australians who strongly opposed immigration to Australia, taking part in an experiment to live like refugees for 25 days. This choice was deliberate on two counts: first, the type of text is a television series, and the aim was to engage reluctant readers; and second, the series would provoke class discussions about compassion, tolerance and intercultural understanding. The committee regarded these texts to be powerful 'transmitters' of what we (the committee) considered as powerful values important to nurture in young people.

The power and authority to transmit cultural values was also at the forefront of my mind when I was leading the compilation of the *Suggested Texts for English Kindergarten to Year 10*, released in 2012, and included the "classics and successful teaching texts with innovative recent works (including) fiction as well as nonfiction, poetry, drama, film, media and multimedia texts" (Board of Studies, 2012, p. 1). The texts on this list were meticulously scrutinised to ensure they did not contain themes and issues potentially harmful or disturbing to the young reader. Any text that included sexual abuse, child abuse, gratuitous violence[7] and drug use was immediately jettisoned, though the tragedies of William Shakespeare were retained, as is the usual practice in all curriculum authorities in the Western world.

The sector representatives and teachers who were part of these two text selection groups were keen to be involved: these roles are coveted in the NSW English teaching profession because they are considered as roles that enable acquisition of 'inside information' and participation in the key function of texts to be studied in all schools across the state as part of a "body of literary works traditionally regarded as the most important, significant and worthy of study" (Dolin et al., 2017, p. 5). While the occasional dispute between committee members temporarily interrupted the process, the selection of texts was considered by the participants as a powerful role, an important role for schools and students across New South Wales.

Conclusion

There appears to be an inherent understanding in the community that texts are powerful transmitters of cultural values. What authors and titles should be included (or excluded) in a curriculum's reading list remain potent media stories, attracting a good deal of public comment. That texts transmit values is very much apparent in the United States at the moment, where specific texts have been banned from school lists in the state of Florida. While these texts (allegedly) cover issues such as gender and sexuality, the United States has a long history of book banning, with *The Grapes of Wrath*, by John Steinbeck; *The Catcher in the Rye*, by JD Salinger; and *To Kill a Mockingbird*, by Harper Lee, all having being banned or at least challenged by school or religious authorities in the past. And all have been staple titles in NSW schools for decades.

Notes

1 This large-scale research was undertaken in the Western European countries of Germany, England, Sweden and Spain.
2 In Australia, the goals of education are outlined in *The Alice Springs (Mparntwe) Education Declaration* (2019), which highlights the importance of the moral development of students (p. 2) and the capacity for students to "act with moral and ethical integrity" (p. 8).
3 The Jonestown mass murders-suicides in 1978 could be argued as constituting charismatic leadership, imposing a perverted version of traditional authoritarian leadership.
4 Over the years, Don has wondered how the mother felt after the encounter and how she wrestled with her decision – an important one for her, with its spiritual implications.
5 Hardy & Clegg's reference relates to individuals who do not occupy executive positions, not specifically teachers.
6 This phenomenon is not limited to one country. See Austin and Selleck (1975); Bliss and Bacalja (2021); Dolin et al. (2017); George and Shoffner (2022); Marshall (2014); McGaw (2005); Poulson (1998).
7 The issue of violence in texts is always tricky, when considering the violence in Shakespearean tragedies and staples of the English curriculum, such as *Lord of the Flies* and *Heart of Darkness*.

Chapter 6

Being an education leader and acting like a dictator doesn't work

Adrian Piccoli

Telling people what to do in education isn't an exercise of power; it is an exercise in futility.

Education is fundamentally the unpredictable art of human interaction. It is about people working with people. Adults connecting with adults, adults connecting with children. It works best at every level, from the boardroom to the classroom when there are the highest levels of common understanding, trust, respect and human connection. True and effective power in education is a currency that has to be earned, whether you are a minister or a schoolteacher.

The trick to achieving both is understanding the difference between having power and having authority and then using both effectively and not wasting or eroding either. Knowing when to use either or both is the delicate art of politics. It took me a while to figure this out.

In education, having power is not enough. You must build authority. All ministers have the hard power that comes with their office. Sworn into office, they have legal powers granted to the minister by various Acts of Parliament,[1] which include the power to introduce new policy into the department.

But this is not the real power ministers need to make change. The true power for any education leader is that which they generate through relationships, the development of trust and, ultimately, by making the right decisions and by explaining the rationale for those decisions well.

Not everyone is going to agree with every decision that gets made, but if there is a clear rationale, based on sound information and sound advice, then even the sceptics have trouble criticising those decisions. Nothing creates power more directly than success and by being right. True power must be earned through trusting relationships with those who have to put into practice the decisions you have made as a leader. And that trust must be earned.

Liberal/Nationals coalition governments do not historically have a positive relationship with the public sector. In education, particularly, there is a long history of very sour relationships between public sector teachers' unions and ministers. Some previous Liberal/Nationals ministers such as the Hon Terry Metherell, a former Liberal Party minister in NSW, clashed ferociously with teachers.[2]

DOI: 10.4324/9781003312451-9

The great advantage I had was that I had no idea what was expected of me. I came from a farming family in rural NSW and had no history of working for governments or for ministers. I had no preconceptions about what my relationships should be, who I should be close to or who I should keep my distance from. I simply believed in listening to everyone and then making up my own mind. To a certain degree, it meant I was naive about many things to do with education, but it also meant I did not come to the role with any preconceived ideas or ingrained prejudices or any axes to grind. Listening to people in education who were doing the work on the front line just seemed to be good manners and common sense.

The other type of minister is the one who comes to office believing they have all the answers. They invent policy out of their office because they think it will play well in the media or with their own stakeholders whom they are trying to impress or appease. I have always thought that the greatest danger to good education policy is the media release. Many failures in education policy have originated out of a minister's office writing a press release first, focusing on the political win from an announcement, and then working out the policy implementation and ramifications later.

I did not realise this until quite some time after I became a minister. The difference between power and authority is not very clear when you have not experienced genuine power. Most of us have not. As a minister, administering a multibillion-dollar budget and having legislative powers to make decisions that have a real impact on people's lives is genuine power. But just exercising power by making decisions and forcing change on people because the law says you can is not enough in education.

I had been forewarned a year or so before I became the NSW minister for education that the only way to effectively make change in education was to work hard to build relationships. You cannot buy or build authority; you can only earn it through relationships.

Having the opportunity to spend two years as a shadow minister for education before being appointed minister gave me a long lead-in time to develop relationships and understand the portfolio. Gary Zadkovich, a deputy president of the NSW Teachers Federation, gave me some very sage advice more than a year before I became the minister. He told me, "The only way you can achieve effective reform in education is if teachers trust you. Otherwise, you can make all kinds of pronouncements and release all kinds of glossy policy documents but if there is no buy-in by teachers then they will put it all in the bottom drawer and won't implement any of it. You will be wasting your time!"

I took Gary's advice and adhered to it as much as I could. I worked on learning about schools, teachers, children and their parents. I understood the power of authority – that people trust what you are saying, that they trust you are acting in their best interests and that they can see from what you are doing, not just saying, that you have listened to them. I worked harder at building and understanding authority than I did building and understanding the hard power I had as a minister.

Challenge the political status quo to source accurate advice

I also challenged those preconceived ideas about who is on whose 'side' in politics. I always winced when I heard people talk about our political 'base'. The base in politics is that 30 per cent of people (it was 40 per cent 20 years ago) are ideologically locked into one of the two major governing parties in Australian politics (the Labor Party or the Liberal/Nationals Party coalition). I never understood when people would tell me we have to do the wrong thing in order to satisfy our base. I would always argue first that it is the wrong thing to do. Second, political history proves that political parties who pander to their base get successfully voted into opposition every time. Of course, any government needs at least 50 per cent of the seats in Parliament, not votes, to govern, so we needed the base plus most of the middle. There was plenty of 'middle' to be gained in education – if we did things the right way and explained it well.

No one really trusted the NSW Liberals and Nationals in education, especially not in public education. I set about trying to change that. Not by what we did. Most of what we did was consistent with our political values of trusting the power of individuals,[3,4] rewarding effort, being financially responsible and having strong accountabilities in place.

What I did was to interact with the primary and secondary principals' associations, Catholic and independent schools systems and the NSW Teachers Federation from the very beginning. They had much to offer. Senior union members visited my electorate while I was in opposition, and I have had some visit my home to meet my family. Over time, we came to know each other very well. But most of all, I visited schools, I talked to teachers, I talked to principals and I listened to what they said they needed. And we delivered. It made me realise that knowledge and understanding of both your friends and your opponents is at the core of generating the power to change education.

While I cultivated relationships with all of the key players in education, I understood that the NSW Teachers Federation required special attention. It has been historically very powerful and very militant and not usually on good terms with education ministers. Especially not Liberal/Nationals ministers. But as Abraham Lincoln asked, "Do I not destroy my enemies when I make them my friends?"

I also believed that the government and the unions could agree on 90 per cent of what was needed to be done in education, so I thought, why not work on that together? We had a shared interest in improving the education of students in our care. We were never going to agree on how much wages should increase or some other industrial issues, so I suggested we set those issues aside and battle those out when we need to. I set about understanding the unions and identifying their strengths. I sought to understand the pressures their leaders were under from their own membership. I recognised that like me, their leaders were elected representatives. I worked to understand the history of their organisations, why they had such poor relationships with some earlier education ministers and the changing nature of their membership. I soon learnt that there were divisions in their organisations, like political parties, and often, governments.

What I did learn from the very beginning was to identify what we agreed on and to clearly define the issues on which we disagreed. In my discussions with the teachers' unions, we agreed that we would work together on the issues where there was mutual agreement and confine our disputes to matters that divided us. And most importantly, we would not let these two things interfere with each other, lest they interfered with our respective roles in providing quality education for children in NSW.

The NSW Department of Education: a snapshot

The NSW Department of Education is one of the largest single education systems in the world and one of the largest single employers in Australia. Countries like the United States, Canada and the United Kingdom have quite devolved public education systems, most often run by local school boards. These school boards operate and manage their schools. They can range in size from a handful of schools up to several hundred schools. The NSW Department of Education, by contrast, is a single organisation with 2,200 schools and more than 60,000 full-time equivalent teachers. While the NSW government operates 2,200 public schools through the NSW Department of Education, the government is also the regulatory authority for 594[5] Catholic schools and 460[6] independent schools plus public schools through the NSW Education Standards Authority (NESA). NESA is the government authority that develops and publishes the NSW school curriculum as well as registers and accredits all teachers in NSW.

I regularly insisted to my office and the department that we involve the unions in those matters of education reform we both agreed were important. Again, the department would often second-guess me on this because of their own historic, often negative, relationship with the teachers' unions. I insisted they leave the politics up to me and simply provide me with the best possible advice and consult everyone – including the unions. The department's role was to give me their best frank and fearless education advice. It was then my role to put a political lens over that advice. I understood from Australian and international experience that unions working against the government can sink reforms, and I was keen to make sure that didn't happen.

Teachers' unions also have their own political element to them. Senior executives of the NSW teachers' union are elected by members, so there is pressure on them to perform in a political way. That is, they sometimes feel compelled to protest about what the government is doing. That protest can be in the form of media criticism and/or large-scale strikes and protests. However, teachers' unions working cooperatively with the government are not necessarily in the political interests of the union. Sometimes, the pressure is for the union to be more aggressive with the government to show their members that they are tough.

I understood the need for the unions to create a public perception about how they deal with the minister for education. But I knew that behind closed doors we could still work together. Four or five times a year, I would arrange an off-the-record breakfast with union senior executives to discuss ongoing issues and to gauge their support for some of my ideas. Our trust levels were very high. I provided them with involvement and trust in decision-making, to which they had never previously had access.

In the second year of the Gonski funding reforms, the department had provided advice to me about how much additional unallocated money was available for the following year. Together with the department, we had to decide how that money would be spent. Would it be distributed to schools, or should we target some of the funding to specific areas of need?

So I asked the NSW Teachers Federation a question few ministers have ever put to them. "How would you recommend I spend $80 million next year?" I don't think the union ever expected that level of transparency and trust from a minister, especially not a National Party one. In the end, they made very constructive suggestions about how best to use that money, and given that it triangulated with other advice we were receiving, we implemented it. We allowed the union to be part of the decision-making, something I am very proud of to this day. We threw off the traditional adversarial relationship in the best interests of children.

I was often heavily criticised by MPs in my own party, powerful conservative media and their commentators because I had a constructive relationship with the unions and other public education stakeholders.

For example, on 29 September 2016, *The Daily Telegraph* ran an opinion piece, titled "Piccoli Launches a War on Parents". The article was critical of my support for a more equitable funding system that funded schools based on the needs of their individual students. The article suggested that I was disrespectful to parents who sent their children to nongovernment schools, as if somehow fairer funding for disadvantaged children denied parents the right to choose where their children went to school.

If I ever did anything that ran contrary to what was seen as conservative ideology, I was immediately labelled a captive of the union. If I sought to give more money to public schools through the Gonski school funding reforms, if I sought to support the work of teachers, principals and school executives by providing them with more time, I was condemned. If I opposed silly, superficial, failed free-market policies, imported from the United States and the United Kingdom, I was condemned. It never bothered me. They were wrong, and I was right.

While at the time it can be very difficult and emotionally draining to deal with this kind of very public criticism, it is important to stay true to your values and trust that good people will stand by you. Bearing in mind the criticism I had endured over the years; I made the point very clear in my final speech to Parliament about at least one way to measure your success as an education minister:

> Measure your success by your enemies and by who your friends are. I list my enemies as Alan Jones, Miranda Devine, Mark Latham and Ray Hadley. But I name my friends as Deirdre Kennedy from Walgett, an Aboriginal lady who taught my children how to make johnnycakes; Thomas George, the member for Lismore with whom I came into Parliament 19 years ago; Phyllis Jones, a truckie from Hay; Jude Hayman, the principal of Griffith Public School; David Gonski; Bishop Peter Comensoli; Labor MP Jihad Dib, whom I have had the pleasure of getting to know; Ben Denkant, who is a timber cutter from Mathoura; Henry Rajendra, a union organiser in Western Sydney. . . . I tell you that I will put my friends up any day against the enemies I have made over my period in Parliament.
> Parliament of NSW Hansard, 13 September 2017

I stayed strong on doing the right thing, and that gave me enormous power to do even more. What the critics didn't understand is what we were achieving together was much more than what we could have achieved under the old rules. We moved the industrial landscape more significantly working together than had we been at odds with each other. We improved the power of principals to improve teaching standards and to remove underperforming teachers from the profession. We even introduced a dress code for teachers, all with the support of the Teachers Federation because we worked closely with them, and we understood each other. It was also in the interest of public school stakeholders to maintain and nurture this positive relationship. At times when the union could have made my life very difficult politically because of problems within the department, they let the opportunity pass.

On one occasion when there were major issues with a new IT system being rolled out to schools, I was made aware that the Greens[7] and the Teachers Federation had agreed not to publicly criticise me because they did not want to give the conservative ideologues an excuse to pressure me out of the ministry. I'm in no way suggesting they liked everything I did, or even most things I did. They certainly preferred the devil they knew. Having said that, on several occasions, the federation strongly criticised me and the government for decisions we had made and policies we had introduced as they should. I just tried to keep it to a minimum by consulting with them and including them in the decision-making. It just seemed like common courtesy and good politics. Plus, I actually liked the people in the union I was dealing with. They really cared about students.

All this matters because it allowed me to make decisions that I deemed to be in the best interest of students and schools ahead of the perceived interests of unions, media or even my own party. My colleagues who were sceptical at first soon started to see that good policy was becoming good politics.

Just prior to the following election, one of my Liberal Party colleagues approached me in Parliament and said how he always thought I was crazy. He thought from the day we came into government that we should just be 'smashing' the union because that's 'just what Liberal/Nationals governments do'. He said for three years he had wondered why I had not done this, and he had thought I was wrong. He now saw that I was right about not just the policy but also the politics. He told me how he now loves visiting public schools. He can go and visit his local schools and is welcomed with open arms by the principal and by teachers. They praised him for the reforms and changes that the government was introducing. He told me that he was wrong, and I was right, and leading up to an election, he was very pleased to have been wrong.

Notes

1 https://sef.psc.nsw.gov.au/understanding-the-sector/westminster-system
2 https://trove.nla.gov.au/newspaper/article/122299149/12994167
3 www.liberal.org.au/our-beliefs
4 https://nationals.org.au/about/what-we-stand-for/
5 *Australian Catholic Education Statistics 2022*, National Catholic Education Commission.   https//:Australian-Catholic-Education-Statistical-Report-2022.pdf (ncec.catholic.edu.au)
6 *Compare schools: Association of Independent Schools of NSW.* https://schoolcompare. com.au/independentschoolsnsw/
7 The Greens are a left-of-centre political party in NSW and at the federal level.

Analytical contemplation

Being an education leader and acting like a dictator doesn't work

Don Carter

In this analytical contemplation, the following points are covered:

- The origins of 'soft power' as a concept related to international relations and its applicability in education.
- Soft power resources: persuasion, strategic narrative, credibility, attraction. How the accumulation of these resources enhances power and authority.

In the previous chapter, Adrian refers to the use of 'soft power' as a means to achieve his goals. We all recognise this term and have probably used it in conversation to explain how and why an event happened and who exerted such power. Although this term is often used in diplomacy and international relations, it is applicable to us when we examine relationships and wielding of power in education. According to Nye (2008), soft power is a type of constructive engagement and "rests on the ability to shape the preferences of others" (p. 95). It is associated with "assets such as attractive personality, culture, political values, institutions, and policies that are seen as legitimate or having moral authority" (p. 95). Soft power is a complex idea (Durrani, 2023, p. 2) and has been used in various ways and, at times, finds itself "stretched and twisted" (Nye, 2006, p. 140). However, what we can say with a degree of certainty is that the use of soft power does not draw on coercion or force but utilises irresistible narratives and credible and attractive reputations and builds collaborative networks (Durrani, 2023; McClory, 2015).

The notion of soft power came to prominence towards the end of the Cold War (Nye, 1990), where it became a core idea underpinning international diplomacy and a method to help explain why the West prevailed in the Cold War and Soviet Russia failed so badly (Cull, 2022). The application of soft power in this era saw countries using it as a kind of cultural influence to promote their national image as a 'brand' (p. 409). This type of cultural influence involved the rise of cultural institutes, an increase in partnerships and exchanges, the use of international broadcasting and, in the United States, the funding of the Fulbright scholarship programme and the "multifaceted global infrastructure of the United States Information Agency" (p. 409). The

DOI: 10.4324/9781003312451-10

employment of soft power has also been evident through the use of sport[1] to achieve political, social and financial goals (Dubinski, 2019) and even through the role of libraries via their promotion of scholarly and grey literature (Bell, 2022). In the broader sense of the term, soft power is "synonymous with non-military power and includes both cultural power and economic strength" (Vuving, 2009, p. 3).

An important consideration is to shed light on how power is exerted through the use of what are called soft power 'resources'. In fact, power cannot be exercised without the use of resources, and sometimes, these resources are not necessarily tangible (Vuving, 2009). Take, for example, a wink from one person to another in a sign of friendship, as an attempt to exercise soft power. In this attempt, the resource is the eye and the movement of muscles that activate a facial expression we label a wink.[2] A further example is when an individual pays attention to another individual and, as a result, wields a degree of soft power over this other individual, which might then manifest itself in some tangible activities (Vuving, 2009, p. 4). While the example of winking as an example of soft power might seem trivial, our point is that in all human interactions, a range of verbal and paralinguistic (nonverbal) resources are at the disposal of the actors involved.

In the following sections, I argue that by combining a set of soft power resources, it is possible to generate a kind of 'attractiveness' or 'attraction' between participants that then facilitates consensus and alignment between those participants. The key resources I discuss are strategic narratives, issues narratives, persuasion and credibility, which together constitute a formidable arsenal of soft power resources. This combination in turn generates a condition called 'attractiveness', which manifests when actors interact. The condition of 'attractiveness' is more complex than the qualities of Weber's charismatic leader and points to a more sophisticated and complex amalgam of resources than mere attraction to another's arguments or personality. And Adrian's recount provides a readymade set of examples of how the utilisation of these resources can be employed.

Strategic narrative as a soft power resource

We all know how tricky and sometimes laborious it can be to convince someone of the worth of our argument. Establishing yourself with others takes time and effort, and as Adrian points out, you cannot "buy authority, you have to earn it". When faced with the task of persuading others, many of us have experienced mentally rehearsing a point of view before the actual discussion and have experienced having to quickly amend and readjust this argument as we interact with the other party in our attempt to convince them. What we do not always realise is that in these attempts, we are using a range of resources to persuade the other party, and one such resource is strategic narrative (Roselle et al., 2014, p. 74).

The use of narrative is as old as history itself. Narratives have played a central role across cultures throughout history and have various functions, including explaining histories and passing down traditions and practices to the next generation. Barbara Hardy's evocative quote "[F]or we dream in narrative, daydream in narrative, remember, anticipate, hope, despair, doubt, plan, revise, criticise, construct, gossip, learn, hate, and love by narrative" (1968, p. 5) captures the centrality of narrative for us all. Narratives tell us about ourselves and about others and their interactions with us and each other. Narratives are developed over time and provide insights into the 'life journeys' of others, what was bound up in their past, what might happen currently and what fate might lie in wait for them (and us).

What we may not realise is that narrative is a soft power resource. And the strategic use of a narrative can be valuable in our interactions with others as a vehicle for the skilful deployment of our ideas, which can in turn be attractive to the pre-existing ideas and values of another person or group. Strategic narratives have been used extensively in international relations (Barthwal-Datta, 2015; Schmitt, 2018) and usually depict the storyteller as the 'hero', and the 'other' is often cast as the rival or sometimes as a collaborator (Chaban et al., 2019, p. 237). One long-running example is the ongoing Russian strategic narrative (Schmitt (2018, p. 497), which has retained cohesiveness and currency over a sustained period of time. Here, the strategic narrative identifies the "good guys" (Russia) and the "bad guys" (the West) (p. 497). This 'plot/storyline' assembles the major events of Russian history as an easily plausible and understandable story against the imperialistic aims of the capitalist West that are designed to embarrass and weaken Russia. The time period for this story involves (according to the Russian account) ongoing Western aggression since at least the 1990s (time), and its context (setting) is the geopolitical context of a "worldwide war for supremacy and occurs in several locations simultaneously" (p. 498). And as Schmitt (2018) points out, the Russian version of this strategic narrative involves more specific settings, including Ukraine, Georgia and Syria, in restatements of the alleged decades-long Western attempt to undermine Russia (p. 498).

In the field of education, strategic narrative plays a key role in the presentation of lines of argument. We can see aspects of strategic narratives in Adrian's recount, particularly his recount of interactions with the NSW Teachers Federation. Traditionally, as Adrian points out, conservative governments and their education ministers have been enmeshed in fraught encounters with the union. And traditionally, the union membership has largely been satisfied to continue in this way. If we consider this relationship in light of specific narrative elements such as characters or actors, setting/environment, conflict or action and resolution (Roselle et al., 2014), we can see parallels:

- Actors/characters – Adrian and union officials/union members (heroes and villains).
- Plot/storyline – ongoing negotiation, traditionally in disagreement.

- Setting – education in general (school funding, teacher pay and conditions, quality learning).
- Conflict – disagreement with the above issues.
- Resolution – elusive, ongoing disagreement, in general.

But it is a little more complex than this because in his quest to secure agreement with the union, Adrian employed a key approach of the strategic narrative – what is called "Issues Narrative" (Rosella et al., 2014, p. 76). This strategy involves an actor explaining why a policy is needed and desirable and what will be required for its implementation and success. As Roselle et al. (2014) explain, issues narratives contextualise government action, highlighting the important actors and identifying and defining the specific issue and how a set of specific actions will resolve the challenge or issue (p. 76). By emphasising a specific issue or issues, such matters can be considered from a "variety of perspectives and be construed as having implications for multiple values or considerations" (Chong & Druckman, 2007, p. 104). By concentrating on a 'reframing' of an issue, actors can develop a "particular conceptualisation of an issue or reorient their thinking about an issue" (p. 104).

What Adrian was able to do was reorient the attention (and opinions) of union officials to the issues upon which all parties agreed. In doing so, he relied on clear and accurate advice from the Department of Education and constructed strategic narratives in which the 'good guys' were the minister, his office and the union. He created a context in which he 'recast' the traditional adversarial roles to new roles which positioned children in classrooms as the 'winners' and both he and the union could accept credit for doing so. Adrian found common ground between the parties, reconstructing and reshaping participant identities, characterisations, reputations and expectations to turn the interactions into cooperative ventures. When he writes about the NSW Teachers Federation that "I also believed that the government and unions agree on 90% of what needed to be done. . . . [W]e shared an interest in improving the education of students", he is able to tap into the values of the stakeholders, and when he notes that "knowledge and understanding of both your friends and your opponents is at the core of generating the power to change education", he is pointing out the alignment of his values and goals at one level with those of the stakeholders – an exercise which builds the "attractiveness" related to the "fulfilment of needs" (Roselle et al., 2014, p. 72) for all parties.

Here, Adrian was, in fact, " 'formulator' and 'projector' of certain strategic narratives" (Roselle et al., 2014, p. 72), and largely because the recipients of strategic narratives are in control of their own "agency, intentions and motivations" (Chaban et al., 2019, p. 238), the results of the interactions were positive, which was important for the public image of both parties. And this positive public perception is a key goal in the use of strategic narrative (Miskimmon et al., 2013, p. 8).

Adrian's relationship with stakeholders was developed over a two-year period when he was opposition spokesman for education and then in his tenure as minister from 2011 to 2017, and he was able to recruit the support of others and establish himself as someone with integrity and good intentions. I do not write these things to aggrandise Adrian or his work as education minister – I point out that his concerted work in developing positive relationships partly relied on the use of strategic narrative.

The 'life-cycle' of a strategic narrative that is anchored in the promotion of a quality education for all children is potentially durable due to its positive and irresistible sentiment. It would only be the most foolish and naive actor who would openly campaign against such a goal.

Credibility as a soft power resource

Credibility, as a soft power resource, is essential and is closely linked to believability. As a concept, credibility has a long history dating back to the ancient Greeks and is partly about keeping a promise (Teles Fazendeiro, 2021). In recent times, there has been a renewed interest in the concept, sparked by the election of Donald Trump[3] as president of the United States (2017–2021) and the ensuing controversies concerning our so-called 'post-truth' era, where terms such as " 'news,' 'fake news,' 'alternative facts,' 'bots,' 'spin,' and 'click bait'" are hotly debated (Self & Roberts, 2019, p. 435). The word 'credibility'[4] has been defined as "believability, trust, perceived reliability, liking, similar concepts, and combinations of them" (p. 435) and works towards establishing "mutually understandable roles" (Teles Fazendeiro, 2021, p. 300). However, we need to understand that credibility is not an "objective" credibility, in that benchmarks of credibility may vary according to the audience and that credibility can be challenged (Cash & Belloy, 2020).

This potential variation in what constitutes 'credibility' in the eyes of the individual sets apart Adrian's successes in developing believability and reliability with stakeholders. And I say this because as Adrian noted earlier, it was rare that a Liberal/Nationals minister would directly consult with teachers' unions, let alone seek advice on how funding should be allocated. It is also remarkable that Adrian and the Teachers Federation were able to agree to occasionally engage in a public media brawl when, in fact, it was to pacify the conservative elements of the media who were highly critical of Adrian's close liaison with the unions. This also points to the trust Adrian was also able to engender with stakeholders and how the transfer of trust to another reduces complexity for the bestower and potentially provides authority and power for the trustee. Adrian's work with stakeholders is also an example of what is called "altercasting" (Teles Fazendeiro, 2021, p. 301), which is the process by which a person engages in 'self-presentation', whereby they present themselves to the world in a way that engenders support and cooperation. Here, Adrian had worked hard to develop trust with stakeholders over many months and, in doing so, would have utilised a suite of 'performance cues' to elicit positive responses from the other parties. These include verbal and nonverbal cues which seek to encourage a "role 'complementary' to one's own" (p. 301), which are linked to "performance – persuasion, pressure and public posturing" (p. 301).

Adrian was able to undertake this kind of 'performance' because he had identified the values, norms and ideas which motivated the actions and views of the different stakeholders. He knew that the teachers' unions were driven by an agenda to improve pay and conditions for teachers as well as ensuring the provision of a quality curriculum for students. In his interactions with stakeholders, Adrian (like all those engaged in negotiations) undertook a "performative endeavour" (Teles Fazendeiro, 2021, p. 302), where the importance of working towards a "coherent sense of self in relation to others" (p. 302) allows the other parties to construct a coherent view of the presenter – that is, Adrian. By working with stakeholders over a concerted period of time and building this consistent person, Adrian was able to "diffuse uncertainty" (p. 305) in the minds of the other parties and establish and maintain positive working relationships. He had established not only credibility with stakeholders but also public credibility.

Persuasion as a soft power resource

A key soft power resource is persuasion (Habermas, 1990). This resource has the capacity to activate cooperation, agreement and improved social relations within and across networks, communities and more broadly. Persuasion as a practice best finds expression in the utilisation of argument, where participants are driven by the presentation of facts and evidence, often based on logic and reason to reveal (in the eyes of the presenter) the 'truth'. Earlier, I mentioned how Adrian's arguments were based on advice from the department. In Adrian's exchanges with stakeholders, we need to remind ourselves that the participants in these exchanges "share a common lifeworld" (Mattern, 2005, p. 595), where common (educational) values are generally shared, making listening, debate and argument possible, and therefore, when the participants engage in discussion and debate, they do so from a position of mutual legitimacy – that is, they recognise the professional histories, a shared language and the associated credibility of the other, making robust interactions possible.[5]

However, persuasion as a resource does not merely rely on argument to be effective. And while it may appear an obvious point to make, *how* a participant expresses themselves is an important consideration. To be persuasive, the coherence of the speaker's linguistic representation of ideas is crucial. While the content of the speaker's presentation is important, the *form* in which it is presented is equally important in building resonance with other participants. To be persuasive, the speaker is required to craft words and sentences into a coherent and compelling account, which can take a number of forms to be presented to the other participants. These forms might include bargaining, presenting a persuasive argument, offering a "negotiable proposition" (Mattern, 2005, p. 598), presenting a literary device such as a metaphor or issuing a "direct challenge" (p. 598), for example. The choice of form is important, although it may not be a conscious choice by the speaker but, rather, a spontaneous choice according to the specific context of the interactions. However, what is required in all contexts is that the speaker accumulate the necessary evidence that will persuade the other participants that the speaker's representation is, in fact, reality (p. 601). The choice of form is an important component of the strategic narrative and its persuasive impact.

Attraction as a soft power resource

We saw in Adrian's chapter his attempts with different stakeholders to find 'common ground'. As mentioned earlier, he knew that there existed commonalities between his agenda and the agenda of the teachers' unions. Adrian well realised that, traditionally, his 'side' of politics – the conservative side – had "not usually been on good terms" with teachers' unions. He also knew that the leadership of the principals' councils had similar goals to his own programme of reform, so he sought to reduce possible tensions between himself and these organisations by creating what is called an "amenable milieu" (Nye, 2011, p. 97). This meant that he worked to establish an environment where the key players were able to communicate openly and honestly. It was an environment where ideas could be discussed and debated, where the traditional political and industrial biases and behaviours were put to the side and a shared programme of initiatives was prioritised.

This situation reflects the proposition that soft power harnesses 'attraction', where agreement between parties is established by something more than rational argument. The irresistibility of an argument or position can be successfully conveyed through a conflation of culture, values and policies (Nye, 2009), presenting that argument or position as both rational and affective, or, to put it another way, to engage both the intellect and feelings of some or all the actors involved. The 'attractiveness' of an argument can be detected where the collective needs and desires of a group are reflected in that argument. For example, the values and goals of a pro-democratic activist group which promotes human rights, the right to protest and free and fair elections potentially provide 'attractiveness' to other organisations and individuals wedded to similar ideals, regardless of the diverse causes that they might be espousing (Roselle et al., 2014).

We can see this at work in Adrian's chapter. While Arquilla and Ronfeldt (2001) assert the importance of "whose story wins" (p. 328), what we see in Adrian's recount is more a case of the coalescence of synonymous and aligning stories. Adrian was able to create consensus around shared meaning[6] – that is, he identified the commonalities in the reform agendas of key stakeholder groups, particularly the teachers' unions and principals' councils. When we look specifically at the central goals and aims of the actors in this chapter, we can identify certain goals that are common to all. Take, for example, the NSW Teachers Federation, which declares in its vision statement that it seeks to maintain a "strong public education system with a well-qualified and supported teaching profession, free from political interference" (NSWTF, n.d.). The Independent Education Union similarly announces to its members that it works "to achieve regular improvements to pay and conditions, by using your (i.e., the members') collective voice to ensure you are heard on education policy" (IEU, n.d.).

These interactions are examples of soft power, where common goals are identified and the 'needs' of those involved are largely satisfied. The aspirations of stakeholders were acknowledged by Adrian, and together, all parties were able to make progress on many issues. And while this type of interaction can produce positive outcomes to the agreement of all parties, there is always some risk present for all involved. This risk is called "representational force" (Mattern, 2005), which is a "coercive form of power that is exercised through language" (p. 583). What I mean here is that this type of force is manifested through the structure of a speaker's use of language in the way they represent 'reality'. This is not the use of physical force; it is the use of language to manipulate another actor to think and behave in a manner that satisfies the goals of the other party. The representational force threatens the 'self' of the other party – it threatens the other party's own self-view, its self-identity, through adroit and manipulative use of language. It threatens to expose or re-create the public persona of the actor in ways that they consider as inconsistent with the ways in which they have previously presented themselves publicly. The use of representational force is always available to the actors involved and was indeed available to Adrian and to the key stakeholders with whom he was negotiating, had they chosen to use it.

Both Adrian and the other stakeholders had well-established public 'images' created through statements, announcements and specific actions and behaviours. The 'mission statements' of the teachers' unions and the principals' councils all pronounce their commitment to quality education. For example, the NSW Primary Principals' Council states that "the NSWPPA has been instrumental in shaping a better public school system for primary students in New South Wales" (New South Wales Primary Principals Association, n.d.), while the NSW Secondary Principals' Council similarly announces that "our commitment is ultimately to enhance learning, teaching and outcomes for every student with whom principals and schools work" (NSW Secondary Principals' Association, n.d.). Publicly available statements of intent which align with public expectations help to establish a positive image and platform, upon which an individual or organisation might further a specific agenda.

Conclusion

In this chapter, I have explored the idea of 'soft power' and how this manifested in Adrian's recount. In doing so, I have explored some key resources of soft power – strategic narratives, issues narratives and credibility – and how these accumulate into an 'attractive' amalgam for those involved in negotiations. The amplification of an actor's credibility can strengthen that actor's legitimacy and that of the government with which that actor is associated (Teles Fazendeiro, 2021, p. 306). We see this in Adrian's recount with a fellow MP expressing his delight with Adrian's work because it meant that colleague was now welcomed by his constituents in a friendly and positive way, reflecting an evaluation of the government's work in education as being in the interests of the community.

Earlier in this chapter, I pointed out that the application of soft power harnesses irresistible narratives, credible and attractive reputations and collaborative networks. In fact, I argue here that the application of effective soft power and diplomacy emanates from the vibrant conflation and deployment of these phenomena, and in Adrian's chapter, we can see the application and effects of these phenomena. Adrian made a point of meeting with key stakeholders while occupying the position of opposition spokesperson on education. He met with the teachers' union officials and even introduced them to his family, demonstrating his 'ordinariness' as a husband, father and community member. In doing this, he was constructing a 'narrative' about himself, which no doubt mirrored the contexts of those officials with whom he met: as a parent of school-aged children, the very people for whom the unions were advocating. Moreover, 'ordinariness' is made possible by everyday cordiality between peers, and these interactions also mirror what the Austrian philosopher Martin Buber (1878–1965) argued in his statement that "true humanity is created in genuine encounters" (Buber, 2008, p. 34).

Adrian's various meetings before and after becoming minister also established his reputation for listening and seeking the advice of stakeholders. This should not be underestimated because "reputation has long been a part of statecraft" (Cull, 2022, p. 411) and the individual standing of princes, presidents and prime ministers. Reputation also plays a significant role in the projection of an image and vice versa, whether this be an image of the individual or the state. During Adrian's ongoing meetings with education stakeholders, he was not only able to develop a reputation favourable to those in attendance but able to project a set of values through the "prism of signalling and the likely responses to threats" (p. 412). What I mean here is that as the stakeholders became familiar with Adrian's values, goals and aims, as well as the types of strategies he was willing to employ to achieve those aims, they were able to gauge and predict how he would respond to certain situations, even to what he might perceive as 'threats'.

While Adrian, as education minister, enjoyed 'authority' and the capacity to make decisions with far-reaching implications for education in NSW, this does not necessarily ensure credibility in the eyes of stakeholders and the general public. In the first analytical contemplation, we explored the notions of 'possessive' and 'situational' authority and how the utilisation of both provides for the projection of strong authority as a type of power; however, the establishment and strengthening of credibility is also a key component of authority and, ultimately, power.

Notes

1 The application of soft power through sport can be controversial, as the LIV golf tournament, as sponsored by the Saudi government in 2023, illustrated.
2 A wink can be used subversively, as well as an indication of friendship.
3 For an insightful analysis of 'Trumpism', see Henry Giroux, (2023). "Trumpism and the challenge of critical education" in *Educational Philosophy and Theory*, 55(6), 658–773. Here, Giroux remarks that "post-truth is pre-fascism and Trump has been our post-truth president."
4 There is an etymological link with 'credit' here, as in extending money or trust/affirmation.
5 We should note that to their credit, the NSWTF did not see Adrian's approach as weakness or attempt to exploit it.
6 It would be interesting to canvass the aims and intentions of the other meeting participants who might employ the same strategy.

Chapter 7

The power that comes with experience

Adrian Piccoli

It is always helpful to have eyeballed a problem yourself

I was born in western NSW. I lived there for more than 50 years. For almost 20 years, I represented a huge piece of southwestern NSW covering more than 100,000 square kilometres. My electorate had some of the richest people in the country but also many of the poorest. I spent a lot of time in rural and remote communities in my electorate helping individuals and participating in community events like debutante balls, school assemblies, protest meetings and celebration events.

I know western NSW very well, and I care deeply about the future of rural and remote Australia. What upsets me deeply is that rural and regional Australia, particularly the provision of education, doesn't get a fraction of the media and policy attention it needs or deserves. When I travelled around western NSW, I witnessed a lot of examples of where their distance from Sydney meant they were often 'missed' or overlooked. Sometimes their challenges were too hard. The local advocates like parents, principals and local government found it difficult to have their issues heard and acted upon. In my travels, I sometimes came across absurd examples of where the 'system' had badly let schools and students down. My experience at Walgett was one such example.

Walgett is a community in the far northwest of NSW, about an eight-hour drive from Sydney. Due to the huge farming interests in the region, it is one of the wealthiest agricultural areas in Australia 'per capita', but for much of the community, it has a long history of disadvantage and dysfunction. There is a very large and proud Aboriginal community living in and around Walgett. As a community, they have very strong views about education and particularly where it falls short in Walgett. Pretty much everything has been tried in Walgett.

I visited Walgett many times, and I love going back every time. The community have been fantastic to me and have been kind enough to take my family and me out to see some of their traditional lands and cultural sites.

In response to this problem of remote schools not receiving enough policy attention, in 2012, we introduced the Connected Communities strategy [61].

DOI: 10.4324/9781003312451-11

The strategy identified 15 public schools in regional and remote NSW which needed extra attention from the department and the government. They all had a very high proportion of Indigenous students and needed some different thinking to help them succeed. Walgett Primary and Walgett High were two of the schools.

As part of the strategy, the department undertook an audit of the facilities at all 15 schools. They are a long way from major centres, and the parents generally lack agency outside of their own community. Many of the Connected Community[1] school facilities had fallen foul of the classic problem for rural and remote Australian schools. That is, they had been left to deteriorate through a combination of being a long way from Sydney, absence of public or media pressure to upgrade them because it was too far for metropolitan journalists to travel to and parents having little capacity to demand that they be upgraded. I took it upon myself to deal with this issue of assets to give these communities schools they could be proud of. I am a big believer that the physical conditions of schools can say a lot to students about how they are valued by society.

During one of my visits to Walgett, I popped in to see a kindergarten class. We talked about the various measures the school was using to engage and teach the children. I noticed that in the back of the classroom was a huge evaporative air conditioner bolted into the window. It was big, ugly, rusted and with at least half the slats at the front of this machine broken or bent. It looked terrible. When I mentioned it to the teacher, she said it looked terrible, but worse than that, she couldn't use it during class. She told me that because it was so noisy, it could not be used when the class was inside. Instead, they had to turn it on in the morning, then turn it off when the children came into class and then turn it back on at lunch and so forth during the day.

Now, it gets hot in Walgett. Really hot. Summer temperatures can reach more than 45 degrees centigrade for days at a time. Even a good evaporative air conditioner[2] struggles to keep rooms cool in that sort of heat, and this one was not a good one. I parked this information in the back of mind, thinking, great, this is exactly the sort of thing the asset audit will pick up.

Two weeks later, I received the audit report and the list of items that needed to be fixed or replaced at each of the schools. "Yes, yes, yes", I said to myself as I looked down the list. Until I got to Walgett Public School. No mention of any air-conditioning issues. The next day at our weekly Minsec meeting (I had a scheduled weekly meeting between myself and my ministerial staff and the secretary of the department and other senior executives of the department), we discussed the outcome of the audit and the source of the funds we were going to use to fix the $35 million worth of issues. It was all fine except that I raised the issue of the air conditioner at Walgett Public and the fact that it was not in the report.

I was told by one of the senior executives in the department, quite patronisingly, "Minister . . . it is all well and good for you to travel around schools, meet with teachers and parents and hear all these stories but they will sometimes show you things that are not quite what they seem."

I said, "I don't think that was the case here. I have seen the classroom and the air conditioner myself, and it looked pretty bad. Something needs to be done." So, it was reluctantly agreed that someone would go back and have a look, just to keep me happy.

The following week's meeting became one of the more memorable in my time as minister. Someone had indeed been back to visit Walgett Public School and visit the very room I had been in. And yes, the air conditioner looked terrible and was indeed very noisy. And yes, I hadn't been given the full story. At this stage, there were lots of raised eyebrows as to what was about to be revealed.

What I hadn't been told that day was that when it gets oppressively hot, the teacher does have to turn the air conditioner on during class. And yes, it is so noisy that students can't hear the teacher. By now the secretary of the department was looking very worried. But it gets worse. Because it has to be turned on and it's so noisy, the school had bought microphones for the teacher and speakers for the classroom, so that students could hear above the racket. There were audible gasps. The secretary did not look amused.

But it got even worse than that. What had been discovered was that because evaporative air conditioners use humidity to cool a room, that very humidity was worsening the otitis media ear infection that many Aboriginal students suffer from. When a child has otitis media, their hearing is already compromised, so background noise is a greater problem for these students. This situation is therefore simultaneously worsening their condition and their ability to hear. As time went by, the teacher had to keep turning up the microphone. You could have heard a pin drop in that meeting as the most senior people in education talked about ear infections in Walgett and the failed systems that should have picked this up years ago. When there are system failures like this, why would we be surprised by poor learning outcomes, angry parents, disengagement by students at schools like Walgett and why it's hard to retain teachers in remote schools?

I wish that was the end of the story. A promise was made to replace that air conditioner and all the air conditioning at the school. When asked when this would occur, I was told it would be done in March. It was now October, and these children would have to endure another summer of this. No way. I directed it be done immediately. By the following week, someone had gone to the Bunnings hardware store in Dubbo and had bought a reverse cycle air conditioner on wheels, and it was now in place in that classroom.

This is, of course, one story, one classroom in one school. It is a system failure. These asset problems should have been picked up much earlier. But the lesson here wasn't about assets but, rather, about the failure of the system to properly support rural and remote schools. If the system wasn't picking up assets problems, then was it also missing more critical issues like child protection and teaching and learning problems? There is a flaw in the system if it requires a minister to visit to see and remedy an individual weakness that should have been fixed years ago.

Knowing detail yourself is essential to build credibility and authority

All the talk in the last decade has been about the power of big data. Big data can tell us a lot about trends in education and can point policymakers towards the root cause of problems and can help illuminate potential solutions. But collecting small data is also essential at every level of education leadership and practice to ground the insights that big data is providing us. I always thought that the best way to test the strengths and weaknesses of the education system was to embed myself with those who operate within that system.

I eventually got a bit bored with being taken on school tours every time I visited a school. It's also not a great insight into what the real problems are in a school or within a school system. Weeks of preparation have gone into a visit. Lawns have been mowed, a special parking spot has been reserved for the minister's car and all the students have been told to be on their best behaviour. Ministerial visits can be a nuisance to schools. In fact, I often just 'dropped in' to schools unannounced if I happened to be passing nearby. Some principals told me that they enjoyed those visits because there was no fuss and no preparation. It also helped that they knew I wasn't visiting to 'inspect' schools. I had a reputation for talking to educators, so I could learn from them what they wanted me to do.

Schools are really proud of their facilities, but the only way to find out what is really going on is to sit down with teachers and principals and let them tell me what they are thinking.

On most occasions, when I would visit a school or a country town, we would gather a group of about a dozen principals, without any other people in the room, and have a good off-the-record conversation about what they were thinking. They would tell me what pressures they were under, what they needed us to do and, just as importantly, what they needed us to stop doing.

These were always very insightful. I am not sure the department liked me doing it because I would often find out issues before they did. It truly empowered me to test and challenge advice I was receiving from the department. I could say that advice provided to me did not accord with the conversations I was having with principals. It was the perfect opportunity to triangulate the advice I was getting to make sure it was correct. On more than one occasion, I was told in no uncertain terms that it was very unusual and not always welcome for the minster to know more about what was going on in schools than some members of the department.

It also let me take the temperature of principals and teachers on areas we were considering reforming. I could road test ideas to see if they had support from the profession, which sometimes ran contrary to the view of their industrial representatives.

One of the measures we introduced to support the wellbeing and mental health of students was to double the number of school counsellors that were employed by the department and allocated to schools. In NSW, we had this arrangement, built up over many years of industrial negotiations, that to be a school counsellor, that person had to be four years trained as a teacher, have a four-year psychology degree and have at least one year's experience as a classroom teacher. Nine years' worth of work and study to be a school counsellor meant they were very hard to come by, especially in regional areas. Doubling the number was going to make this impossible under existing rules.

Principals made it very clear they wanted more counsellors available to their students, and most agreed that the onerous credentials were unnecessary. After getting that advice from principals, I set about changing the rules. I wanted these rules changed so that to become a school counsellor, all a person needed, as a minimum, was psychology or psychiatry qualifications. This was a major departure from the policy that had been in place for many years. I was advised against it because the union had negotiated these conditions, and they would guard them ferociously.

The odd fight with the union as far as I was concerned wasn't going to hurt my reputation with the more conservative elements of my party, so I was up for it – especially because the policy change was right. I could defend it all day. But I also understood that lots of principals thought these rules were ridiculous. They were especially open to relaxing the rules if it meant giving their students more access to school counsellors. I knew I could persuade practitioners to support the change, and I knew I would win the public debate.

The union did take it to the industrial court. I was adamant that even if they won the legal battle that Parliament should pass legislation to override the decision. The court ruled in favour of common sense, and the rules were changed.

Please sue me!

It is important to fight for what you think is right even at the expense of unpopularity.

I was once threatened with a defamation action by a university vice-chancellor because I had introduced a policy that made it more difficult for university students to enrol in undergraduate teaching degrees. The policy change was that students entering teaching degrees directly from school had to meet minimum requirements in their year 12 examinations and assessments.

In NSW, the end of year 12 credential is called the higher school certificate. We introduced new measures that meant that a teacher would not be registered to teach in NSW if they had not achieved at least a designated minimum score in three of their six HSC subjects. In NSW, each subject is scored on a band between 1 and 6, with 6 being the highest. We made it a requirement that a student must have achieved at least three band 5 results, including English, to be eligible to teach in NSW. This had the effect of stopping universities taking any undergraduates straight from school who did not meet this requirement, as it would mean they could not teach when they graduated.

One university vice-chancellor saw that as a threat to his business model and so sent his chancellor to tell me that the vice-chancellor was going to sue me. I told the chancellor that I would welcome a legal case being made by a university against an education minister for increasing the academic standards of students going into teaching.

A vice-chancellor suing an education minister would be big news. I salivated at the thought of doing TV and radio interviews telling the public how I wanted academically capable teachers standing in front of every child every day and that a particular university doesn't think that's a good idea.

This would have been a public relations gift for me and the government – me arguing for higher standards, a university arguing for lower standards.

He never sued.

Public servants are great, but they are only human

Ministers can't be and are not expected to be across every detail of the agency they are responsible for. It is not the minister's job to micromanage their department.

The secretary of the department is the chief executive officer, and they have the operational responsibility to run the department. As a result, ministers rely on the advice from public servants, especially in very big agencies. That advice often comes in collectives of senior public servants, who have usually decided beforehand what they will advise the minister. It is one of the foundations of the Westminster system[3] of government, and it's a system that works well. But the public service has its own internal politics, and its own agenda, and public servants make mistakes.

The public service wants ministers to think that everything is under control, all is well and that there are no problems that cannot be handled. Ministers should not make the mistake of thinking that everything they are being told is accurate or true.

Advice given collectively is often different to advice given separately

To get around or test the collective advice, it is essential to form individual, personal relationships with people who will tell you 'off the record' exactly what is going on.

Apart from talking directly to teachers and principals as described earlier, I would often visit the head office of my department and just walk around on my own, popping in to visit staff to ask them questions to improve my understanding or even just to say hello. I would stroll in without a tie, and I am sure, on occasion, people thought I was the delivery guy. I would ask to be introduced to individuals or groups of staff. Some of the people were amazed. Some who had been working in that building for 30 years said they had never seen a minister in the building before. I'm not sure if they thought I was checking up on them – I wasn't – but the public servants always seemed pleased that I took the time to visit and see what they were doing.

I just thought it was a good way to find out what was going on. I learnt a great deal from those little fireside chats. The secretary of the department joked that she was going to set up an alarm system to warn her when I was inside the building.

Like any good leader, I was keen to learn as much as possible and to get as wide a range of opinions as possible. I didn't want just one source of information and advice. I wanted as many as I could get my hands on.

During a ministerial visit to Dubbo in western NSW early in my tenure, I had some time to spare in between meetings, so I decided to pop into one of the local primary schools, unannounced, to ask them how the rollout of a new IT system was going (it was called the Learning Management Business Reform (LMBR), and it wasn't going well). I rocked up to the front office and asked if I could talk to the principal.

I introduced myself, and not surprisingly, the receptionist had no idea who I was. She went to see the principal but didn't come back. When the principal came out, she was very apologetic that no one had recognised me. No apology was needed, of course, and I explained that I had chosen her school just because it was the closest to where I had to go next. We went on to have a great chat about LMBR and various other things that were going on at her school. I left with a bit more knowledge, and all was good.

A week later, I was to attend a function in Broken Hill, 750 kilometres west of Dubbo. I was told that an email had gone around to all of the public schools in western NSW to be on the 'lookout' for the NSW minster for education.

> The email said, "If someone comes to the front office of the school in the next two weeks and says that they are the Minister for Education, then they probably are."
>
> It was a sweet story.

Being a minister can also be fun

I went to hundreds of events during my time as the NSW minister for education. However, the two events I enjoyed the most every year were the annual conference dinners for the NSW Primary Principals Association and the Secondary Principals Council. While I was kindly invited to speak at the conferences during the day, it was the conference dinner and a few drinks afterwards which were always the most enjoyable – and enlightening.

For a start, the nights were fun. It was lovely to catch up with the many principals I had become friends with over the years. We would have a laugh, and as the night got later and people became more and more relaxed, the more I would learn about what was 'really' happening across education in NSW. I heard all the gossip, and I heard exactly what principals thought I should do as minister, as well as what they thought about me, the government and the department. And I am sure I probably shared my own opinions about the very same subjects. On several occasions, I was the last to leave the function centre with the last few die-hard principals.

Principals really appreciated the fact that I not only went along but that I stayed because I wanted to stay, not because I had to. I genuinely enjoyed the time we spent together.[4]

Using evidence is a powerful sword and a very useful shield

Any significant change in education policy or practice should have evidence – research and data – to support that change. It seems flippant to say, but putting facts and evidence behind the reasons for change is essential to build the support for reform, particularly from the teaching profession. Teachers will always ask, "Why are we doing this?"

Evidence is the sword used to make the case for change and to guide the policy response and cut through the resistance. Evidence is also a very useful shield. While we used evidence to guide the policy development work we were doing in NSW, we also used the power of evidence to resist reforms we knew were wrong.

In Australia, the Commonwealth government does not run any schools. It provides direct funding grants to government and nongovernment school systems and directly to independent schools. But it does not operate any schools or employ any teachers or other school staff.

The Commonwealth seeks to use its funding power to influence education policy at a national level and to force systems and independent schools to implement the Commonwealth government's reforms. NAPLAN, operated by ACARA, is an example of a national reform, as is the adoption of National Teaching Standards, administered by AITSL. These organisations have education specialists running them and included on their management boards. It's when policy comes from the minister's office through press releases and political motivations, rather than education motivations, that everyone starts running for cover.

Independent public schools and vouchers are two such examples. Some political parties and free-market commentators advocate for these types of reforms as a way of using market forces to drive improved outcomes in schools. The idea behind independent public schools, or charter schools, is that handing all the responsibility of running the school, hiring staff and so on to a school council or, in some cases in the United States, to a private company will lead to better outcomes than if they are operated by a government department.

The theory is that competition will cause teachers to teach differently and students to behave differently. The idea that an underperforming school would close and another new school would spring up around the corner just sounded so neat and plausible. It sounded as if they were talking about a hardware store. Education is far more complicated and, fortunately, much less Darwinian than that.

Or vouchers. The theory is that if government-funded vouchers were handed out to parents, they could choose which school they want to spend their children's government-funded education on. Again, all fine in theory, but the responsibility of education for governments is to consider the education of all students, not just those who would use this and head off to another school. Further, concentrating disadvantaged students, whose parents/carers generally have less personal agency and less ability to move, in certain public schools is the wrong direction to take a country's education system. I wouldn't be part of it despite the pressure from my own political party because these market-based approaches align with the free-market ideologies of centre right political parties like the Liberal/Nationals.

We resisted these reforms vigorously, and we used evidence to do that. These 'silver bullets' all sound so plausible in theory, but the evidence didn't match the enthusiasm advocates had for these reforms. In the United States and the United Kingdom, where they have been in place for years, there is no evidence that they lift the performance of any system. Yes, individual schools perform better, and some perform worse, but on average, there is no improvement.

Instead, there seems to be nothing but constant scandal coming from the United States about operators taking advantage of taxpayer funds, exploiting teachers and exploiting children.[5] The other form of evidence we used was to look at what the best systems[6] in the world do. Countries that continuously outperform Australia on multiple measures have not implemented these kinds of reforms. They have not commercialised their education system. They attempt to treat all their students fairly and equally, and their results show this to be the most effective approach.

We have given public schools more decision-making authority, roughly matching the authority that Catholic school system principals have. It's the authority to change their mix of staff within their budget as well as have a greater say in staff recruitment. We trust principals to make the right choices for their students, but we have kept the best elements of a system in place.

We retained a staffing system that provides a powerful incentive for teachers to work in remote communities on the proviso that, in future years, they can apply for a priority position closer to a place of their choice. This system rule helps ensure that every student has a high-quality teacher in front of their class even in difficult-to-staff parts of the system. Yes, it does mean that, in some cases, schools in more desirable locations don't get to select all of their own staff, but the intention of this compromise is to ensure every child is treated fairly, not necessarily equally.

We maintained the strengths of a system while freeing individuals to make their own decisions.

Sometimes, the most honest decision a minister can make is to break a promise

Governments breaking promises is a cliché and synonymous with politics. Promises are often made, especially during election campaigns, that subsequently prove to be very wrong and a very bad idea. Sometimes, these promises are very bad policy ideas or involve very inefficient use of public funds. Governments are then locked into these promises and are very reluctant to be seen as 'backflipping' on a promise. Broken promises can see political capital and public support for the government erode very quickly.[7]

But sometimes, when things change or new facts are introduced, 'backflipping' is essential for the sake of good policymaking and in order for taxpayers' money not to be wasted. Rather than be vilified by commentators, it should be applauded when it is the right thing to do.

One of the major election promises made by the NSW opposition in the lead-up to the 2011 NSW election was to target the literacy and numeracy performance of students from kindergarten to year 2 through the appointment of 900 literacy and numeracy teachers. The reform was called the *Literacy and Numeracy Action Plan* (LNAP). Overseeing this commitment would be a *Ministerial Advisory Group on Literacy and Numeracy* (MAGLAN) to provide the best advice to the government on the implementation of the plan.

The purpose of LNAP was to improve the learning outcomes of students from kindergarten to year 2 through changed teaching practices and from sustained and whole school professional development. There were essentially two initial promises made prior to the election. One was that 900 additional literacy and numeracy teachers would be employed across the state.

The second promise was that a ministerial advisory group would be set up to advise the government on how to effectively implement the promise.

A third promise crept in as we got closer to the election. As the election got closer, I was asked for more detail about how the 900 teachers would be allocated across the state. I was asked how many would be allocated to the Illawarra, how many to Newcastle and so forth. Because opposition parties simply don't have the resources to work out exactly how promises like this are best implemented, we estimated the allocation of those teachers. We promised that they would be allocated proportionately, based on population. For example, I promised 60 numeracy and literacy teachers for the Illawarra. Not surprisingly, after the election, the government was then pressured to allocate the teachers exactly as had been promised.

The problem was that the advice from MAGLAN[8] was not to allocate teachers in this way. MAGLAN was of the view that improvement in literacy and numeracy was dependent upon a changed approach to classroom practice among existing teachers in targeted schools and that this would not be achieved by the simple injection of a new batch of 900 teachers sprinkled across the state's schools.

On the advice of the expert members of MAGLAN, we therefore proposed that the 900 FTE should be regarded not as 'people' but as a funding resource, which could be used in large part to employ instructional leaders to provide the professional development of existing teachers in the use of new literacy and numeracy teaching practices.

This posed a problem for me as minister but also for the government, as the 900 FTE teachers was an election promise and very much in the public domain. I was persuaded by the MAGLAN advice but had to respond regularly to opposition and media calls for information on the progress of appointing the 900 teachers. For the first three years or so, as the programme took shape, I had to manage this difficult issue publicly and in Parliament. One *Sydney Morning Herald* headline read, "O'Farrell (Premier) Accused of Dumping Literacy and Numeracy Pledge".[9]

Evidence, however, is not just a sword but also a shield for changing direction. It would have been easier and indeed politically expedient to simply allocate 900 additional positions across schools in NSW in the way we had promised, without any regard for potential impact. In fact, there would have been political 'reward' for having implemented the promise we made, even though it would have been bad policy and a poor use of public funds. That reward would have come in the way of positive coverage by media, positive announcements in MPs' electorates and a big tick for having 'delivered on an election commitment'. But it would have been wrong.

Instead, we broke our promise and provided $261 million between 2012 and 2016 (funding equivalent to 900 full-time teaching positions) to target students in kindergarten to year 2 at risk of not meeting literacy and numeracy standards in 448 schools across NSW. That funding focused on instructional leadership, diagnostic assessment, differentiated teaching and tiered interventions in each school.[10]

But just using evidence doesn't solve the political problem caused by breaking promises. Having evidence – the advice of experts and the research they relied on – in this case, was necessary but not sufficient.

What was also essential was taking the time to effectively communicate that evidence and advice to internal stakeholders like the NSW Teachers Federation and the principal representative groups as well as leaders from the Catholic school system and independent schools. Simply announcing a decision to break a promise is politically reckless and diminishes trust, an essential element of a minister's authority.

By considering the best evidence provided to me by MAGLAN, we broke our promise and communicated the decision clearly, without losing my authority as a minister.

No one criticised the decision.

Notes

1 education.nsw.gov.au/public-schools/connected-communities/connected-communities-strategy
2 In addition to the new air conditioner, more than $8 million was invested in rebuilding the Walgett High school campus and refurbishing the Walgett Primary School campus. In addition to capital works funding, Walgett High School and Walgett Primary School received significant increase in recurrent funding thanks to the "Gonski" school funding reforms, parliament.nsw.gov.au/Hansard/Pages/HansardResult.aspx#/docid/HANSARD-1323879322–67962/link/9
3 sef.psc.nsw.gov.au/understanding-the-sector/westminster-system
4 If I can offer new ministers one piece of advice, it would be this – do not drink alcohol. I never drank alcohol at any of these events or even at home. To be an effective minister, even at social events, requires the attention of every sense we have, so don't dull any of them with alcohol. Many ministers have been brought down by stupid decisions or stupid comments they made after having had a few glasses of wine. Alcohol tends to shut your ears and open your mouth. It's just not worth it.
5 news.yahoo.com/americas-biggest-teacher-principal-cheating-scandal-unfolds-atlanta-213734183.html
6 Measured using PISA, TIMMS and rankings.
7 The best example of this phenomenon was when Australian prime minister Julia Gillard introduced a carbon tax after having promised only months earlier that there would be "no carbon tax under a government I lead", smh.com.au/national/

pm-says-no-carbon-tax-under-her-govt-20100816–126ru.html; Australian prime minister Tony Abbott suffered a similar fate, smh.com.au/national/then-and-now-the-abbott-governments-broken-promises-20140514-zrcfr.html

8 Members of MAGLAN were invited to join on the basis of their experience and expertise: Dr John Ainley (deputy director, ACER), Professor Peter Freebody (Sydney University); Dr Meredith Martin (private consultant and member of the Board of Studies); Cheryl McBride, Jane Cameron and Tina Rowarth (all public primary school principals at that time); Mandy Westgate (Catholic primary school principal); Robin Yates (AIS and a representative of the Exodus Foundation). Dr Ken Boston was appointed chair.

9 smh.com.au/national/nsw/ofarrell-accused-of-dumping-literacy-and-numeracy-pledge-20130311–2fwct.htmlandparliament.nsw.gov.au/la/papers/pages/qanda-tracking-details.aspx?pk=49502

10 https://pre65.education.nsw.gov.au/content/dam/main-education/literacy-and-numeracy-strategy/media/documents/literacy-and-numeracy-strategy.pdf

Analytical contemplation

The power that comes with experience

Don Carter

In previous chapters, we have seen how the accumulation of power resources has enabled the holder to retain and exert power and authority. Resources such as possessive and associative authority, credibility, persuasion, strategic narrative, for example, have allowed the holder to generate trust with and between others and, ultimately, generate authority and power. In this analytical contemplation, I explore how power and authority are manifested through specific discourses anchored in the following:

- The power of 'evidence-based' discourses in education and 'what works'.
- The power of the 'datafication' of education and some of its effects.
- Problems and challenges associated with 'evidence-based' and the datafication of education.

The power of knowing the facts

In his chapter "The power that comes with experience", Adrian points to the importance of 'being on the ground' to witness conditions personally. This first-hand experience of events and people is invaluable, and as Adrian indicates, stands to strengthen credibility and trust. A minister for education who travels the state, visits schools and witnesses the conditions of those schools builds 'field knowledge', enabling them to draw their own conclusions. This is a common-sense approach to developing knowledge and understanding and possible solutions to challenges and problems. For Adrian, seeing the conditions in Walgett was a major driver for the development and implementation of the Connected Communities[1] programme, from which school improvements strengthened the working and learning conditions of staff and students. As he points out, "[K]nowing detail yourself is essential to build credibility and authority."

Knowing the facts and being across the detail is akin to the collection of data. It provides a solid basis to argue a position, refute the arguments of an antagonist, evaluate current policies and make decisions for the future. The collection of evidence and its ethical and effective use underpins all aspects of

DOI: 10.4324/9781003312451-12

our lives, particularly in health, transport, education, nutrition and the built and natural environments. The following section is an exploration of not only the importance of an evidence-based approach in education but also some of the nuances, complexities and inconsistencies inherent in the term 'evidence-based' that may not be apparent in the first instance to the casual observer.

The power of evidence

In his previous chapter, Adrian discusses the power and importance of 'evidence' and labels it a "very powerful sword and a very useful shield". The importance and power of data collection in education is well recognised by governments, teachers and the public, as evidenced by the establishment of a number of Australian government agencies to collect, analyse and publish information on educational data. For example, in New South Wales, the Department of Education agency, the Centre for Education Statistics and Evaluation (CESE), has responsibility for the "in-depth analysis of education programs and outcomes across early childhood, school, training, and higher education to inform whole-of-government, evidence-based decision making" (Centre for Education Statistics and Evaluation, n.d.). At the national level, ACARA, responsible for the national curriculum in Australia, collects student data to calculate socio-educational advantage (SEA) and data about students for whom English is a second or other language.

All Australian states and territories have their own agencies for data collection on issues, including student socio-economic status, performance in standardised tests, attendance and cultural and linguistic background, and these data help to maintain a current profile on the students in Australian classrooms. The collection, analysis and dissemination of educational data is essential to the establishment and maintenance of a responsive and responsible education system and extends to the collection at all "levels of educational systems (individual, classroom, school, region, state, international)" (Jarke & Breiter, 2019, p. 1), as well as providing a solid platform for decision-making, which can form the basis for increased student achievement and planning for the future (Schildkamp, 2019). At the local school level, data collection has been normal practice for decades. Teachers collect data on a daily basis, using the results of formal tests and assessments, through to observation and anecdotal records, to 'assessment for learning'.

However, an international movement away from trusting teacher judgement about the performance of students has been apparent over the past two decades (Daliri-Ngametua & Hardy, 2022; Daliri-Ngametua et al., 2022), as digital technology has made possible the compilation of data sets about student performance through what is known as 'big data'. This term refers to the vast amount of data now available to organisations and businesses to inform and improve their performance and outcomes. There are different types of big data, with the first type including structured (text) data, such as "transactions that can reside in databases, and unstructured (non-text) data, such as videos, photos, social media content, and Internet of Things (IoT) data that can exist in many format types" (Parise, 2016, p. 186). Big data is now considered as essential for organisations in the twenty-first century just as physical assets such as money, labour, machines and material were seen as essential in the past (p. 186).

And this shift to a reliance on large-scale data collection in education has seen an attendant shift in rhetoric. Currently, the terms 'evidence-based education' (EBE) and 'what works' in classrooms are two ubiquitous and powerful terms which act as discourses[2] to shape our thinking. According to the French philosopher and critic Michel Foucault, power and knowledge are communicated by discourses which shape our lives and manifest themselves in what we say, do and think, constituting a "regime of truth" (Coloma, 2011). Discourses are apparent in the style of language used by individuals, which, in turn, represent the specific sets of principles and beliefs of different groups, institutions and organisations. Although Foucault uses the term 'discourse' in different ways (Ball, 2013), it is possible to identify educational discourses through the use of interrelated terms. For example, conversations and written texts that use terms such as 'achievement', 'assessment', 'standards' and 'qualifications' (Oliver, 2010) create an educational discourse (Bourke & Lidstone, 2015, p. 835). When a discourse is established, a key question is, "[W]ho produced the statement and with what authority?" (p. 835), which allows the investigation of the underlying bases of power and authority inherent within the discourse.

The power of evidence-based education

A current and powerful discourse is 'evidence-based education', which has made its way into a range of disciplines, including architecture, allied health professions, law, management, public policy and education. Its origins lie in medicine (Biesta, 2007), and its importance can be traced back to England in the middle of the twentieth century, when a progressively more centralised and nationalised public sector was under increasing budgetary pressure and scrutiny, particularly regarding resources invested in the National Health Service (Lawn, 2013; Whitty, 2008). As a result, the government sought to redress expenditure blowouts through increased efficiencies via the adoption of an evidence-based approach to medicine based on large-scale, randomised, controlled trials (RCTs) (Crafts, 1996).

Since the 1990s, the discourse of evidence-based in education has been apparent in the use of RCTs as a way of and managing education budgets and the allocation thereof (Bridges et al., 2009; Hammersley, 2007; Thomas & Pring, 2004). Specifically, EBE refers to the "development of school policies and classroom practices based on systematic reviews of experimental research evidence" (Boaz et al., 2002, p. 25), and its principles see a movement away from tradition and intuition to scientific evidence, findings from published scientific research, organisational evidence, data, facts and figures (Barends et al., 2011, p. 223). This line of thinking in education was promoted by academics and policy researchers, who considered education an appropriate site for policy development and the trialling of interventions (Eacott, 2017), with the rationale behind the RCTs being to "measure the progress of students participating in an educational intervention against that of a control group of equivalent students who are, most typically, continuing as normal" (Connolly et al., 2018, p. 277). There have been substantial investments into the implementation of EBE, with the "No Child Left Behind" (2002) and "Every Student Succeeds" (2015) acts in the United States and the "What works network" (2013) in the United Kingdom.

Evidence-based education is intended to identify and utilise effective interventions to reveal 'what works' in education, often through large-scale testing and assessments. This approach has been apparent in the United Kingdom over the past decade, where the government promised to reform the education system based on the "evidence of what works" (Department of Education, 2016, p. 73), and is exemplified by the promotion of the Educational Endowment Foundation (EEF) as the "designated What Works Centre for Education" (Department of Education (DoE), 2016, p. 39). This type of intervention is based on the idea of the "New Science of Education" (Furlong & Whitty, 2017), which promises improvements in education through the implementation of RCTs and systematic reviews of the data gleaned from the tests which are then often promoted as "seemingly infallible empiricist research" (Hordern et al., 2021, p. 144).

The point about 'what works' and EBE discourses and their current ascendancy is their power to influence and shape thinking, discussion and actions of policymakers, politicians and the general public. While discourses can facilitate discussion and understanding of salient issues among professionals in the same field, discourses also have the inherent power to make it almost "impossible to be outside of them; to be outside of them is, by definition, to be mad, to be beyond comprehension and therefore reason" (Ball, 2013, pp. 20–21). This can exclude those from outside a profession from participating, and for those within a profession, discourses have the power to "constrain, enable, writing, speaking and thinking" (p. 19). The following section elaborates on some of the problems and complexities related to the 'what works' and EBE discourses.

Problems with 'what works' and EBE discourses

In this section, I point out problems with the 'what works' and EBE discourses. In doing so, I acknowledge that some research into RCTs in education have identified useful and meaningful contributions to knowledge and theory (see Connolly et al., 2018, p. 289). In addition, I acknowledge that data can be used to glean insights into the processes of learning, how pedagogies are used, curriculum design and learning over time, particularly as researchers develop increasingly fine-tuned technologies and methods (Lang et al., 2017; Piety et al., 2014). Moreover, data may be used to predict outcomes, detect risks and 'personalise' the education system around individuals' needs (Bulger, 2016).

However, it is also important to acknowledge the numerous criticisms of the 'what works' and EBE discourses. The first criticism on the 'what works' discourse focuses on the idea that an effective model of successful teaching and learning, identified through an RCT, can be replicated across numerous settings. This line of thinking has been challenged because it ignores the inappropriateness of establishing "universally and replicable laws" (Hodkinson & Smith, 2004, p. 151) and also overlooks context and individual difference through the adoption of "deterministic, patterned, universalizable, stable, atomised, objective, controlled, closed systems of law-like behaviour" (Morrison, 2001, pp. 72–74).

Critics point to the difficulties of capturing the complexities of school and classroom environments in the tightly controlled context of laboratory-like settings (Cartwright, 2013; Dekker & Meeter, 2022; Ma, 2021), arguing the diversity of student cohorts, the (un)availability of resources for schools and school systems and the overall nuances of different educational settings are largely ignored in RCTs. Plus, the cultural and linguistic diversity of student cohorts render generalisations and generic conclusions about 'what works' as problematic (Dekker & Meeter, 2022). At the simplest level, for example, it is quite reasonable to expect that students in a Sydney metropolitan high school have different learning needs from students who are enrolled in a remote rural school, thus supporting the idea of what works in one setting may not work in another setting. These criticisms reflect the claim that RCTs "ignore context and experience . . . (and) generate simplistic universal laws of 'cause and effect' . . . and are inherently descriptive and contribute little to theory generation" (Connolly et al., 2018, p. 277).

Second, the discourse that stems from the implementation of RCT findings is promoted by advocates as 'evidence-based education'. However, critics assert that the improvement of educational practice is based on the investigation of the "conditions for realising a coherent educational process in practical contexts" (Elliott, 2004, p. 176) rather than the imposition of one set of practices from one context to another. In short, the criticisms of EBE approaches in education can be summarised in this way: it is not possible to undertake RCTs in education at the practical level because RCTs ignore context and experience and seek to generate universal laws of 'cause and effect', which are inapplicable in all contexts, and that RCTs are, by nature, descriptive and contribute little to theory. (Connolly et al., 2018, p. 278).

What I am pointing out here is that the use of the terms 'what works' and 'evidence-based' is often used uncritically and unproblematically by different actors to promote their claims, which are usually related to 'rigour' and 'robustness' in education. Orland (2009) sums up the problem by stating:

> [E]ducational research is much more likely to be paid attention to by educational policy leaders when it buttresses arguments about particular policy directions or prescriptions already being advocated, thus furthering a particular political/policy position. It is research as ammunition not as knowledge discovery.
>
> (p. 118)

The presence of 'what works' and 'evidence-based education' are examples of two current and powerful discourses in education, which continue to shape policy and discussions.

Here, I am advocating for a more judicious use of the terms 'what works' and 'evidence-based', in the hope that we can avoid the situation where "politicians and policymakers borrow strategically and selectively from evidence, choosing some forms of evidence while ignoring others" (Gerarrd & Holloway, 2023, p. 38). I also want to emphasise that evidence to track and improve student learning is compiled from multiple sources and acknowledge that a research investigation is subject to possible influences such as the ontological[3] perspective of the researchers, the research questions under review, the methodical approaches, how the data are analysed, interpretation of the data and the degree of impartiality of the research funding body or the researchers (Garner & Kaplan, 2021, p. 310). And before research can be deemed 'evidence', it must be independently peer reviewed and published in a respected relevant academic journal.

Therefore, I am advocating that governments and school systems take responsibility for the following:

1 Raise answerable questions, search for evidence, assess it and carefully apply it to practice (Dekker & Meeter, 2022, p. 7).
2 Fund local-classroom research initiatives that drive learning outcomes for students in similar contexts – that is, that governments and school systems provide funding to develop tailored research into their local schools and classrooms and disseminate the findings to other local schools. Where data can be extrapolated to other settings, then that happens.
3 Promote the idea of the 'teacher as researcher' in local and wider contexts to assemble data as the basis for decision-making at those levels.
4 Reduce the level of administrative tasks that currently burden teachers. Free up time to allow teachers to do what they were educated to do – teach.

The datafication of education

Another powerful trend in education is what has been called the 'datafication' of education. While data clearly form a major part of everyone's life, each time we log onto a device, visit a website, purchase items online and even during the time our cursor hovers over a piece of information, data is being collected. And, of course, this is in addition to our personal details being stored by insurance companies, telecommunication organisations and government departments such as health authorities. One particular story about data that demonstrates its power – and, in this case, what is called 'predictive analytics'[4] – comes from a story in the *New York Times*, written by Charles Duhigg,[5] in 2012 (Duhigg, 2012). In this story, Duhigg recounts a father visiting a Target store to complain that his daughter had received coupons for maternity clothing and baby products. The father was incensed that his daughter had been receiving advertising about these products which she had not requested. However, after a brief investigation into the matter, it became clear that Target knew before the family or anyone else that the daughter was pregnant. What had happened was that Target had compiled data about the daughter's purchase history for some 25 products, which, after analysis, produced a 'pregnancy prediction' score. This story created quite a storm and brought 'big data' into the public arena, with the realisation that personal data had become a valuable commodity that is traded among commercial entities and data compilers.

The collection of massive amounts of data is now known as 'datafication' – a term popularised by Mayer-Schoenberger and Cukier (2013). Datafication refers to the transformation and commodification of digital interactions into collections and compilations and involves three broad characteristics: the production of digital data, the processing of data and the subsequent (re)use of data and its associated social, cultural, economic and political consequences (Pangrazio & Selwyn, 2021, p. 434). The fact that many young people are enthusiastic users of various social media platforms means they are subject to the generation and collection of substantial amounts of personal data (p. 432) that can be used and traded by commercial interests. In addition, data collected through online standardised tests in education, the dissemination of health and psychological data by government platforms, the sharing of children's[6] data on social media by parents and networked games and toys all combine to generate large amounts of data that provide insights into the interests, habits and capabilities of young people.

Of course, there are positives about collecting data for educational purposes. In a small-scale study of 14 teachers in two Australian schools, for example, Bolea Jover (2019) identifies several benefits stemming from the data provided by the national standardised literacy and numeracy tests, NAPLAN. The benefits include schools being able to compile more information about student progress in literacy and numeracy and the capacity to make quick comparisons about how different students or groups are performing in these two areas, as well as the capacity to establish an informed picture of the worth of the school's literacy and numeracy programmes. Bolea Jover reports that teacher responses when asked about working with digital data suggests that they "appreciated and somehow enjoyed some of the benefits afforded by the increasing use of digital data" (p. 47).

However, teachers in the study reported numerous negatives to working with data. First, they felt they were increasingly "enmeshed in a system which risked transforming their roles and diminishing their professional authority" (Jover, 2019, p. 47). These teachers reported that their working lives were being reconfigured by working with data, finding themselves in a situation where they were attempting "keep data on track" but were in fact being "kept on track by the data" (Lewis & Hardy, 2017, quoted in Jover, 2019, p. 47) and felt that they were required to collect different types of quantified data to prove they were "doing their jobs" (p. 47). The teachers also reported that their workload was increasingly directed to tasks focused on collecting data, indicating a shift away from what has been traditionally known as a 'good teacher' to a "new type of individual" formed "within the logic of competition" (Ball & Olmedo, 2013, p. 88), immersed in the data production as a record of the progress their students have made.

These observations reflect pressures teachers can experience as part of an unrelenting drive to raise student performance, while the data generated to measure student performance are used to compare schools, teachers and even nations (Apple, 2005; Steiner-Khamsi, 2003). The focus of these processes is the reshaping of "complex educational processes into data points that can be used to sort, order, benchmark, compare, and rank" (Stevenson, 2017, p. 538). In contemporary education, the measurement of all aspects of education is central to the notion of success of schools and school systems, which is increasingly portrayed in terms of targets achieved and by the application of metrics to evaluate performance (Grek, 2009, 2015; Ozga, 2009). As a teacher increasingly assumes the role of a data collector, they become

> reconstituted as a self-entrepreneur who adds value to his or her self and school, as teachers understand and conduct themselves in terms of operationally defined standards, numbers, and performance indicators set by for-profit and non-profit vendors, testing companies, and bureaucrats,
> (Holloway & Brass, 2018, p. 378)

where statistics assume a form of "objective reality" that is apparently beyond question (Taubman, 2010, p. 209). Subsequently, teachers experience an increase in their workload, compounded by a growing sense of alienation as they are forced to focus on outputs over individuals (Allen, 2014).

Conclusion

These considerations raise a series of questions, including how much data is enough? Is comparing schools, school systems, teachers and even nations based on the results of standardised tests worthwhile or desirable? If so, are there any unintended negative outcomes? These are just a few questions that are central to school-based education that require further exploration. While I believe there is a place for data in education (see Fischer et al., 2020; Livingstone et al., 2021; Simionescu et al., 2021), education systems have been seduced by numbers in the crucible that has mutated into educational accountability. And while I also believe in the importance of tracking a child's development in literacy and numeracy, I am also of the view that childhood is a precious time of life and should be full of rich and exciting discoveries rather than the relentless slog of testing and assessment. I also consider the role of the teacher not only resides in being accountable for student learning but also thrives on the joy of allowing a child to "reveal an intelligence to itself" (Rancière, 1990, p. 28).

Notes

1 The Connected Communities Strategy "began in 2013. It was created because it was clear that a new approach was needed to how we deliver education and training in our most vulnerable communities, and to how we link to other related services, such as health, welfare, early childhood education and care, and vocational education and training." NSW Department of Education. Connected Communities Strategy (nsw.gov.au).
2 Other dominant discourses are associated with 'quality teachers' and 'quality teaching', both of which are problematic due to their lack of clarity and openness to interpretation.
3 Ontology, in its widest sense, relates to the theory of being. What we mean here is that the way researchers might categorise entities and phenomena can influence the way research is conceived and conducted.
4 See Mishra, N., & Silakari, D.S. (2012). Predictive Analytics: A Survey, Trends, Applications, Opportunities & Challenges. Predictive analysis is an advanced branch of data engineering, which generally predicts some occurrence or probability based on data.
5 Duhigg, C. (2012). How Companies Learn Your Secrets. *The New York Times* (nytimes.com).
6 The phenomenon of parents sharing details of their children's lives on social media has been labelled "sharenting" by Blum-Ross and Livingstone (2017).

Chapter 8

Accumulating, keeping and renewing power

Adrian Piccoli

The importance of saying no

Morning talkback hosts, or shock jocks,[1] can be big, bad and ugly. Alan Jones[2] from Sydney's 2GB radio station was one of the biggest and one of the toughest. They have been an influential and controversial part of Sydney and indeed Australian politics for decades.

When I had been the minister for only a few months, an issue arose involving Gosford Public School. Gosford Public School was right in the centre of the business district of Gosford on the NSW Central Coast, about 80 kilometres north of Sydney. Because of a proposed development of the Gosford central business district, the previous government had decided to move the school to a new site next to the nearby Henry Kendall High School,

Not surprisingly, when there is a proposal to move a school, there is always a great deal of community angst about it. In the lead-up to the election, as the opposition spokesman on education, I had said that a new government would review the decision, and we did. I went to Gosford and had a look, took advice from the department and spoke to local people. There were some challenges with parking and various other matters, but it was the right decision to make, and we backed the previous government's decision.

A few days after my visit to the school, I was asked to appear on Alan Jones' radio programme to talk about my visit. There I was standing at the airport in Griffith, in my electorate, in the freezing cold at six o'clock in the morning talking on the phone with the biggest shock jock of them all, and I knew he was going to come at me with all guns blazing. There had been extensive community consultation about the proposal, the decision had been reviewed several times and I had been to visit the new site to see for myself what the issues were. After all this, I had reconfirmed that the new government was going ahead with the plan to move the school.

But Alan Jones had other ideas. The owner of his radio station had interests nearby,[3] and I can only presume that was his motivation for opposing the plan to move the school. But nobody opposes Alan Jones! He had me on the phone and proceeded to tell me how wrong and terrible I was. All standard

DOI: 10.4324/9781003312451-13

procedure so far. Then he brought in the head of the Gosford Public School Parents and Citizens Council on the phone for a three-way tirade. Every point he made about the plan I defended, and I explained why he was wrong.

Shock jocks have several tricks up their microphone. One of their tricks is to ask a loaded question or make a claim. If you refute it or provide facts which prove that their claim is wrong, then they do not engage further in that line of questioning, and they certainly never concede to being wrong.⁴ Instead, they immediately move to the next line of attack. The other trick is that if you argue with them, their microphone overrides yours. So you might think you are giving as good as you are getting, but all the listeners can hear is the shock jock talking or yelling, and it sounds like you are sitting back, meekly listening to the tirade.

Jones was doing what he does, shouting half-truths and avoiding inconvenient facts. But every allegation he put to me, I was able to respond to. He reached a crescendo at the end of the interview, where he demanded, "Minister, you must promise me one thing, that you will have this decision reviewed."

I said, "No! The decision has been made, and we are moving on!" Well, the condemnation, the insults, the abuse. Jones began his rant, "Goodbye, goodbye. That's Adrian Piccoli. He's gone as education minister. You're gone. There's one casualty. No use talking to the bloke. . . . (He) couldn't care less about the local community, couldn't care less about anyone." It was quite amazing, and I must say quite liberating and empowering. He had nothing. He was angry because I had blunted his power and made him look like a fool.

I do not think I even got the chance to politely thank him for the interview. He just hung up. More importantly, when I returned to the office that day, I saw some people from the department, and I learnt something that I did not know at the time. I learnt that staff in the department had listened to that morning's radio interview, as the radio clip had been emailed around the department by their media monitors. I didn't realise at the time that the department staff listened to almost every word I was saying publicly to gauge what sort of minister and leader I would be by the way I responded, particularly to political pressure. That is where they were getting their signals about how I operated as a leader. It is where they determined either consciously or subconsciously what I would be like as a leader.

One senior executive told me, "Had you said, 'Yes, we'll review it'", it would have shaped the way the bureaucracy would provide advice to me in the future, knowing that the minute I get a bit of pressure put on me, I would change my mind. In effect, they worried I would stop taking their frank and fearless advice. People you are leading are listening and watching to see how you can be strong-armed as a leader.

I did not know that at the time, but I am glad I answered "No" – whatever Alan Jones might have said about me for the following five years. It can be tempting to accommodate significant media personalities or media outlets because they are without doubt influential. They are important communication channels for leaders and can make life difficult if you 'disobey' them. It can be tempting to think that accommodating the media can lead to more favourable future media coverage. As an aside, it was often easy to pick those ministers or MPs who leaked private conversations to the media, as they were often the ones who received 'soft' coverage in return. In fact, one MP was nicknamed 'the pillow' because he was shaped by the last person who sat on him.

It is also important to remember that the media has no direct power in education. Journalists simply have no authority. They are a crucial communication outlet and cannot be ignored, but they cannot force ministers to make decisions. It is only when ministers bend to their will for fear of incurring their wrath that they gain power.

The only power people like Alan Jones have is the power that ministers give them when they roll over and do their bidding. When ministers roll over, they are simply spilling their voter-derived power and authority, and self-respect, on to the ground. Occasionally, shock jocks and journalists are right, but usually, they are wrong. But they are always emboldened when ministers cave to their demands. It is their way of operating. Get their callers enraged, and then they savage a minister who then accedes to their demands for a change in decision or a review of a decision. Makes them look very powerful.

My Alan Jones experience taught me an invaluable lesson about retaining one's power. I never forgot it.

Trust brings people together for the common good

> I have been a teacher and a school principal for 35 years and I have never known everyone to be heading in the same direction until now. Principals, teacher Unions, the Department, The Minister, Catholic and Independent schools. Everyone is on the same page, there is no brawling – everyone is just working towards the best interests of children.
>
> (Unknown teacher 2016)

This is the finest compliment I ever received as the NSW minister for education. It says a lot about the relationships we developed over the years, the understanding that had emerged between previously competing parties in education in NSW. This was an acknowledgement that we had the environment for change right. We were creating an environment of trust and cooperation that had seen other systems around the word change and thrive. It was an acknowledgement that when everyone works together for the common good of education, children are the winners.

The relationship with the union was the one most in need of repair. We nurtured and developed our relationships with other key groups in education, all of which had a significant contribution to ensuring we made sound decisions in education. It wasn't just about my relationship with each group but their relationship with each other that also needed repairing.

NSW has three schooling sectors – 2,200 public schools, a large system of 600 Catholic schools and 500 independent schools. The three sectors were often at odds with each other – at odds with each other over funding, over performance and over enrolments. The three sectors had different accountability rules and even had different school registration rules. The sectors were not on equal regulatory footing, funding was a mess and the relationships were not great. As a government, we wanted to put every school on the same footing and treat every sector the same. That is a fundamental principle that helps to ensure that every student is treated as fairly as possible irrespective of which sector they are in. If the same rules apply to all schools and to all students, then we can start to think of our education system as being fairer and more equitable. In 2011, it was not either of those, and it still is not where it should be.

School funding is the most obvious. The Gonski[5] reforms went a long way to rebalancing some of the historic inequities that had emerged over several decades.

But it was much more than just funding. In 2012, we created a Schools Advisory Council, which had as members the heads of the Catholic and independent sectors as well as the president of the NSW Board of Studies (now the NSW Education Standards Authority). This group brought together issues that were common to all three sectors, including countering violent extremism, the issue of teacher accreditation, developing professional practice hubs, as well as using their employee powers to force universities to increase the standards for accepting students into initial teacher education courses.

Again, the strength of this group is that we focused on the shared issues where we could make progress, and we dealt with more contentious issues like school funding separately. We still had our fair share of very public brawls about those contentious issues. In the past, the minority of issues that divided the three sectors kept them from resolving other common issues that they had.

Inclusive decision-making makes everyone more powerful

The Council of Australian Governments[6] was formed in 1992 as a formalised way of bringing state and territory governments together across various areas of government responsibility. All the premiers and the prime minister would meet quarterly, as would treasurers, ministers for health and so forth. They were designed to bring all governments together to help solve significant national policy challenges.

Education ministerial councils were held every quarter, and they brought together Australia's education ministers from all states and territories, the Commonwealth minister for education, as well as the heads of all of their departments. Also included were the heads of the national education agencies such as the Australian Curriculum Assessment and Reporting Authority (ACARA) and the Australian Institute for Teaching and School Leadership (AITSL). Any policy, funding or curriculum reform with a national focus came to these meetings for discussion and decision.

These were strange meetings for a minister to appear at. I was the minister for education in NSW and was being asked to make decisions that impacted all schools, public, Catholic and independent, as well as early childhood education and care. I had the power to make decisions at these meetings whether it was to approve changes to the national curriculum or the minimum hours of early childhood care that would be offered to preschool students or changes to the way Australia accredits teachers.

What I wanted for those meetings was the authority to speak on behalf of all the education sectors in NSW, not just the Department of Education. So, prior to each of these ministerial council meetings, I would host a meeting of all the education stakeholders in NSW, together with the department, and we would go through the meeting agenda in advance.

As we went through the items, I would get their view on contentious issues and seek their opinion on whether I should support various recommendations or not. We would sit around the boardroom in my office, with the president of the teachers' union sitting next to the head of the independent school sectors, sitting next to the head of the Council of Catholic School Parents. Those meetings allowed everyone to have their say about the direction of education in NSW for the sake of all children, not just in their own spheres of influence. On almost every aspect of education policy, including funding, there was generally a consensus. Even when there was not complete consensus, the meetings were useful to understand the position of stakeholders and to understand where the friction points were.

The most powerful outcome from those meetings was the authority it gave me to speak on behalf of the totality of NSW education later in the week during the actual meeting with all the other ministers. To be able to say that every single stakeholder in NSW, the largest state in the country, holds this position, and this is the position NSW insists on was very powerful. We always got our way. It was the exercise of power created by trust, cooperation and a common desire to serve the interests of children.

This level of inclusion for stakeholders was unprecedented in NSW. This generated a desire to work for the common good amongst and between stakeholders. Of course, those discussions before and after these meetings in my office led to a better understanding between what had often been competing stakeholder groups. Every time we met, it improved the harmony across the education sectors and, therefore, enhanced my reputation as a leader.

We trust, but we verify

Part of the motivation behind building and nurturing those strong trusting relationships was the recognition that no one knows everything. "We trust, but we verify" was one of US president Ronald Reagan's great Cold War quotes after the Russians complained to the Americans that, despite a signed arms reduction treaty, the Americans were still flying spy planes over the Soviet Union. Not in the same league as Cold War diplomacy, but I applied the same rule. The department provided me a great deal of advice, as they should, of course. But I also road tested a lot of that advice. And I tested it with everyone.

One of the first reforms we introduced involved redesigning the way public schools received their funding. We inherited a system where staff were paid centrally and then schools would receive funding for anywhere up to 600 different programmes. They ranged from programmes to support literacy to supporting Aboriginal students, sports programmes and so on. Every one of these separately funded programmes had to be acquitted individually, and the school had to account for and evaluate every single one of them. Schools were not allowed to spend any money left over from these programmes on anything else in the school. This meant schools often had small amounts of money on their books with which they could do nothing.

As part of the changes to the way schools would be funded, I had been told that this was fixed.

Visiting Finley High School, a school in my rural NSW electorate, I was having a chat with the principal, Bernie Roebuck, about his school, and I asked him how he was finding the new funding arrangement. He told me it was still a pain in the neck because he had all these little buckets of money with which he could do nothing. He took me to his office and showed me the details. The problem had not been fixed. Needless to say, upon my return to the department, I made it very clear that schools could not operate like this, that we had made a commitment to schools to fix this problem, so we would fix it. I subsequently referred to these reforms as the Roebuck reforms, named after Bernie Roebuck, the principal of Finley High School at the time.

Everyone is a stakeholder in education

I also cultivated very strong relationships with individual teachers and parents, as well as my individual parliamentary colleagues. We consolidated that power by bringing the various interest groups together based on a shared interest in equity and focusing on children.

Vicki Brewer is a very well regarded high school principal in Sydney and very sceptical of ministers – especially conservative ones. I knew of her by reputation. She is a fierce advocate for education and an especially fierce advocate for public education. Early on in my tenure, I spoke at a Secondary Principals' Conference and detailed some of our reform plans around giving principals more decision-making authority, changes to the way schools managed their finances, as well as outlining our preliminary thoughts on what we could do to support and improve the teaching profession. When it came to questions from the floor, Vicki Brewer stood up and asked me a question that was right on the mark. She asked, "Minister, how will you know if these reforms are working?"

It was a question that I would keep going back to in my mind every day. I told her the truth – "I don't know." I told her they are based on the best evidence we have at our disposal but that only in time will principals and teachers be able to answer that question for me.

The question constantly brought me back to the potential impact of the reforms. It also helped to motivate me. I like tough people who stand for what they believe in and fight to make sure the right thing happens. That's Vicki Brewer – and I like her! So, I was keen for the answer to her question to be "Yes, they are working to improve students' results and students' wellbeing." But I could not answer it on the day because they had not had time to take effect.

I shocked Vicki about a year later when I called her school out of the blue on my way back home after a week in Parliament. When I spoke to Vicki, I reminded her of her question, and I asked her how she thought the answer was going. She was stunned that I recalled her question, and she was surprised that I would take the time to seek her advice. The answer was positive, but it was not all glowing. She pointed out things that needed improving, which I took away and added to my list of things to do. During my time as minister, I called her every year after that, at her school, on a random day, to ask her how the reforms were going.

In February 2017, Vicki wrote a letter to me at the end of my time as minister:

Your work was important and ground-breaking. And your leadership – the vision presented, the negotiation with all stakeholders and the necessarily nuanced interpersonal skills to compete with conflicting priorities and people –was critical. It takes a deft hand to woo vastly different stakeholders in the cut and thrust of so many diverse needs without losing sight of the main game or the end point. You are one of the few people to understand and apply the adage that "the things that matter most must never be at the mercy of the things that matter least". Your reforms will be lasting. They were meaningful and right. Your pursuit of Gonski, for example despite the odds and controversy, was inspiring. We would not be in a position that we are today without your insistence on its place in our history. Its future status is unknown but without you we would never have known its possibilities. For that we are grateful.

I know her question remains unanswered, but her letter gives me heart that the decisions we made and the approach we took to the profession and reform were the right ones – that we are heading in the right direction and that those whom I was leading were on board.

No one likes change

Change, by its very nature, requires upsetting some of your friends and most of your enemies. The trick is to not upset them all at the same time.

It seems every person has an opinion about education. From parents who see schools through the prism of their own experiences decades earlier or media who focus on either test results or sensationalist headlines or politicians who know education is an important political issue for elections. It is also tricky because education is an almost entirely human enterprise. People dealing with people is an imperfect art. There are many divergent opinions about what should happen, when and why. There are many people with a very strong stake in education and often a very strong stake in the status quo.

To suggest that someone can come in and simply direct people to do things differently and succeed with that approach is wrong. It takes an understanding, built from a lot of one-on-one conversation and trust. It is also important to understand what stakeholders in education want and what pressures they are under.

Early on in my tenure, we introduced a series of reforms called 'Local Schools Local Decisions'.[7] NSW has historically had a very centralised education system. Everything was very tightly controlled by the centre. Staff were employed and allocated centrally. Almost every funding allocation, and the purposes for which it could be used, was allocated centrally. Principals often complained that they had very little leadership discretion in their decision-making.

It was not an education reform as such. It was an administrative reform. At no stage did anyone claim that this reform on its own was some kind of silver bullet to improve educational outcomes for children. It was simply a change in the way the NSW education department distributed resources and people to schools, and it gave principals a greater say in the way their schools were run, especially as to how their budgets would be spent.

The reforms would give public school principals in NSW similar decision-making authority that principals in Catholic and independent schools had enjoyed for decades. We were very careful to use the word 'authority'. This was not an increase in 'autonomy' but, rather, an increase in authority. It did not mean that schools within the public education system could go off and do what they liked. Schools still operated under the Department of Education's policies and rules, but they had greater decision-making authority within those rules. They were unable to grant themselves pay raises, but they did have a greater authority to choose who they employed in their school and what mix of staff they could have at their school. For example, if a school preferred to have an extra literacy teacher ahead of having a librarian, then the principal could make that decision based on what their students needed. Schools were also given a lot more discretion to bring in external services to their schools, again based on the individual needs of their school.

The media and politics in general had become obsessed with the results of NAPLAN tests as well as PISA and TIMSS results. Pressure was being applied to teachers, principals and schools to 'improve these results'. When I became minister, principals made it very clear to me that if they were going to be accountable for results, as they increasingly were, then they needed the flexibility and authority to make decisions to allocate staff and resources to best influence those results.

Principals were right to insist on greater flexibility around who they appoint to their staff and how they allocate the school budget to suit the individual needs of their children. All these were legitimate concerns, and something we were determined to improve. The teachers' union, on the other hand, prefers a very centralised system. They see it as their role to tightly control what happens in schools, especially about staffing. They prefer schools to be allocated staff entitlements rather than allowing schools to choose their own mix of staff. In that way, it is much easier for unions to influence what happens in schools because they only need to influence the decision-making of one department, not 2,200 individual schools.

This reform looked like it was going to get ugly. But I knew the principals wanted this. I also knew that public opinion was on my side. The public perception of public schools is that they are very tightly regulated schools, with little discretion around staffing. They were not free to hire and fire, and as a result, they were being held back.

The union declared war on these reforms, but they were still being included in the negotiations about what they were ultimately going to look like. I knew I had this battle won during a conference of the NSW Primary Principals Association (PPA). I was asked to sit on a panel of three people during that conference. It was to be myself, the president of the PPA and the president of the teachers federation. As we discussed the *Local Schools Local Decisions* policy, the president of the PPA made it clear that his members liked the idea of having greater decision-making, while the president of the federation raised his concerns that principals couldn't be relied upon to use these powers properly and that it would create too much administrative burden. The union president was reminded that 95 per cent of principals were members of his union, although principals made up only 5 per cent of his membership. They started to more or less argue on stage between themselves about the merits of this reform. Had the union and the principal groups both opposed these reforms, then we would have been in real trouble. I was very happy to have the principals on side.

Notes

1 According to the Oxford Online Dictionary, the term 'shock jock' refers to "a person who presents a radio programme and who often says things during it that are not considered acceptable by most people".

2 Alan Jones is a controversial former radio broadcaster with Sydney radio station 2GB from 2002 to 2020.
3 realestate.com.au/news/john-singo-singleton-ready-to-start-the-gosford-development-boom-with-bonython-tower/
4 For an interesting paper on Alan Jones, see Vredenburg, J., & Spry, A. (2019). *Shoving a sock in it is not the answer. Have advertisers called time on Alan Jones?*
5 Led by businessman David Gonski, a review into Australian educational funding was released in February 2012. The review was commissioned by the then–Gillard federal Labor government designed to reform school funding and lift outcomes for less privileged students through a new needs-based funding model.
6 From 1992 to 2020, the Council of Australian Governments (COAG) administered and managed relations between Australia's states and territories, with the federal government focusing on matters of national importance.
7 Launched in 2012 by the NSW Department of Education, the *Local Schools Local Decisions* (LSLD) education reform aimed to give NSW public schools more authority to make local decisions to best meet the needs of their students.

Analytical contemplation

Accumulating, keeping and renewing power

Don Carter

In this analytical contemplation, I explore Adrian's experiences through the lenses of the following:

- Symbolic power as a potent version of power in education.
- Power in the form of capital: economic, social and cultural.

(Bourdieu, 1990)

Education is an emotional issue for many of us. We have all been to school, and many of us have children who currently attend a school or who have passed through the schooling system. On any given day in Australia, education will figure somewhere in the media, whether it be a focus on student test performance, school fees, teacher shortages or educational equity. And one specific issue that is bound to arouse interest is the location of a new school or, as we saw in Adrian's chapter, the proposal to relocate a school – Gosford Public School. This type of issue is one that can spark controversy, and as we read in the previous chapter, the plan to relocate the Gosford Public School attracted the interest of radio broadcaster Alan Jones, an influential figure on Sydney radio from 2002 to 2020.[1]

Over this period, Alan Jones wielded substantial influence and enjoyed ready access to politicians, bureaucrats, sportspeople and businesspeople. During his career, Jones courted numerous controversies,[2] appeared in court on several occasions to defend himself and was never far from controversy as he "ducked accusations; and prevailed in the face of storms and juggernauts" (Kampmark, 2020, p. 3). Jones' audience over the years grew considerably, and he subsequently won consecutive radio ratings, which, in turn, attracted increased advertising revenue for the hosting radio station, 2GB. This positioned Jones as an influential figure; however, this status did not necessarily require him to rely on robustly factual material in his interviews (p. 3). Rather, he often utilised confrontation as a type of performance theatre and, at times, resorted to questionable sources of data as a means to counter the arguments of his interviewees (p. 4).

DOI: 10.4324/9781003312451-14

Being interviewed on a cold winter's morning at a regional airport is not ideal, and particularly when the interviewer has at his disposal an array of technical landmines to cut the interviewee off at any moment. This reminds us that hard power is not always limited to military operations and physical force, and as we saw in an earlier analytical contemplation, politicians are able to use hard power in the allocation of funding to states and territories, and a radio shock jock can wield hard power like a blunt instrument. Many of these broadcasters are adept at inciting controversy and provoking agitated responses from their audiences, or, to express this more eloquently and comprehensively, the shock jocks transfer "the capacity of non-elite, poorly resourced actors to challenge institutionally located power through strategic actions, many of which rely on symbols with cultural or historical resonances, in order to circulate their messages within and by the media" (Lester, 2010, p. 591) – in other words, inciting the listener to react and challenge issues which the broadcaster wishes to promote or nullify.

Adrian's refusal to acquiesce to Jones' demands that the school relocation plans be abandoned is relevant to our exploration of power, particularly with regard to retaining power and authority. Much of the literature on power centres not only on the acquisition of power but also on the accumulation and retention of power (Buzan & Lawson, 2013; Enloe, 1996; Rathbun, 2007). Of course, the retention of power as a theme is not new; if we were to turn our attention to the current state of international relations (as well as to history), we would see many examples of authoritarian figures and their regimes attempting to retain and consolidate power, with Russia's Vladimir Putin and North Korea's Kim Jong Un being two obvious examples.

While Russia and North Korea are large-scale international examples, the exchange between Adrian and Jones constitutes an example closer to home. Both men came to the interview with an accumulation of resources: Jones, with his broadcasting popularity, financed by the incoming revenue stream from advertisers, with a team of producers and researchers and the upper hand, technically, in that he could cut the conversation short and talk over the top of his guest. Adrian came to the interview with the legitimacy and authority of being a minister in a democratically elected government and with the sizeable education budget for the state of NSW. Both men were also practised at utilising their accumulated soft power resources of strategic narrative, issues narrative, persuasion and credibility. However, given the fact that this book is focusing on education, we will leave the analysis of Alan Jones and his power to others and, instead, return to education.[3]

Symbolic power

In this analysis, I explore the notion of symbolic power as a type of invisible but compelling version of power. I also investigate the accumulation of power resources as a compilation of different types of 'capital' and, in doing so, draw on the work of the French sociologist Pierre Bourdieu (1930–2002), whose influence extends across disparate investigative fields, including accounting research literature (Malsch et al., 2011), the relationship between social class and consumption practices (Longhurst & Savage, 1997), higher education (Di Maggio, 1979), the sociology of music (Prior, 2011) and the analysis of artistic behaviours (Danzon-Chambaud & Cornia, 2023).

As we have seen in previous chapters, the accumulation of power resources is essential to the acquisition of power. However, the notion of 'symbolic power', which basically means the power to "constitute the given" (Bourdieu, 1990, p. 170), is less visible and apparent, but it permeates our lives in different ways throughout the duration of our existence. Symbolic power is the capacity to make the outcomes of our actions and all forms of human endeavour appear inevitable and natural, as though they have always existed in a particular way. So much of our everyday lives is based on practices that we take for granted – gaining a licence before driving a car, paying for utilities such as gas and electricity, queuing in the supermarket to pay for goods and so on. We accept certain rules and practices that underpin our daily routine and the general fabric of our lives. As we go about our daily business, adhering to well-worn routines, we often 'miss' seeing the power behind our practices in our 'taken for granted' world. What we do not realise is that symbolic power threads its way throughout all aspects of our lives and is anchored in practices, including state-sponsored regulation, codification and classification, all of which to the average citizen can appear natural, desirable and enduring.

It is, therefore, much easier to recognise overt examples of power. For those of us (including the authors) who have incurred a speeding ticket or have been issued with a parking infringement, we know that the specific carriers of power (police and parking officers) apply legislated power as do democratically elected governments and their representatives. But overt power is different from symbolic power because the latter *mis*recognises power since it appears, *prima facie*, that *no* power is being wielded at all (Bourdieu & Wacquant, 1992, p. 168). What this means is that we fail to see the power behind the rules and regulations that govern our lives, shape our attitudes and rule our behaviour. Symbolic power is dissimilar to other forms of organised power such as military, ideological, economic and political power, of all which have their own unique systems of interaction and institutions (Mann, 1986). Symbolic power, on the other hand, is a kind of *uberpower*, imbued with the capacity to "enframe" (Mitchell, 1990, p. 569) practices, schemes and categories as "non-particular and unchanging" (p. 569) and presents these practices as benign and ever present.

The accumulation of symbolic power is most readily available to those who already occupy state-sanctioned positions, as those in elected governments and in state-authorised agencies such as departments of education. As education minister, Adrian wielded symbolic power through his responsibilities as a decision-maker in policy and decision-making processes of the government that are central to government action. As a member of the NSW cabinet, he played a key role in the formulation of new legislation, the appointment of staff, budgetary changes and other work.[4] In the community, he was generally afforded respect in meeting with constituents and in engaging with stakeholders. This is typical for representatives of legitimised governments and organisations which have a special status in the community.[5]

In addition, symbolic power resides in other organisations including teachers' unions, parent groups and teacher professional associations, which are able to wield symbolic power due to their democratically based constitutions, and their publicly acknowledged legitimacy is based on the "right to be and do something in society – a sense that an organisation is lawful, admissible and justified in its chosen course of action" (Edwards, 2000, p. 9). The representatives of such organisations act as the transmitters of symbolic power, naturalising practices and the traditions of the state (or their own specific organisation) and presenting those practices as those "which goes without saying" (Bourdieu & Wacquant, 1992, p. 168).

The state itself incrementally accumulates symbolic power through its administrative activities, which, over time, become accepted as 'part of life' and remain largely uncontested. This accumulation occurs as it administers apparently benign activities such as census data gathering, the issuing of birth certificates and establishing weights and measures (Tilly, 1992). Most of us would not think twice about the requirement for parents to register the birth of their child because the registration is a mere backdrop to the actual birth, but as a practice of bookkeeping, the birth certificate formats "our first point of entry into the information systems that are the atmosphere of so much of what we do in the world" (Koopman, 2019, p. 40). While many data collecting activities appear 'natural' and neutral, historically, these activities originated as a set of practices linked to the financing of war preparations called consecutive "extraction-coercion cycles" (Tilly, 1992, p. 70), which shaped the modern state through the need to establish complementary organisations, including supply chains of armaments, food and uniforms, treasuries to raise revenue and logistical structures to enforce conscription. These cycles constituted mechanisms to extract taxes from the general population for these preparations (Tilly, p. 92) and represent the normative, often invisible, practices of the state. They also represent the symbolic power of the state.

Symbolic power and education

While this might appear remote from what we encountered in Adrian's reflections, we understand that his work as education minister involved a host of administrative functions within a large and complex education system, both in NSW and nationally, reflecting Weber's contention that bureaucratic administration is "at the root of the modern Western state" (1978, p. 223).

Adrian's work entailed liaising with a host of complementary organisations, all of which demand different types of compliance requirements. Indeed, currently in Australia, there is a complex network of education organisations. For example, at the national level, we have the Australian Institute for Teaching and School Leadership (AITSL), the Australian Curriculum Assessment and Reporting Authority (ACARA), the Australian Education Research Organisation (AERO), Education Services Australia (ESA) and the National School Resourcing Board (NSRB). At the local state level, the Department of Education, the New South Wales Education Standards Authority (NESA) and the three school sectors (the department, the Catholic Education Commission and the Association of Independent Schools).

Each of these organisations wields symbolic power in one way or another. Take, for example, the NSW Board of Studies (BOS), which had been responsible for NSW curriculum development, the external higher school certificate examinations, home schooling and the registration and accreditation of non-government schools. In 2014, the BOS merged with the NSW Institute of Teachers to form the Board of Studies Teaching and Educational Standards (BOSTES) and broadened its powers to include the accreditation of teachers and the administration of the NAPLAN tests. In 2017, the organisation was renamed the New South Wales Education Standards Authority (NESA) as an "independent statutory authority reporting to an independent Board and the NSW Minister for Education and Early Childhood Learning".[6]

What is of interest here is how a series of reforms and a merger of two agencies[7] have the capacity to build and strengthen power and authority[7] in an example of the accumulation of power resources. NESA is now responsible for the responsibilities outlined earlier, plus the registration and accreditation of teachers in NSW, as well as the accreditation of the higher education providers (universities) that deliver teacher education programmes in NSW. A broadening of powers is evident in the NESA website statement that asserts that it "works with the NSW community to drive improvements in student achievement" (NESA, n.d.), signalling that more than curriculum development, the agency is charged with the improvement of student learning performance. If we reconceptualise these responsibilities as power sources, we can see that the resources necessary for the accreditation of teachers, which, in turn, are necessary for the employment of teachers in NSW, and the operations of universities offering teacher education courses are now present in one agency.

This represents the stockpiling of power resources. One might argue that this creates administrative efficiencies and is convenient for teachers, schools and universities to seek advice and accreditation from one organisation; however, another might counter that this consolidation of resources constitutes the accumulation of power in the form of regulatory requirements for teachers, schools and universities. In addition, the cycle of regulatory requirements imposed on teachers, schools and universities 'naturalises' and embeds these requirements into the routine and landscape of education, thus rendering them as inevitable, unavoidable and, to a degree, invisible and, in doing so, enhances symbolic power, authority and status.

While symbolic power is one means to ensure status, authority and power, the accumulation of what Bourdieu labels as "field-relevant capital" (1990, p. 112) is another. There are four types of capital: economic capital (financial), social capital (social networks), cultural capital (educational and cultural background) and symbolic capital (an accumulation of the other types of capital) (p. 112). Capital helps define "what is and is not thinkable and what is do-able . . . or not" (Grenfell, 2012, p. 222) and ascribes value to what is rare and sought after and that which is "most common (and) is of least value" (p. 222).

In the following section, I explore how different levels of capital affect the accumulation and maintenance of symbolic power by drawing on the work of Bourdieu.

Economic capital and power

The accumulation of economic capital as a power resource equates to the accumulation of authority and power. This is inevitable in school-based education due to the size and social significance that education plays in nations where sizeable and substantial education bureaucracies have been assembled, funded by large sums of taxpayers' money.[8] Compulsory schooling for children is a relatively recent (and expensive) phenomenon in the Western world and is intricately tied to notions of childhood, economics and the aspirations of the state.[9] In contemporary education, we can see parallels with Tilly's (1992) argument about complementary organisations because with the advent of compulsory schooling came the establishment of an array of organisations, associations and bureaucracies underpinning schooling, responsible for a range of functions, from the recruitment of teachers and administrative staff to the procurement and distribution of resources.

In NSW, the establishment of the Department of Education in 1863 (known then as Secretary of the Board of National Education), initiated an organisation that today controls a budget of more than A$8 billion and over 2,240 schools, with a total enrolment of almost one million students. In contemporary education, parent groups, teachers' unions, teacher professional associations and commercial interests, all lobby and vie for attention and resources to ensure their views are heard and agendas fulfilled. In addition, each Australian state and territory has its own department of education and curriculum/accreditation agency. As noted earlier, Adrian was responsible for a substantial NSW education budget, and no doubt, the other key organisations in education, including the teachers' unions, also were responsible for administering sizeable budgets. The access to and administration of sizeable economic resources is an example of economic capital and signals access to authority and symbolic power.

Social capital and power

The notion of social capital relates to our interactions within the networks of organisations and social relationships and the value we and others ascribe to those interactions. Specifically, social capital is "the actual or potential resources which are linked to possession of a durable network of . . . relationships of mutual acquaintance and recognition" (Bourdieu, 1997, p. 51). The resources of social capital provide "members with the backing of the collectively-owned capital, a 'credential' which entitles them to credit, in the various senses of the word" (p. 51). In other words, we accrue social capital with not only the number of influential people we know but also the volume of capital each of them possesses.

As outlined in the previous chapter, Adrian had invested a great deal of time as opposition spokesperson for education and then as the minister, developing relationships with a range of individuals and organisations. He was able to establish, as power resources, trust, credibility and authority. But these resources can easily be lost or surrendered in exchanges with others – as could have happened in his exchanges with Alan Jones.

Following the radio interview, Adrian expresses surprise when he realised that departmental personnel listened to every word he uttered in the interview (and all interviews), fearing that if he had acquiesced to Jones' demands, an urgent reconfiguration of policy would have ensued. This may well have also entailed a diminution of his standing in the eyes of senior bureaucrats and his parliamentary colleagues. Adrian notes, "[T]he only power people have is the power that Ministers give them when they roll over." This observation is reminiscent of Bourdieu's observation about a window that breaks because a stone is launched at it:

> Just as we should not say that a window broke because a stone hit it, but that it broke because it was breakable.
>
> (Bourdieu, 2000, p. 148)

Adrian is signalling the idea that it is easier for capital (i.e., power) to be surrendered by the holder to another party than it is for the other party to seize that power. Authority is easily eroded or given away when it appears as though you are controlled by other people. Had Adrian changed direction and ceded to Jones, he would have been effectively transferring a level of his own (symbolic) power to Jones and those audience members who supported Jones' position. He would have eroded some of his other resources, including credibility, which he had worked hard to establish and enhance with the department and beyond. As a result, the symbolic power of the ministerial office held by Adrian could well have been undermined. In addition, the surrendering of his power resources (credibility and trust) would have signalled a diminution of what Bourdieu calls the "logic of distinction" (1997, p. 47), where an individual occupies a unique position, and no one else can lay claim to that symbolic value.

Cultural capital and power

The term 'cultural capital' refers to the social assets of an individual, including intellectual capabilities, level of education, style of speech, modes of dress and so on. Cultural capital is acquired through the "systematic cultivation of a sensibility" (Moore, 2012, p. 108), meaning that the longer an individual is exposed to a certain asset of practices and attitudes, for example, the military or priesthood, the more likely it is that the individual will be predisposed to "express dispositions of a particular kind" (p. 108). Cultural capital impedes social mobility and embodies three types of capital relevant to our discussion: embodied, objectified and institutional capital, as we explain.

'Embodied capital' includes a range of socially acquired behaviours, skills and forms of conduct and generally requires a good deal of time to develop (Crossley, 2012). Often, these practices are inherited from parents and reinforced by the social group with whom we spend our time. Taking an interest in and going to the opera provides a type of embodied cultural capital just as going to the football to support one's favourite team is another example of cultural capital. A child who has been raised to respect and value education in their schooling and who studies hard to achieve good results has a level of cultural capital that is not readily available in the first instance to those who have not had the opportunity to acquire experience of Australian education.

Objectified capital refers to the possession of cultural goods such as books, paintings and other art works, while institutionalised cultural capital refers to the value of institutional qualifications in the labour force and the associated employment opportunities. Increasingly, over the last four decades, the importance of qualifications has been emphasised as part of a move to ensure that ability, training and experience are the key drivers in economic rewards and are free of bias involving questions of ethnicity and gender (Garcia et al., 2011, p. 433).

Cultural capital and education

Cultural capital is an important quality available for those who hold privileged positions. If we return to Adrian's presence at the Council of Australian Governments meetings, we would expect that the participants were all qualified in one way or the other or occupied positions of significance in education. The necessary qualifications or experience in education, in turn, qualifies the individual for participation and input and represents *institutional capital*.

As Adrian indicates in his recount, he prepared for the council meetings by doing what he had done for a number of years previously – listening. He assembled NSW stakeholders and talked with them to compile their views on relevant issues to enable him to advocate on their behalf at the council meetings. What Adrian had established over a period of time as opposition spokesperson on education and then as minister was his own specific *practice*. This means he had implemented a set of behaviours imbued with a "practical sense of what is appropriate, legitimate, and effective in a particular context" (Edwards, 2009, p. 252). Adrian's practice involved canvassing stakeholder views through listening and asking questions and then representing those views in the appropriate forums and, in doing so, over time, he built up his *social capital*.[10]

However, listening is only part of the picture. Adrian also acted as a 'disruptor', interrupting established patterns of behaviour (e.g., the traditional union vs. a conservative government) and related expectations of those involved in negotiations. Previously, negotiations in education relied on what we might call the usual 'practice' – that is, conflict and disputes between opposing political forces (government and union). Eventually, 'practice' becomes accepted because it is seen as appropriate, legitimate and effective in specific contexts and gradually becomes a "set of durable dispositions developed and inculcated over time" (Edwards, 2009, p. 252). Adrian's ongoing negotiations with stakeholders, based on listening – and also challenging established attitudes and behaviours – disrupted the educational environment and the traditional ways things were undertaken.

His presence at these meetings evoked discomfort because, as Adrian notes, he was an education minister, responsible for public education in NSW, and these meetings focused on Australia-wide education issues. Adrian's attendance was a unique opportunity to shape education policy beyond the NSW state borders. But it was also a potentially complex task because, as Adrian points out, he was being asked to make decisions about education across the public as well as Catholic and independent sectors and in early childhood education. However, the meetings constituted a unique opportunity for NSW education 'voices' to be heard at a national level, and to achieve this, Adrian embarked on a programme of consultation with NSW education stakeholders that informed his contributions at these national meetings and, in doing so, strengthened his authority as education minister – and his symbolic power.

Conclusion

Education concerns people, whether it be children in a classroom, teachers, administration staff or stakeholders. To build positive relationships, one has to build social capital using the resources of credibility, persuasion and trust. And to sustain one's capital, consistency, with a degree of predictability thrown in as reassurance for those with whom one is interacting, helps to maintain and extend the relationships and the issues under scrutiny. The accumulation of resources and capital enhances symbolic power and strengthens status and prestige.

Notes

1 Jones' radio audiences were consistently high during his tenure and increased his ratings during the pandemic in 2020 (2GB's Alan Jones' ratings surge during coronavirus pandemic (smh.com.au).

2 For a comprehensive account of controversies involving Jones, see Jenna Price (2019) *Destroying the joint: a case study of feminist digital activism in Australia and its account of fatal violence against women*, thesis submitted to fulfil requirements for the degree of doctor of philosophy, University of Sydney.

3 The book *Jonestown: The power and myth of Alan Jones* (2006) by journalist and author Chris Masters created controversy even before the book was published – and certainly after publication. One reviewer wrote that the book is an account of "how Jones wields and abuses his power as a broadcaster makes for profoundly disturbing reading" (Matthew Ricketson, *The Age*).

4 According to the Parliament of NSW website, "[T]here is little reference to the Ministers by title in the New South Wales Constitution". Roles and Responsibilities of the Premier and Ministers (nsw.gov.au)

5 I am not arguing that Adrian's role as minister did not entail argument and antagonism. I am arguing that his role as minister afforded him a unique status that is unavailable to the ordinary citizen.

6 New South Wales Education Standards Authority: Our story | NSW Education Standards.

7 Note how the rebranding included the word 'authority'. This term was also used when, at the national level, the National Curriculum Board (2008) was renamed the 'Australian Curriculum, Assessment and Reporting Authority' in 2009.

8 In the 2022–2023 Australian federal budget, approximately $125 million has been allocated for early childhood and school education. 2023–2024 Budget – Department of Education, Australian Government.

9 For a readable and comprehensive account of the rise of schools in Australia, see Campbell and Proctor's *A History of Australian Schooling* (2014).

10 I would also argue that his interactions with Vicki Brewer (principal) and follow-up with her strengthened his social capital (and credibility).

Chapter 9

Having clear guiding principles generates its own power

Adrian Piccoli

In education, decision-making is easy. Change is much harder.

When I look back at the six years I spent as the NSW minister for education, I admit there were many times when I was tempted to simply make decisions and get things done rather than take a slower, more deliberate approach of consulting and accumulating authority before making a decision. Having had that experience as an education minister – sometimes choosing the former path but mostly the latter, it is my view that to be effective, a minister needs to spend 50 per cent of their time on policy and 50 per cent on diplomacy. Too little time spent on diplomacy, and a minister can't get anything done; too much time spent on diplomacy, and a minister won't get anything done.

Having observed education leaders over the years both in Australia and around the world, unsuccessful leaders see their role as decision-makers first. They seek to impose their power on teachers, schools or government departments. The tyrant education leader, be they a minister or principal, who turns up expecting to make everything change overnight might succeed in making things different, but they will not succeed in making things change. Like a mediaeval castle siege, the occupants will usually wait them out until they pack up and leave.

Successful leaders in education, by contrast, see their role as leaders first. They bring those whom they lead along with them. Successful leaders also see their role as being joint decision-makers with those whom they lead. Very little change in education is affected by passing laws or issuing media releases or giving hectoring speeches listing everything that is going wrong.

Decision-making is the easy part of leadership. Generating true change is the hard and elusive part. It is the part that needs an underlying and long-term commitment to core values and principles. People need to believe in their leader. They need to understand and be included in the development of the values and principles of their leader. They need to be listened to and feel that their own values and principles are incorporated into the grand plan of the leader. They need to believe the purpose and direction of their leader, and they need to feel included. They don't need to agree with every decision,

DOI: 10.4324/9781003312451-15

but they need to understand why and how the leader's principles are what they are.

Leaders also don't operate and should not operate in isolation. They are part of a leadership team. In my case, our team included the secretary and deputy secretaries of the Department of Education and the CEO of the NSW Education Standards Authority, as well as my chief of staff, policy and media advisers and the other support staff in my office. Together, we formed a very effective and powerful leadership team.

Below are some of the principles our leadership team applied to guide our decision-making.

Principle: the interests of children always come ahead of the interests of adults

The key overriding principle we applied to every decision was to put children at the centre of all our decision-making. While that seems unremarkable, it's not an easy principle to apply in education because children tend not to complain about decisions, but adults definitely do.

I heard far too many stories about underperforming teachers who remained in the profession, teaching children, but who should have been performance managed out of their school. However, because they were only a year or two away from retirement, the school was waiting for them to retire rather than go through the difficult performance management process. They did this to protect themselves and the teacher; however, it was at the expense of the children in the school.

I know from the personal experience of my own children at one of their schools where a teacher had been deemed, through several performance management processes, to no longer be suitable to teach but was left in the classroom because the system they were in wanted to protect his 'spiritual wellbeing'. Wow, how about the children's spiritual and educational wellbeing? Children don't complain! Using an ethical framework that puts children at the centre of all decision-making makes difficult decisions, like removing teachers, very easy.

In education, we are so often kind to adults and hard on children. The best interests of children often run contrary to the perceived interests of adults in the media, in political parties and indeed in the teaching profession and those who advocate for them. It really needs to be the other way around.

Principle: students, teachers and parents should be proud of their schools

It is certainly true that the squeaky wheel gets the oil, and in education, it's no exception. It was one of the factors that really irritated me and unfortunately causes much of the inequity we see between schools and between systems.

If a heat map of where the most powerful people in Australia lived and then a map of every overfunded school, government and nongovernment, was laid on top of it, then I have no doubt there would be a very strong correlation between the two.

Conversely, the least powerful schools, those with a parent group not well connected, tend to be the ones that miss out the most, particularly in relation to the quality of facilities. The funding system was unfortunately skewed in NSW even between public schools.

Schools in country NSW and especially remote communities are usually the worst off. No metropolitan newspaper photographers go to remote schools and report on the physical conditions of these schools because those outlets don't care and because it's generally not of interest to their readers or their viewers. So I went out there instead. I lived in western NSW at the time, so I was already familiar with remote schools and small towns missing out on what schools and communities in bigger cities took for granted.

During my fourth visit to Walgett in far northwestern NSW, I was being shown around Walgett Primary School when I asked the principal why no one had ever taken me to see Walgett High School. Despite the many visits I had made to the town in the time I had been minister, I had always been taken to the primary school but never to the high school.

He didn't even pretend to conceal the truth. He told me that everyone was so embarrassed about the condition of the high school that they didn't want to take me there. I immediately said, "That's the very reason we should go and have a look." So, he took me there. And he was right. It was an embarrassment.

Here was a school built for 500 students in its heyday, 30 years earlier, but now the school's enrolment had dropped to 150, with fewer than half of the students turning up on any given day. The school was cavernous. It was a two-storey school, with concrete buildings and what looked like a prison exercise yard in the middle of it. What struck me was the noise. Because it was so big and had so few students, you could hear yelling occasionally or swearing but couldn't see who it was. It was eerie. There were broken drainage covers, holes in the ceiling with exposed wires, graffiti. It was a mess. The girls' toilets were disgusting. It's the little things that say a lot. The toilet roll holders were made of welded four-millimetre rusted steel plate with a big padlock at the end of the roll holder to keep the holder in place. There were doors missing, and the place stank. I wouldn't have turned up either if I was enrolled at that school. I was shocked.

After this visit, I set about doing something about the condition of not just this school but all the schools in the *Connected Communities* programme. I told Parliament in 2013, "It is true to say that we as a community have treated Aboriginal people like rubbish, particularly those in some remote communities where they are hidden from view."[1]

In a front-page story in *The Australian* newspaper on 26 September 2013, I urged the media to hound me about Aboriginal education. I complained that I get regularly hounded about irrelevancies in education like whether skipping had been banned in a particular inner-city school or whether ethics classes would be expanded but never about the state of Aboriginal education or the condition of schools like Walgett. Journalists thought it was either brave or crazy, for a minister to invite criticism of himself, but I never did get hounded about Aboriginal education despite the invitation.

Now I don't blame the previous principals for the condition of the school. I sympathise with principals in schools like Walgett, who deal with every sort of trauma coming through their gates daily. The physical condition of the school is probably the last thing on their minds. This is the reality for many schools which service very disadvantaged students. Just getting to the starting line with these children and these schools is a battle. Getting high-quality, experienced teachers to come to these schools is a huge challenge, and often, they just have to take what they can get.

I am often disappointed about the difficulty these schools have attracting staff, when there are thousands of teachers in metropolitan areas of Australia looking for a permanent job. And these jobs provide a golden opportunity to make a massive impact on young people's lives, especially Indigenous students. While tens of thousands of people walked across the Sydney Harbour Bridge in solidarity with the rights of Indigenous people, Walgett couldn't get anyone to come and teach maths to year 7 children.

So, as part of the *Connected Communities* programme, the department undertook an audit of the school facilities, and we soon announced a $35 million investment into the school facilities, including an almost entire rebuild of Walgett High School. Those works have now been completed, and the children have moved in. As I walked around the new school during a subsequent visit, I was walking through what was previously the area I described as the prison exercise yard. It has now been converted into a covered outdoor learning area with synthetic grass, some lovely landscaping and a few buildings removed to open it up into a bright and welcoming space.

As I walked along, I could hear the sound of a piano playing. I followed the music until I found a classroom where two Aboriginal girls were playing two electric pianos. They didn't see me look around the corner, but there they were, having a great time, lost in the music.

It was one of those moments when you see the culmination of many people's work leading to those wonderful moments of learning and joy. There is still a lot of work to be done, and the problems are far from resolved, but what I saw could not have been a more stark and wondrous contrast to what I had seen three years earlier.

Early on as minister, I was taken to visit schools in some of the most disadvantaged suburbs in western Sydney. One of those schools was Tregear Public School. Being from western NSW, I didn't even know there was a suburb called Tregear.

As soon as we pulled up out the front, the first thing I noticed was the fence around the school. Presumably, the school had been the subject of break-ins and a fence had been built around it, but it was one of the first fences built around schools in NSW. Back in those days, they built the cheapest fences they could, which was a chain mesh fence, with three strands of barbed wire running along the top. How awful it must be for children to turn up to a school that looks like a prison. I imagine parents didn't feel particularly empowered dropping their children off in such an intimidating environment. It looked like a cross between a prison and a war zone. The amazing thing, of course, is that people just got on with it. These communities had just got used to it, but I wasn't going to accept that. How can you tell a child that they are valued and that we have high expectations of what they can achieve but then have a barbed-wire fence around their school?

There were about 30 schools with barbed-wire fences around them scattered across western and southwestern Sydney, and I was determined to do something about it. But again, it wasn't easy. We had to carefully navigate our way around this issue. There were many, many other schools which did not have a fence at all, so we had to consider whether it was appropriate to spend almost $250,000 per school replacing an existing fence rather than building more fences around more schools. And we didn't want to be accused of spending money on something that was not a priority for the school. In the end, every principal was contacted, and they all agreed it was the right thing to do.

I'm not sure how many people in these schools noticed after a week or so that they now had new, modern security fences equal to any other school in the state, but I am sure students turn up to those schools and in the back of their mind see that people do actually care about them.

Principle: listen to the people doing the work – support the teaching profession

One of the key principles that became embedded in my mind was the need to take the profession along with me if we were going to affect change. I was determined not to be belligerent towards teachers and public education. The power to influence change is magnified the more people you can bring with you.

Liberal/Nationals governments have come to be feared and loathed by teachers and public education advocates for decades in Australia and indeed around the world. I have never understood the policy or political logic of Liberal/Nationals government ministers who insist on denigrating teachers. Apart from anything else, there are 300,000 teachers and principals in Australia, plus all their families, spouses and friends. If one considers that in Australia, there are 150 federal electorates meaning there are 2,000 teachers on average in each federal electorate and given that at every election, several electorates are determined by just several hundred votes, it just doesn't make political sense in Australia or anywhere else for that matter to turn such a large part of the population against you.

It doesn't make sense from a policy perspective either. The status of the teaching profession is a significant weakness in many systems around the world, including in Australia. Teachers struggle for the respect that the profession enjoys in other higher-performing countries. It is counterproductive for leaders to undermine the profession through lazy political rhetoric. Publicly stating that 10 per cent of teachers can't read or write is not correct and not helpful. All it serves is to cynically throw red meat to the conservative base. That's dumb!

From the experiences in Finland, and Ontario, Canada, particularly, it was clear that in successful jurisdictions, two factors needed to be kept in mind. First, that change takes a long time in education. It is critical to set a course and then stick to it. That's not a universally understood fact. There is enormous pressure from politicians, media and treasuries to see immediate improvements in test scores from any policy change and especially any investment of new money. There is no silver bullet in education.

It continues to frustrate me that we don't expect a multibillion-dollar investment in a new train line to start carrying passengers from the day the first sod is turned, yet that's the expectation with schools. In Sydney, the state government started building a new $8 billion rail line at about the same time the state started investing increased amounts of money in school education through the Gonski funding reforms. Building a new train line costs an enormous amount of money and takes many years before a single passenger is carried on the new line. Even then, it might take years to get to its expected capacity. No one seriously suggests that halfway through construction of that rail line, when billions of dollars have already been spent, that we stop and do something different because the train line isn't carrying any passengers and is therefore not working.

It is easy to conceptualise the staged construction of a train line but much harder to do so with education. In education, we expect to see results leap forward within a year of any change. That's the test of patience and staying the course that education leaders need to explain more clearly to the public.

Second, change will only come if the profession is on board with the reforms in a positive, inclusive and constructive way. A constructive relationship involves getting ideas for improvement from the profession itself, supporting the work of the profession but then engaging the profession in the implementation of reform.

Many school leaders warned me about change without ownership by the profession. Teachers will say all the right things and then do what they have always done if they don't believe in the changes. They will ignore or resist the change and carry on as before. So I worked closely with teachers, not against them. I spent many, many hours talking directly to teachers about how I and the education system could best help them do their work.

Principle: influence at scale – focus on system change

Looking at the successful transformation of other systems around the world, it is also very clear that concentrating on sustainable, systemic and scalable reform rather than one-off programmes was essential.

This principle was about staying away from one-off programmes and looking instead at the systemic levers that can be used to change all schools. There are 2,200 public schools in NSW and 1,100 Catholic and independent schools. True reform, true change has to come from system-wide changes to what happens in the classroom. There were one-off examples of great practice and great teaching, but it was patchy. How could we turn these great teaching practices into system-wide embedded practices?

Again, the best performing and most improved systems around the world experienced a cultural change in their classrooms but more importantly in their staff rooms, which drove much of their improvement. The role of governments and systems is to provide the right environment for that cultural change to happen. Valuing the teaching profession, funding and setting high expectations are essential elements to driving that change.

Not every teacher is excellent.

I know it's not very politically correct to say, but there are some teachers who are not very good at their jobs. Maybe they were, and they have now lost the passion they once had. Perhaps there are some who should never have become teachers. That's true and indeed true of every single other profession. There were and perhaps still are teachers who worked in public education who believe they are employed by the union rather than the NSW government. On one occasion when the NSW secretary of the Department of Education sent an email to all staff, she received replies demanding to know how she got this person's email address and others demanding that she stop sending them emails. One teacher wrote in response to the secretary's email, "You must have mistaken me for someone who gives a shit!" While minor infractions as that in any other profession might lead to dismissal, it does highlight a disconnect between what some teachers are doing in the classes on a day-to-day basis and where they see themselves in an organisation and as part of a profession.

The idea that all teachers are excellent and that all the problems in education are caused by externalities like workload, curriculum and so on is holding back reforms to the teaching profession and to the reputation of the profession.

Principle: create a fair school education system

Being fair is not easy because it means different things to different parents.

Parents are very powerful stakeholders in education decision-making, particularly when it comes to issues involving school funding. Nothing excites the passions in education like debates about money, especially if money to any school or school sector is going to be reduced by governments. And the schools which tend to be overfunded or at least have sufficient funding tend to be the schools where parents have the most agency. These parents have the greatest access to MPs, the media and other powerful community members.

For any government even thinking about cutting or changing the funding mix between schools and school systems, the subject must be approached very carefully, or the political fallout can be severe.

I knew things were getting serious when I heard that priests had started criticising government funding cuts from the Sunday pulpit. The funding split between government and nongovernment schools has always been a very divisive issue in NSW and Australia. When the NSW Liberal/Nationals state government was elected in 2011, the state budget was a disaster. The costs of running the government were increasing at almost double the rate that revenue was increasing. Government departments had been exceeding their budgets almost every year. The government of which I was a part came into power on a promise to bring the NSW budget back into balance. To do that, we needed to cut costs – not an easy thing to do for any government. Given that education formed almost one-quarter of the state budget, there were going to have to be significant cuts to the education department's budget, and some very contentious decisions would have to be made.

Cutting a budget for an agency like education doesn't necessarily mean the actual dollar amount of funding is going to decrease. It usually means it's going to be increasing at a slower rate than previously anticipated. What drives funding in government budgets are enrolment growth and teacher salary increases. Both of these were going up, so the budget naturally goes up. In 2011, the NSW budget expenditure was increasing by 7.6 per cent[2] a year, and the new government needed to bring that growth rate down closer to 3 per cent. That small percentage change required cuts of $1.7 billion over a four-year period just from the Department of Education budget.

Not an easy or popular thing to do. But every agency in the government had to do it. For NSW education, it was especially important. The Gonski school funding report had been commissioned in 2010 by the then–federal minister for education, the Hon Julia Gillard, and was due to be handed to the federal government in 2011. The NSW government knew this report was coming, and we knew that NSW would be expected to have to make a financial contribution to the funding reform to leverage more money from the federal government. This was a critical moment – we had to get the NSW budget back on track, or we wouldn't be able to support the Gonski funding reforms.

The question was, of course, where to cut funds from. I had made a policy decision that no funds were to be cut from inside the school gate. That quite literally meant that we would not cut the funding of any activity that took place inside the gate of any school. No cuts to teachers or programmes, no cuts to administration staff employed in schools.

Instead, cuts came from reducing the size of the state office bureaucracy, rentals (the department had offices all over the city) and other costs from the department. There were significant savings that could be made, so the department set about finding them.

One of the key decisions we made as a government to help find the required savings was to also reduce the funding the NSW government allocated to nongovernment schools. In 2011, the NSW government provided more than $800 million in grants to nongovernment schools. This represented close to 10 per cent of the NSW education budget. We could not ignore this significant element of the budget from our savings measures. If we didn't cut funding to nongovernment schools, then we would have had to cut even more from public education, and there was simply no justification for that.

Premier Barry O'Farrell, treasurer Mike Baird and I agreed through the expenditure review committee process that to reduce funding only to government schools was unfair. The fairest thing to do was to reduce the funds given to nongovernment schools by the same percentage value as was being cut from public education. This had never been done before. There had been plenty of cost-cutting in public education by both Labor and Liberal/Nationals governments, but no one had previously cut funding from nongovernment schools.

This was going to be very, very noisy. To ensure the entire cabinet was on board, I took the proposal to the cabinet. Cabinet approved my proposal that the cuts would be made from nongovernment funding in the same proportion as for public education and that I was authorised to consult with the sector about how to achieve these savings. The issue was how to manage this. Later in the day, I met the two sector heads, Brian Croke from the NSW Catholic Education Commission and Geoff Newcombe from the Association of Independent Schools, in my office.

Needless to say, they weren't happy about the proposed cuts, but then neither was I. No one likes being in a cost-cutting environment. I told them the details of the decision we had made, and they agreed to come back to me with their views about what they could do. I was asking them to find savings within their own bureaucracies in order for the cuts not to have an impact inside their own schools. They also asked if they could advise the chairperson of the independent and Catholic sectors. I agreed on the basis that confidentiality be maintained.

They both advised their chairpersons, but before long, the proposed cuts became public, and a campaign by the nongovernment school sector against the government began. This meeting had been held on a Thursday, and by the next day, it was all over the media. We gave government MPs advice to say that no decision had been made because that was correct. It had been agreed that I would consult the Catholic and independent sectors about how we would make these cuts to funding. It didn't have to be cuts to schools – no cuts behind the school gate. We weren't doing that in public education. We were reducing the costs of the bureaucracy, and it was my firm belief that the nongovernment sector could have done the same to meet their savings requirements. But it was not to be.

Bishops called the premier. Bishops called the federal leader of the Liberal Party, Tony Abbott, a strong Catholic, and he called the premier. The pressure was on. On that following Sunday, some Catholic priests were urging their parishioners to campaign to have these cuts reversed. I was very disappointed as both a minister and a Catholic. Surely, I thought, if it was good enough for the government school system to tighten their belts, the nongovernment sector could do the same. If we hadn't taken money out of the nongovernment school sectors, then we would have had to take even more money out of the government sector, and I wasn't prepared to do that – as a minister and as a Catholic. What we were proposing was completely fair.

The following week was a Parliament sitting week. By this stage, the media were in a tailspin about it. The media knew how explosive an issue school funding is with parents. So did government MPs. This had all the drama needed for a political time bomb. MPs had been lobbied by angry parents who had been whipped up by their schools and from the pulpit. Parents were being told their school fees would have to rise by thousands of dollars as a result of this decision – which wasn't true. Priests and bishops had been calling MPs and other prominent members of both the Liberal and National Party. People had called for me to be sacked. The Labor opposition were keeping their heads down.

On the Tuesday of a sitting week, the Liberal and National parties have what's called a joint party room meeting. Members from both parties sit in this meeting, where they are briefed on the week ahead in Parliament, including proposed legislation to be debated and any other major issue. Clearly school funding was a major issue.

At these meetings, ministers stand up at the front of the room; they give a few minutes to summarise the issue and then take questions. The briefing plus questions usually lasts no longer than five minutes. This briefing lasted one and a half hours. Every question imaginable was thrown at me. People were very angry. "This is our base", I was told. "The Bishop called", another MP told me. That meeting has the power to vote down any proposal that is put before it.

I stood there for an hour and a half taking a barrage of questions and acrimony. Leaning up against the desk at the front of the room, I thought to myself that if I get rolled here – that is, the decision to cut nongovernment school funding gets overturned by a vote of the joint party meeting – then I am going to resign. In all good conscience, if the party of which I am a member cannot recognise the inherent fairness in what we are doing, then I cannot remain a minister. If we reject this decision to fairly apportion budget cuts between government and nongovernment schools, then I am going to walk outside and resign. Not just from my ministry but also from Parliament. It was a very close-run thing.

I am certain that the majority in that room agreed it was the fair thing to do, but the majority thought it was politically the wrong thing to do. To his eternal credit, Premier Barry O'Farrell saved the measure and saved me. The premier stood up and told the MPs that we needed to do this. We needed to fix the budget as we had promised to do and that we had to do it fairly.

What most of my colleagues didn't appreciate is the respect that we as a government garnered from this decision. Never had nongovernment schools been asked to take the same pain as government schools. The government sector appreciated the fact that if they had to take some of the pain then that pain should be apportioned equally, and it was. There was not a single day of industrial action as a result of those budget cuts because it was fair.

We explained why we were doing it, and we explained how. No cuts inside the school gate. No teachers to lose their jobs. All sectors would be treated the same. And that we were doing this so that if and when the Gonski funding reforms were introduced, we would be in a financial position to make a contribution. Those funding reforms did eventuate. We did have the capacity to contribute, and they have profoundly changed schooling in this state and across Australia ultimately for the better.

The courage to make decisions for the long term, decisions based on fairness, can reward governments handsomely. If we had not made these savings, there would have been no deal signed between the Commonwealth and NSW, which kept the Gonski funding reforms alive. In the end, the funding agreement we signed with the federal government ensured that all three sectors had record funding growth not even two years later. Funding distributed on a needs basis, with funding certainty. We now have a funding system in this country, while not perfect, that is the envy of the world.

Notes

1 parliament.nsw.gov.au/Hansard/Pages/HansardResult.aspx#/docid/HANSARD-1323879322–75252/link/9
2 parliament.nsw.gov.au/Hansard/Pages/HansardResult.aspx#/docid/HANSARD-1323879322–43691/link/40

Analytical contemplation

Having clear guiding principles generates its own power

Don Carter

In the previous chapter, "Having clear guiding principles generates its own power", Adrian provides a series of principles which helped to guide his actions and programme of reform as minister for education. In the following analysis, I refer to several incidents Adrian recounts, focusing on the following:

- The difference between 'power to', 'power with' and 'power over' and how these matter in the exercise of power.
- The formation of a 'dominant coalition' to drive change.
- The importance of phronesis (practical wisdom) to effect change.
- Resisting change – how different 'cultures' of resistance are evident in education.

Versions of power

Adrian's case study highlights several key points related to power, including 'power to', 'power with' and 'power over'. The terms 'power to' and 'power over' were first coined in 1993 by Hannah Pitkin in her investigation of Wittgenstein's later "ordinary-language" philosophy. In this study, Pitkin suggests that a study of power begins not with a definition of power but with the examination of how power is exercised:

- 'Power to' refers to both 'capacity' and 'empowerment'. This means that an individual is able to do or achieve something by acquiring and retaining the resources needed to make power relations effective (Göhler, 2009). 'Power to' relations can also represent forms of resistance that individuals and groups may use to try to counter a dominance model (Weaver, 2001).
- 'Power over' means the ability to force one's will over others and presumes that an actor has more power than another actor and over processes and procedures (Pitkin, 1993).
- 'Power with' refers to power as an "empowerment model where dialogue, inclusion, negotiation, and shared power guide decision making" and drive dialogue and action (Berger, 2005, p. 6). All three are central to Adrian's recount.

DOI: 10.4324/9781003312451-16

Power as capacity and empowerment – 'power to'

In his seminal work on power, Parsons (1963) argues that power is the "generalised medium of mobilising resources for collective action" (p. 108). Haugaard and Lentner (2006) offer a broader definition, asserting that "there is no single essence that defines the concept but there are a number of overlapping characteristics" (p. 9). In both cases, however, power involves the acquisition and retention of resources, and for a minister for education, resources relate not only to the financial and regulatory type but also to credible sources of advice. And in his role as minister for education, Adrian was not only able to draw on the substantial resources of the Department of Education when required, he also had ready access to key education figures within and beyond New South Wales. The capacity to access and utilise resources provided the basis for the initiation of key education programmes while Adrian was minister. As minister, Adrian possessed "'webs' of powers" (Ribot & Peluso, 2003, p. 154), where the material, cultural and political-economic resources were at his disposal, providing the impetus for reform and the capacity to forge partnerships. And when the individual actor aligns power, authority and resources with other similarly equipped actors, a new force of 'irresistibility' is created, as I explain in the next section.

Dominant coalitions

Adrian was also able to assemble a team of key people in education. By gathering these people, he had assembled a "dominant coalition" (Cyert & March, 1963; Grunig, 1992). Such coalitions are often employed as 'specialised teams' to engage in joint decision-making when organisations are too large for one individual to control and manipulate (Hage, 1980). And typically, in these groups, decision-making processes reflect what is called "reciprocal interaction" (Göhler, 2009, p. 31), where one source of power engages with another "counterpower" (p. 31). The result of this interaction is that the power of both (all) parties is strengthened, resulting in a type of mutual dependence on each other, where the maintenance of exercise of power is undertaken jointly, underpinned by pragmatic agreement. This is related to the notion of 'possessive authority' that is already inherent within a legislated and publicly legitimated position such as a government minister (see chapter 4).

Although Adrian does not divulge details of the meetings of this dominant coalition, conventional thinking around the operations of such groups maintains that within the group, the power to influence decisions is drawn from various sources, including the authority invested in group members by virtue of their senior positions as well as personal qualities such as "charisma, expertise, information, reward, and sanctions" (Berger, 2005, p. 7). Interactions between members focus on the shaping of organisational decisions, the interpretation and allocation of resources and potential effects on organisational structures (p. 7). The interactions of group members reflect the idea that power is an individual characteristic or ability, although it can also be considered as departmental or organisational – or, in this case, group centred (Grunig, 1992). Interactions between members of "dominant coalitions" are reminiscent of the parallels between power and money – where power acts as the circulating medium through which "obligations are exchanged within a political (or group) system" (Göhler, 2009, p. 32).

Dominant coalitions and the 'power over'

Membership in a dominant coalition encapsulates the capacity to exercise 'power over' – that is, the ability to make decisions and effect change due to the position one holds in the coalition and access to resources plus membership in other associated organisations. But this explanation of 'power over' does not fully explain the idea of 'power over'. Foucault considers power as a means of domination; as 'power over', however, he argues that power must not only be defined (and, therefore, not confined) to the sovereignty of the state or the law, it needs to be understood as a "multiplicity of force relations immanent in the sphere in which they operate and which constitute their own organisation" (1990, p. 92). He asserts that power is "everywhere" (p. 93), omnipresent and coming "from everywhere" (p. 92), "permanent, repetitious, inert, and self-reproducing" (p. 93).

However, defining power – or access to power – in this way, does not completely explain the ways in which power is manifested or used by individuals or organisations. Thus, Foucault contends that power is not an institution, or a structure, nor is it a "certain strength we are endowed with" (p. 93). In fact, power is the name given to a "complex strategical situation in a particular society" (p. 93) and is exercised from "innumerable points" (p. 94) in concert with other relationships such as economic, knowledge and sexual that have a "directly productive role, wherever they come into play" (p. 94). Power is also exercised with "calculation . . . [including] a series of aims and objectives" (p. 93).

Adrian, as minister, was able to draw on the legitimised power of his position. He was able to use this position to assemble resources when required: form the dominant coalition group, seek advice from key people within the Department of Education and groups and education jurisdictions and access and allocate funding, as we saw in the previous chapter, for the rebuilding of Walgett High School.

His actions were also guided by a series of principles, where he developed relationships by engaging in what he terms as 'diplomacy'. He ensured that he engaged with collaborators to harness their support, and for some of his colleagues in the Liberal Party and for members of the teachers unions who were traditionally engaged in political 'warfare' with Conservative governments, he was able to "traverse the local oppositions and link them together" (Foucault, 1990, p. 94), activating "redistributions, realignments . . . and convergences of the force relations" (p. 94). Adrian and his coalition were able to make decisions effecting change through the use of what Foucault calls "tactics" (p. 95).

'Power with' and tactics

The issue of tactics in power is inherent within a version of power called 'power with' – the capacity of all individuals to share power and engage in collaborative decision-making. Here, interaction, dialogue, cooperation and relationship building are highlighted as the means to achieving the aims of the individual or group. The success of the dominant coalition was ensured by a shared vision and mutual respect for each other's expertise and experience. The sense of collaboration between members also reflects the acknowledgement of each other's record of achievements in education and also each other's capacity to influence – that is, each individual's capacity to influence others within their own organisational structure and beyond. As one seminal work in the theory of power argues, "Power is the capacity to exert influence. Power does not have to be enacted for it to exist, whereas influence does; it is the demonstrated use of power" (Dahl, 1957).

Throughout this book, Adrian has outlined his vision for education and, in the previous chapter, specified the principles which drove his ministerial career and allowed him to exert influence in his dealings with others. When we read principles such as "the interests of children always come ahead of the interests of adults" and "students, teachers and parents should be proud of their schools", it is difficult to argue that these are not worthwhile or worth pursuing.

Having said that, part of the strength or the irresistibility of power is its potential. It seems reasonable to me that stakeholders would react favourably to Adrian's principles and overall agenda. And when the holders of this potential power are acknowledged experts and office bearers in the education system, they also wield what is called "epistemic power" (Audi, 2008, p. 3). This refers to those who exert influence on what is considered as worthwhile (or not worthwhile) knowledge. Generally, experts are considered as the social category who possess epistemic power, where they possess the power to persuade, to exert influence over the thinking of others by virtue of the capacity that makes them experts. The dominant coalition, comprising recognised experts in education – or, at the very least, the capacity to tap into expertise whenever required – held expertise in several crucial domains: financial resources, demographic data and forward planning, building and architectural resources and personnel/workforce data and analyses.

The notion of 'power with', as we have seen, was central to Adrian's recount in the previous chapter and, in fact, most of his recounts throughout this book. His ability to influence and persuade through sustained and strategic engagement helped to achieve a series of specific aims and goals. His willingness to be patient and work towards goals, rather than take a 'machine-gun' approach of small and rapid reforms, saw him focus on "sustainable, systemic and scalable reform" rather than the smaller, media-friendly reforms and perhaps, ultimately, less effective and short-term reforms.

The power of phronesis (practical wisdom)

A useful concept in understanding the work that Adrian undertook as minister is the idea of phronesis, which has been translated as practical wisdom in dealing with both routine decisions and unexpected contingencies (Fowers et al., 2021). Phronesis has become an area of study across psychology, philosophy, professional ethics and education (Kristjánsson et al., 2021). However, there continues to be debate as to what constitutes phronesis (Grossmann et al., 2020; Kristjánsson et al., 2021), with some considering it a "skill" (Stichter, 2018), others as a type of intuitive artistry (Dunne, 1993), while others as just one virtue among others (Peterson & Seligman, 2004). Using the definition of practical wisdom as the "capacity to integrate the many virtues into a coherent and worthwhile life" (Fowers et al., 2021, p. 7), it is possible to contemplate that without practical wisdom, an individual could not live well consistently, because the "complexity and contingencies of life would be overwhelming" (p. 7). Practical wisdom has three characteristics: content, a quality of person and a form of action (Frank, 2012, p. 48).

Phronesis and content

More than just 'knowing the facts', a person who is able to apply phronesis has the capacity to identify what is most important in a given situation so that the "relevant virtue or virtues can be activated" (Fowers et al., 2021, p. 7). This kind of person understands that most situations are complex, requiring the integration of "multiple moral considerations" (p. 7) into decision-making and actions. This integration is particularly important when there is a degree of conflict between the virtues or one virtue needs to be prioritised over another one.

As Fowers et al. maintain, the individual who embodies phronesis uses their knowledge of situations and the world in general to "weigh various concerns against each other" (2021, p. 8) and use this balance in transforming their knowledge into practice. Without a perspective on what is 'good', there is no basis for a balanced interpretation and "no standard by which to evaluate various translations into action" (p. 8). In short, the criterion for judgement is absent.

Adrian's acknowledgement that education stakeholders would find the prospect of budget cuts unwelcome is an example of phronesis. He took action and met with stakeholders to explain the situation and, in doing so, combined honesty, compassion and transparency. It was an acknowledgement of the complexity of the situation and the need to recruit support for the cuts and a calculated risk in that it reflected the need to "balance the benefits and burdens that accrue in a situation" (Fowers et al., 2021, p. 7). Another consideration in the application of phronesis is that the individual making the decisions has an "understanding of what is good, which can be thought of as having a blueprint for a good life" (p. 8). This sees the 'practically wise person' understanding what is good aligning with particular situational features in what is called the "benchmark of salience" (p. 8), denoting the capacity to identify the important issues and act on them.

Phronesis and action

The point here is that an individual's capacity to hold and judiciously apply phronesis has manifold benefits for that individual and those for whom the individual is acting. Phronesis enables the individual to hold concomitantly what are sometimes seen as disparate and unconnected emotions: "empathy, awe, guilt, and anger regarding injustice" (Fowers et al., 2021, p. 8). We saw in Adrian's recount a combination of these emotions in his reaction to the state of decay at Walgett High School and his subsequent moves to improve the situation. The activation of practical wisdom makes it possible to imbue these emotions with reason, which allows for the individual to reflect and direct their emotions towards moral actions that are appropriate to the circumstances and consistent with the individual's overall understanding of what is important (Fowers et al., 2021). The practically wise person's emotions and actions must be guided by reason because without this connection, the individual may be liable to act impulsively or irrationally and fail to follow the appropriate course of actions to resolve the situation wisely.

Adrian's principles acted as the 'bedrock' upon which he acted. Shocked at what he encountered at Walgett High School, he resolved to rebuild the school to ensure it became a place of learning where both students and staff were happy to attend. As minister, he challenged the media to hold him to account with regard to Indigenous education, inviting scrutiny and accountability and demonstrating a commitment to his portfolio.

Cultures of resistance

Throughout this book, I have mainly concentrated on what worked for Adrian and me in our recounts of experiences of education. We have focused on the application of different power resources associated with authority and legitimacy. However, throughout his recounts, Adrian has commented on resistance to his endeavours from specific stakeholders, whether these be teachers' unions or even his own parliamentary colleagues. As he points out, not all ventures were successful, and not all actors in their interactions with Adrian were persuaded or convinced. It is also the case that not all individuals (or organisations) will cooperate and contribute to negotiations in education and other domains, and some will actively resist change and innovation. And it is this concept of resistance that I wish to scrutinise in the following section, because resistance aims at upsetting power's "maintenance of the quiescence of the non-elite" (Gaventa, 1982, p. 4).

Three cultures of resistance

Investigating the concept of resistance involves exposing the processes and assumptions underpinning 'taken for granted' phenomena such as authority in managerial structures (Courpasson & Dany, 2009). Such an investigation must also address the attitudes and actions of individuals and groups that often take place in the background – behind the scenes. Actors operate within the structures and cultures specific to their organisation, often in subcultures of cohesion (Scott, 1990), and are obliged to apply interpretation when opacity and ambiguity impede immediate understanding. Three cultures of resistance are apparent in the literature:

1 Cultures of defiance (Burawoy, 1979; Fantasia, 1988).
2 Cultures of appropriation (Vallas, 2006).
3 Cultures of contestation (Lisett et al., 1956; Osterman, 2006; Marquis & Lounsbury, 2007).

Cultures of defiance are the most commonly researched forms of resistance and have been undertaken in a range of industries, including manufacturing and construction (Fantasia, 1988). Central to this culture of resistance is indignation, opposing censures and restrictions imposed from above, reaffirming workers' skills and rights against an employer, vision of expertise and status recognition (Vallas, 2006, p. 1697). The outcome of cultures of defiance is a reaction against what the workers see as organisational elites and a subsequent 'shutting-down' of worker interactions with employers. Suspicion of the 'elites' fosters suspicion that workers are being deprived of rightful recognition of their skills and material resources (rightful pay and conditions). This type of culture tends to reproduce and perpetuate the authority structures it strives to change, affirming rather than changing existing power relations (Courpasson & Dany, 2009, p. 340).

This type of culture is also prevalent in the teaching profession. Teaching in schools is "anything but straightforward or simple" (Neri et al., 2019, p. 199), and teachers are required to "make sense of a plethora of often short-lived and conflicting interventions, prioritising those that improve teaching and learning and resisting those that do not" (p. 199). In this fluid and complex context, teachers seek to reduce uncertainty about the advantages and disadvantages of a proposed change through engaging in five decision-making stages: the *knowledge, persuasion, decision, implementation* and, finally, *confirmation* stage (Rogers, 2003). For many individuals, a decision not to support an innovation takes place at the at the *persuasion* stage, which centres on emotions and feelings, where knowledge of the proposed change initiates a positive or negative attitude towards the change that may influence the adoption of or resistance to the innovation. And this decision is often made at the persuasion stage, where the individual determines that they have not been persuaded to embrace the proposed change (Rogers, 2003). While some individuals are 'early adopters' of a change, others may delay their approval and, in doing so, embrace the role of 'late adopters', while others may completely reject the proposal.

In cultures of defiance, employee responses may generally acquiesce to the boundaries within team structures, with individuals holding a view of "fatalism and resignation" (Vallas, 2006, p. 1694). Workplace ambitions can be restricted to the maintenance of job security and securing pay increases as well as investment in "status gradations, clinging to particularistic identities that sometimes reject management's insistence on flexible team operations" (p. 1694). This type of dispute is often at the centre of a dispute between a trade union and an employer, where the union attempts to exercise power through the mobilisation of its credibility and capacity to organise industrial action, if required (Darlington, 2014).

The second culture of resistance is called *cultures of appropriation*, which is characterised through engagement with managerial structures, norms and mores (Vallas, 2006). The resistance in this culture stems from individuals fearing exclusion from new processes and programmes utilising employee expertise. Related to this is the blurring of boundaries, which define roles, responsibilities and expertise, sometimes creating friction and tension between employees and management. This type of resistance has been apparent in numerous campaigns led by the New South Wales Teachers Federation in support of better pay and conditions for teachers and also in campaigns to improve job security (Gavin & McGrath-Champ, 2017), while Carter et al.'s (2010) troika of strategic approaches (rapprochement, resistance and renewal) theorises the response of teachers' unions to neoliberalism, through rejecting neoliberal influences via militant or industrial means, or accommodating some aspects of neoliberal influence through more participatory and partnership-focused strategies.

The third culture of resistance relates to *cultures of contestation*. This refers to the individual's sense of self-worth, their social status in the hierarchy and capacity to assert their views and individuality and engage in acts of contest to assert themselves (Osterman, 2006). In this culture, scepticism towards authority is encouraged, and members are trained to "refuse unilateral power" (Göhler, 2009, p. 341). This kind of resistance is related to a view of contestation as "professional scepticism" (Endrawes et al., 2023, p. 383) and can be considered as both a "mindset and an attitude" (Nolder & Kadous, 2018, p. 2). Allied to this view, is the importance of the individual having an inquiring mind and the ability to conduct critiques and evaluations of information and data. It also involves maintaining a balance between trust and suspicion, with a slight emphasis on 'alertness' but without dispensing with trust (Endrawes et al., 2023, p. 383).

Professional scepticism is probably more common than we might expect. As Adrian points out, if you fail to bring teachers 'with you', then they will ignore you and just get on with their work, with their scepticism most likely strengthened. Teachers' unions, however, have since the 1990s, shifted their approach from a traditional industrial mode to a more professional mode of unionism (Gavin, 2019), where unions concern themselves more with matters relating to the "'other half of teaching', namely pedagogy, policy and professionalism" (p. 22). In this way, teachers' unions have accumulated potential power resources over the past 30 years: economic regulation (the attempt to secure the highest possible wages and workplace conditions), job regulation (jointly constructed rules and regulations for the workplace) and the exercise of power through the provision (or withdrawal) of labour and expertise (Darlington, 2014).

Conclusion

Power and authority are manifested at the individual, group and organisational levels. While the positions of education minister and high-level education bureaucrats are invested with the authority and prestige of legislated appointments, reform agendas can be circumvented or even jettisoned without careful and considered application of phronesis by individuals and members of groups and organisations. Harnessing the power and authority of a dominant coalition serves to potentially further an agenda, provided its proponents are aware of the nature of likely resistance and have the capacity to work effectively and positively with the different cultures of resistance.

Chapter 10

The two faces of education

Don Carter

I have been in education for just over four decades now. I have worked as an English and history teacher and head teacher in rural and metropolitan Sydney schools, both government and nongovernment. I have worked as an English as a Second Language consultant for the Department of Education, as a project manager for a year 12 cognitive science syllabus that the Board of Studies (BOS) was proposing to release in 2003,[1] as a senior curriculum officer in English, as inspector of English and then as a registration and accreditation inspector. And now, as a teacher education academic. I feel that these varied roles have provided me a 'bird's-eye' view of education and a set of unique experiences.

Each one of these roles provided a certain perspective on education. The daily grind of the classroom was both rewarding and at times frustrating and certainly threw up challenges in dealing with unruly students (and their parents), as well as making sure students were performing well. Teaching in schools and leading a faculty was the best introduction to knowing how schools 'work' – from the staff on the front desk[2] to colleagues in other faculties, the Parents & Citizens Association, the school counsellor and more – it is the 'on the ground' experience that can alone provide the insights into schools and their daily business.

However, once you step out of the classroom into a promotions position, your priorities change. Budgets become important, recruitment of the right people, forward planning and managing colleagues move to the top of the list. And as you move into more bureaucratic roles, budgets and the allocation of resources are paramount. This makes sense. Educational programmes cannot run on the smell of an oily rag, and schools need funds for maintenance, programmes and other resources. In the following recount, I want to illustrate two faces of education: resources and budgets as the 'hardnosed face' of education – permeating all dimensions of education – and the face of education, captured by the child.

DOI: 10.4324/9781003312451-17

The hardnosed face of education – multiple-choice questions in English examinations

When I left the BOS[3] in 2014, I did not expect to become embroiled in controversies, and I certainly did not expect to be critical of my former employer. I thought that I would enjoy my new role in higher education and embark on a research and publication trajectory – a pathway I had wanted to undertake for some time. My work as inspector had been both taxing and rewarding, but it did not entail the research I longed to immerse myself in and did not provide opportunities for writing – beyond ministerial briefing papers and memoranda for senior management. One important part of my role as an inspector was to ensure that English remained as a core subject in the curriculum and that English subjects[4] continued to facilitate student ability to use language as the "centre of the development and expression of our emotions, our thinking, our learning and our sense of personal identity" (Marshall, 2023, p. 29).

Many battles about the content and status of English as a subject in New South Wales were fought within the walls of the BOS. Robust and sometimes fiery discussions were held regularly, particularly in times of financial austerity. One associated suggestion from a senior officer in 2008 was to introduce multiple-choice questions as part of the final HSC English examination. The reasoning was that the multiple-choice questions could be marked by a machine to reduce HSC marking costs, which were, by all accounts, substantial. However, this suggestion was met with horror by my curriculum officer[5] and myself. We saw this as an outrageous betrayal of the intentions of English: to develop a student's capacity to express themselves in well-written and thoughtful language. We believed that multiple choice would reduce examinations in English to a 'pick and choose' subject and cancel the opportunity for a student to demonstrate their knowledge and expertise in writing.

A series of robust meetings then took place between my curriculum officer, the two senior managers and me. We explained as forcefully as possible that this was a retrograde step, one that English teachers would actively and vociferously oppose.[6] We explained the ahistorical and antithetical nature of the proposal – how it contradicted the aims of the subject and betrayed the history of English as a subject in New South Wales. A central point in our argument was that if multiple-choice questions became a key component in the examination, then teachers would tailor their teaching to instructing students on how to answer these types of questions efficiently and abandon the teaching of the broader skills of reading and writing. It was more complicated than this, but that was the basis of our argument. A series of tense meetings took place, but finally, senior management relented and withdrew the proposal. We were not sure which part of the argument won the day, but both of us saw the face of one of those executives change at a point in the conversation. Perhaps it was the prospect of hordes of angry English teachers besieging the board with complaints. I am not sure we will ever know.

The hardnosed face of education – development of the Australian curriculum

Developing any curriculum is complex and sometimes messy. You not only have to deal with curriculum models and their benefits and deficits but you also have to deal with people, their ideas, priorities and agendas. I can say that during the period of the development of the Australian curriculum, it was a particularly sensitive time to be an inspector at the BOS. In New South Wales, legislation dictates that school-based curriculum must be developed by the NSW Curriculum Authority, and this had been the case over many decades.[7] The prospect of an Australian National Curriculum had been envisaged for decades but had not eventuated, although in 2006, the federal government, led by John Howard, brought it back to the table. A major argument for a national curriculum was to establish curriculum consistency across the country to assist the children of itinerant workers and national servicemen and servicewomen. This seemed a flimsy rationale for a national curriculum to me, but it proved to be the impetus for further explorations on the possibility of such a venture, culminating in the release of a "National Curriculum Development Paper"[8] in June 2008, which set out the remit, contents and standards of the proposed curriculum and the membership of the organising body, the National Curriculum Board.[9]

However, in Australia, the planning for and the development and implementation of a national curriculum was never going to be straightforward because reforming the curriculum was traditionally a "protracted and complex" (Savage, 2016, p. 835) process, emphasising the "always contentious" (Brennan, 2011, p. 259) nature of curriculum. In the past, when the likelihood of a national curriculum was tabled, the Australian states and territories launched a defensive counterattack, which "jealously guarded their curriculum sovereignty, overtly or passively resisting attempts to engineer national approaches" (Reid, 2005, p. 15, in Hughes, 2019). In addition, the long-lasting tension between the "nation-building aspirations" (Reid, 2019, p. 199) of the Commonwealth government and the "constitutional responsibility" (p. 199) of the states provided the background for an intricate blend of various educational ideologies and practices, acting as "curriculum gatekeepers" (p. 199). Inevitably, the issue of "States' rights sentiments" (p. 203) continued to feature during the Australian curriculum's development and proved to be a dominant feature of the attitudes at the NSW BOS.

With the development of draft curricula in English, mathematics, science and history by ACARA, the board inspectors (BIs) were asked by senior management to comment on the drafts and recommend changes. Over a two-year period, I compiled the feedback to the draft National English Curriculum, and my fellow inspectors worked on the other subject areas. What we saw in those early drafts was worrying for several reasons, and our responses were captured in an official BOS response in 2010.[10] However, what I found more interesting was the attitude of one of the board's senior managers to our collaborative work with the ACARA officers, as demonstrated by the following recount.

Over 2009 and 2010, BIs had been encouraged to work with the ACARA officers to assist them in the development of a quality curriculum. In September 2010, we were invited by ACARA to a meeting to discuss what was a series of concerns raised by the BIs following months of evaluating draft ACARA syllabuses. The discussion with the ACARA senior officers centred around draft content included in the draft syllabuses for English, mathematics, science and history, with the BIs specifying areas of the content that required strengthening and providing recommendations on how this might be achieved. The discussion was amicable and collegial, with the ACARA officers seeking specific advice on the content for each of the syllabuses. In each subject area, they asked particular questions about how the wording or ideas could be improved. As a BI from New South Wales, it was reassuring that senior officers from the federal agency appeared to be genuinely interested in feedback from NSW curriculum experts. The meeting continued over a two-hour period, with ideas being exchanged and discussed. We felt we had provided the ACARA officers with many worthwhile suggestions and strong advice.

The meeting concluded with an assurance from the ACARA officers that our feedback would be conveyed to the curriculum writers. However, after the ACARA officers had left, the BOS senior officer closed the door of the meeting room, turned to us and snarled, "Do you want to lose your f****** jobs?" We sat there in shock. In a career in education spanning 30 years, I had never experienced a leader speaking to colleagues in such a way. This senior officer believed that our advice to the ACARA team was naive – that is, we were unwittingly providing their curriculum writers with sound advice for the compilation of the national curriculum that might supersede the NSW curriculum and thus render us unemployed.

To sum up the reactions of the BIs following this incident, I can safely say that this senior officer lost our respect and, to some degree, our loyalty. Our interactions after this incident would be wary and suspicious; after all, we as BIs attended the meeting at the request of this particular senior manager, and we had been working with ACARA staff over many months, at the request of BOS senior management. The incident added another layer of complexity to an already delicate relationship between the two organisations and undermined what was previously a healthy relationship between BIs and this senior manager. I understand the risk of surrendering our roles to ACARA, but as mentioned earlier, curriculum in NSW is the responsibility of the local curriculum authority, the Board of Studies. Our view on the outburst was that this officer was gratuitously using a higher position in the public service as a mechanism to assume a position of greater wisdom and superiority. The effect was to alienate four previously loyal and senior subject area experts.

The face of the child in education – "I'm scared of NAPLAN"

No one in education will ever declare that children are not at the heart of their decisions in school-based education. No one would ever concede that the 'child' has become a ghostly but continuous presence, rendered little more than an abstraction in official documents but sometimes 'distant' to the education professional working on the administrative side of education. And during my career in education, I was driven by a strong belief that the child must be at the centre of decisions in education at all times, personified when one child told me, "I'm scared of NAPLAN."

When a ten-year-old girl from a southwestern Sydney primary school said this to me during an interview for a research project I was leading a few years ago, it really touched me. I wondered how many other children felt like this and how many parents had heard this type of statement from their children. The context was a series of classroom observations and interviews with students and teachers from four schools about improving the writing skills and confidence for both students and their teachers.[11] The interview with this specific student took place outside her classroom. I had just finished observing the teacher in the classroom undertaking a lesson on writing. It was inspiring, and the classroom itself was a warm, colourful and inviting space for the students. I had been impressed with this teacher's approach to ensuring that all children felt comfortable with taking part in discussions and offering opinions. I had also been impressed with the teacher's approach to writing, where a series of engaging 'provocations' sparked discussions amongst the students before they began to jot ideas into their books and then transforming those ideas into more sustained pieces of writing. When the student left the classroom and sat with me just outside, I had not expected these words to be the first she uttered. After a slight pause of surprise, I asked her why she felt this way. Her response was direct, stating that:

> [W]e (the students) don't come to school to be tested all the time. We come to learn but practising for the (NAPLAN) tests takes up so much time. Our teacher is great, but she makes us practise too much. I don't like it. It makes me sad.

No other student in this series of interviews spoke directly to NAPLAN in this way,[12] though I did ensure I gathered their views on NAPLAN. The above student pointed to a dimension of standardised testing that is often overlooked when results are released – the effects on students. Anecdotally, I hear stories of schools spending inordinate time rearranging school timetables to accommodate NAPLAN, setting up classrooms to administer the tests and 'drilling' students on the types of questions they will face in the tests. The 'human face' of the tests is the child, like the one I interviewed. And I would expect the reverberations of her nervousness to be felt in her home. This specific interview stayed with me, and when the former CEO of the New South Wales Education Standards Authority, David de Carvalho, wrote a piece in the *Sydney Morning Herald*, titled "Busting some of the HSC literacy and numeracy myths",[13] extolling the virtues of NAPLAN, I felt compelled to respond. To me, David's opinion piece was a vivid example of what I have just described: the abstracted child, considered from a distance, with decision-making 'benevolently' applied in the child's 'best interests'. I wondered how much exposure policy makers had in classrooms, talking with and observing students, talking with their teachers and so on. I wondered about the extent to which they had read the literature on NAPLAN and the negative effects of the tests and if they had read international reports on the effects of mass standardised testing.

I decided to do something about it. I penned a response to David's piece, titled "'I'm scared of NAPLAN': The consequence of a reductive view of education",[14] which was published two days later. It caused a stir, with me being interviewed on numerous radio stations, David posting a response to my article on the curriculum authority's website accusing me of creating a 'straw man' by criticising NAPLAN. I also received numerous emails from strangers congratulating me on my stance. I felt vindicated about publishing the piece. I felt that I was supporting the young girl who had said this to me and those students who felt the same and also felt I had finally shaken the last vestiges of the education bureaucracy from my shoulders and was back in the world of schools and their students. And now I was in a position to say what I thought about education and actually contribute to debates in a robust and informed way.

Notes

1 In 2003, a suite of new years 7–10 syllabuses was released, and the board decided not to overload teachers with a new senior syllabus.
2 Many teachers will tell you that the staff on the front desk in a school are the most important. This is very true.
3 By 2014, the nomenclature 'Board of Studies' had changed to the 'Board of Studies, Teacher Education Standards'. By 2017, the name changed again to the 'New South Wales Education Standards Authority'.
4 The suite of English subjects included Advanced, Standard, Extension 1 and Extension 2, for example.
5 My colleague went on to lecture in English at a metropolitan university. In 2017, the multiple choice in English examinations was again suggested. Several academics and I (and others) spoke against this in the media. The proposal was abandoned.
6 We do wonder, however, had this change been implemented, if the next generation of English teachers would accept the multiple-choice questions as normal, routine practice in English.
7 Previous to the Board of Studies was the Board of Secondary School Studies, and before that, the NSW Department of Education was responsible for curriculum

development. For the chronology of curriculum in NSW, see Campbell and Proctor (2014) in the reference list.

8 https://docs.acara.edu.au/resources/development_paper.pdf

9 The National Curriculum Board was the organisation originally charged with developing the curriculum and was superseded by the Australian Curriculum Assessment and Reporting Authority (ACARA) in May 2009.

10 *New South Wales response to the draft K 10 Australian curriculum for English, history, mathematics and science* (2010), www.boardofstudies.nsw.edu.au/australian-curriculum/pdf_doc/nsw-response-to-draft-k-10-aus-curr-eng-hist-math-sci.pdf

11 See reference list: Carter and Yoo (2022) and Yoo and Carter (2017).

12 Following this initial interview, I asked other students (× 22) about their views on NAPLAN. None was positive about their experiences.

13 *Sydney Morning Herald*: www.smh.com.au/opinion/busting-some-of-the-hsc-literacy-and-numeracy-myths-20170329-gv9832.html

14 *Sydney Morning Herald*: www.smh.com.au/opinion/im-scared-of-naplan-the-consequence-of-a-reductive-view-of-education-20170404-gvdaf2.html

Analytical contemplation

The two faces of education

Don Carter

This analytical contemplation is based on my case study in the previous chapter and briefly investigates the following:

- The power of tradition: how organisational/pedagogical, epistemological and curricular traditions constitute power.
- The key mechanisms of filiation, persistence and routinisation.
- Specific changes to English as a subject established in the early twentieth century.
- Power as manifested in different typologies, including Nyberg's (1981) *force, finance, fiction* and *fealty.*
- Historical notions of childhood as the basis of contemporary views on childhood and their continued presence in contemporary curriculum documents.
- The gap between the rhetoric contained in documents, which outline the 'big picture' aims of education, and the actual experience of some students, as captured by the young girl who told me she was 'scared' of NAPLAN.

Tradition as power

The exercise of power and authority is not always limited to the activities of human interlocutors. In fact, both can be detected in the concept of tradition, which, although a difficult term to define (Williams, 1976), can be considered as "particular sets of practices or embodiments of practice that seek to inculcate certain values and norms [and which] . . . attempt to establish continuity with a suitable historic past" (Hobsbawm, 1983, p. 1). Over many decades, social scientists, philosophers and theorists have identified the often seamless and subtly inscribed power of tradition interwoven into different aspects of our lives and its "irrepressibility and irreducibility, [indicating] what cannot be done away with, or that which must be faced" (Bruns, 1991, p. 12).

In the previous chapter, I explain how the proposal to adopt multiple-choice questions in the HSC English examinations was deeply concerning to a colleague and me. To illuminate why we thought the proposal was a bad idea,

DOI: 10.4324/9781003312451-18

I draw on three traditions in education (Halpin et al., 2000) and aspects of Shils' (1971) seminal theory of tradition, which sees the maintenance of tradition as the result of filiation, persistence and routinisation. I also briefly draw on Yadgar's (2013) work, which highlights the role of language and narrative in upholding, perpetuating and even renewing aspects of tradition. Thus, my intention is to show how the power of tradition shapes beliefs and practices in English teaching and how this renders the multiple-choice proposal as irrational and illogical.

Tradition and education

Tradition remains a powerful force in education, with three kinds apparent: organisational/pedagogical, epistemological and curricular traditions. Organisational and pedagogical traditions refer to the traditions related to the structure of schools and how learning is delivered in a school. For example, one organisational tradition is the comprehensive school, which is based on egalitarian ideals and enrols students regardless of gender, socio-economic, and cultural, religious and linguistic background. Another organisational tradition is the faith-based school, while yet another is the 'grammar' school tradition, which is linked to meritocratic ideals (Halpin et al., 2000). Associated with the organisational tradition is the pedagogical dimension which is related to how groups of students are organised to learn. For example, are the classes streamed into ability groups? Or organised into mixed-ability classes? What overarching approach is adopted? Is it a 'progressive' or child-centred approach, as one might witness in a Montessori school? Or a more traditional approach, which places emphasis on the delivery of curriculum content and emphasises student performance in tests and examinations.

The second approach, epistemology, is the "branch of philosophy concerned with the theory of knowledge . . . the scope, nature and derivation of knowledge and the reliability of claims to knowledge",[1] and epistemological traditions refer to the practices of different disciplines of knowledge and how this knowledge is organised. This tradition selects and represents the knowledge and texts to be included in a curriculum, privileging some knowledge over others. Examples of this are evident in the New South Wales curriculum of the early twentieth century, which foregrounded knowledge of the British Empire and its most significant (mostly male) figures. More recently, in school-based curriculum, a shift has seen knowledge relating to Aboriginal and Torres Strait Islander histories and cultures assume a stronger presence in the curriculum.

Finally, curricular traditions refer to different approaches to education and its aims. In English, for example, Cox (1991)[2] refers to six models: cultural heritage, personal growth, cultural analysis/critical literacy, skills/adult needs and cross-curricular models. Particular models often have lobbyist groups who push the particular ideological agenda of the group. This was particularly apparent at the turn of the nineteenth and twentieth centuries, when specific groups such as the 'practical educationists', 'social reformers', the 'naturalists', the 'Herbartians', the 'scientific educationists' and the 'moral educationists' were all vying for ideological advantage in curriculum and school funding issues (Selleck, 1968).[3] All types of traditions exert power and authority in specific contexts, as I explore later.

Reshaping tradition in education

During the first 15 years of the twentieth century, a series of changes and reforms in NSW education took place as a reaction against the educational practices of the nineteenth century. Education – known as the "old education" (Selleck, 1968, p. 19) – had previously emphasised the "Three R's" (p. 25) ('reading, writing and arithmetic') and been considered as "a matter of packing as much information as possible into vacant and supposedly receptive minds" (Cunningham, 1972, p. 102). There was an emphasis on memorisation and repetition, followed by pupils undertaking activities to apply those facts, with an attendant belief that by 'training' a pupil, the transfer of acquired skills to other activities could be achieved (Cunningham, 1972, p. 102). In this era, there was a belief that a linear, "lock-step" approach to classroom learning was the most efficient way to 'educate' pupils (pp. 103–104). However, this approach to learning was increasingly considered as "outdated, no longer relevant to the needs of society" (p. 106).

The power of organisational and pedagogical shifts

At the beginning of the previous century in New South Wales, a new approach to school education and the ways in which students were viewed was underway. This was called the "New Education" movement, which had gained impetus in the late nineteenth and early twentieth centuries in the United States, Britain and Australia.[4] The New Education drew on the work of Johann Friedrich Herbart (1776–1841), Friedrich Wilhelm August Froebel (1782–1852), Jean-Jacques Rousseau (1712–1778) and Johann Heinrich Pestalozzi (1746–1827) (Carter, 2016).

These educationists shared strong convictions about the importance of a holistic approach to education, with an emphasis "on spontaneity, creativity and self-activity in learning" (Sellars & Imig, 2021, p. 1152), as well as the "'funds of knowledge' that young people bring from parents and others in the 'family circles' of their students, and the focus on whole child development – intellectually, practically and morally" (p. 1152). This view of the child and the teacher's role as nurturer became more entrenched as the focus increasingly highlighted the value of the child's own personal experiences and the harnessing of those experiences as 'stepping stones' into new learning experiences.

These shifting attitudes began to disrupt the tradition of organisation/ pedagogy in schooling. By 1913, in NSW a new system of secondary schooling[5] was introduced, which included high schools, intermediate high schools, district high schools, superior public schools and evening continuation schools. While these schools were charged with the mission of developing students' employability skills, they were also the sites of pedagogical practices that sought to enlist the creative talents of students as they worked their way through the curriculum.

One example of this is the influence of the British educator H. Caldwell Cook (1886–1939), whose work in educational drama was acclaimed in Australia and internationally (Howlett, 2019). Cook promoted collaboration between, and with students, imaginative drama games including role plays and simulations and a view that the "basis of educational method must be a regard for the pupil's interests" (Cook, 1917, p. 45). He used drama as the main methodology for teaching English so that students transformed prose, poetry and Shakespearean texts into dramatic action based on their understanding of the Elizabethan stage (Bolton, 2007). His approach also sought to integrate learning across the curriculum as exemplified by the example of using a daffodil which his students could use as a nature study in biology, the singing of songs in music, an exploration of Wordsworth's poem and the drawing of botanical specimens in art (Cook, 1917). This approach, which aligned with the apostles of the New Education, took root in English teaching, in both Australia and England, where self-expression and the study of literature became central to English teaching (Ball, 2006).

These changes constituted a shift in traditions: from a view of students as 'empty vessels' to be filled with content knowledge to the student as an individual with a set of rich and valid life experiences to be nurtured and extended through classroom work which acknowledged and built on those experiences. The integration of education drama into classroom work became a staple of the English teacher's pedagogical toolkit and remains an important part of teaching today (Fleming, 2017; Zhou & Chen, 2020). And what was happening in classrooms, reflected changes in curricular traditions, as I outline later.

The power of curricular shifts

The power of the New Education discourses was apparent locally. In New South Wales, the director of education in 1905, Peter Board,[6] was heavily influenced by the New Education's approaches to learning. In that year, Board introduced a new primary school curriculum, which placed English at the "hub" of that curriculum (New South Wales Department of Public Instruction, 1905, p. 2), with "historical and literary topics the central focus" (Meadmore, 2003, p. 384).

In both the primary and secondary curricula, Board introduced practices which reshaped the narrative of school education and introduced reforms that have largely remained in place for over a century. The first practice relates to writing in the English classroom, where both the 1905 and 1911 curricula advise that the starting point for pupils' writing was the individual contexts of pupils and their own experiences. The idea was to engage pupils, to allow for self-activity and self-direction through the selection of textual passages for discussion "to be chosen by the pupils themselves" (New South Wales Department of Public Instruction, 1911, p. 18). In addition, the teacher was advised in this syllabus to "rouse interest" in the pupil to "create enjoyment", ensuring that "all methods employed in teaching the subject should be planned with this end clearly in view" (New South Wales Department of Public Instruction, 1911, p. 18).

During their studies, pupils were required to maintain a notebook for jottings, musings, recordings and compilations (Carter, 2016), and the syllabus advised to "discern what he (sic) should record in the form of notes", followed by "how such notes should be made". Last, the pupil should "distinguish the outstanding and most suggestive features of the subject" (New South Wales Department of Public Instruction, 1911, p. 4). These practices and approaches to education and classroom teaching gathered momentum in the following decades as teachers and school systems embraced aspects of the New Education. And these approaches were further strengthened by the key mechanisms of establishing and maintaining tradition: filiation, routinisation and persistence.

New traditions established through filiation, routinisation and persistence

The increased popularity of the New Education approaches to curriculum design and classroom pedagogies were aided by a powerful feature in the theory of tradition, labelled "filiation" by Shils (1971, p. 127). This feature refers to a process of transmission – the "handing down" of beliefs, practices, appreciations and attitudes (p. 127) and involves the "structures of conduct and patterns of belief" (p. 123) repeatedly transmitted over several generations or over a long period of time in organisations, corporations and associations. This process is apparent in the adoption and passing down of New Education attitudes and practices to succeeding generations of English teachers. In addition, the 1921 inquiry into English teaching, conducted in England and commonly known as the "Newbolt Report",[7] was influential in Australia among English teachers (Manuel & Carter, 2019) and promoted the study of literature through children writing their own poems and stories and engaging in drama activities. The report emphasised the "regional dialects within the English-speaking community" (Hodgson, 2019, p. 82), placing value on the language experiences of children, anticipating the work of John Dixon as a promoter of the 'personal growth' approach to English teaching in the 1960s (p. 82). These emphases also anticipated the growing multicultural nature of Australia over the coming decades.

These approaches were passed on to succeeding generations of English teachers through the process of filiation (Shils, 1971, p. 127), which is often manifested through individuals referring to the past as the way things 'have always been done' and, by doing so, attaching authority and legitimacy to those actions. English teachers adopted a child-centred and holistic approach to education in general and English teaching in particular (Beavis, 1996; Green & Hodgens, 1996). The repeated 'handing down' (i.e., filiation) results in the "routinization" (p. 129) of those beliefs and practices, and the constant cycles of repetition normalises and standardises actions and beliefs. By nature of the fact that repeated filiations occur over time, the sets of repeated filiations are characterised as persistence. And persistence over long periods of time ensures the permanence of what is being routinely and repeatedly transmitted. This routinisation and persistence of practices in English teaching ensured that the child-centred approaches endured well into the latter part of the twentieth century before the onset of other approaches such as critical literacy and the genre approach sparked robust debates about the best way to teach English (see Christie et al., 1989).

Tradition demands agency, meaning that for an individual to be part of a tradition, that individual must "enact some further stage in the development of that tradition" (MacIntyre, 1988, p. 11). This assists the maintenance of some features but also opens the tradition up for development with others who are engaged in enacting the "next chapter of this narrative" (Yadgar, 2013, p. 463). This is a kind of "heightened agency" (p. 464), where partici-pants constantly shape and reshape the tradition through the use of a "practi-cal system of significations" (Yadgar, 2013, p. 457) – that is, the words, terms and expressions used in the filiation process. Thus, the speakers of a particular language become its "shapers and reformers" (p. 460) and as a community "live it and live by it" (p. 460). Tradition is only realised when it is "compre-hended, interpreted, loaded with meaning, internalised, and applied or prac-ticed by its bearers" (Yadgar, 2013, p. 468).

Language use as a powerful agent of tradition was also evident in the teach-ing of English. The changes in education in the early part of the last century were accompanied by a change in syllabus language, which would ultimately become a constant over the decades of the twentieth century and help guide teacher classroom practice and beliefs about how English teaching should be enacted. The syllabus of 1911 used terms such as "self-activity", "self-direction" and "self-regulation" (NSW Department of Public Instruction, 1911), all of which encouraged a greater degree of autonomous learning than was implied in previous iterations of the curriculum (Carter, 2016).

The new syllabuses of the early twentieth century highlighted Rousseauian concepts of growth, the romantically inflected concept of the "child as artist" (Mathieson, 1975, p. 56) and the principles of " 'creativity', 'self-expression' and 'child-centredness' " (Sawyer, 2009, p. 72). For English teachers, the use of specific terms helped create a language that, in turn, sustained a tradition of literary-child-centred teaching. Increasingly, terms such as 'autonomous', 'child-centred', " 'individuality', 'freedom', and 'growth' " (Green & Cormack, 2008, p. 261) gained currency over the last century so that by the 1960s and '70s, they constituted the "legitimation of a traditional belief and set of practices . . . [that are] accepted as valid" (Shils, 1971, pp. 135–136) in the teaching of English. This set of practices became known as the 'personal growth' model of English teaching, championed by the likes of John Dixon, and became an influential model for English teachers in the second half of the last century. This 'personal growth' approach to English teaching – and I would contend that its roots are apparent in the 1911 English syllabus – retains a strong influence on today's English teachers (Goodwyn, 2020; Sawyer, 2009).

For English teachers, these practices were more than 'the way we do things', in that the persistent routinisation of these beliefs and practices shaped the stories about how English teaching should be undertaken so that these practices would become 'normalised'. Additionally, for English teachers, the importance of literary studies, developing student autonomy and facilitating student self-expression through writing and drama became deeply inscribed, so much so that increasingly, English teachers assumed the mantle of what Mathieson termed "preachers of culture" (1975, p. 56). English teaching had created its own 'narrative' by embodying specific practices and representations of what the profession stood for and the ways in which it enacted its responsibilities. This is reflective of a view which promotes the idea that "every institution [and profession] . . . is a narrative" (Yadgar, 2013, p. 462).

Promotion of student-maintained journals was also apparent in the NSW Department of Education's 1987 *Writing K–12* syllabus, as was promotion of the idea that students should begin writing based on their own experiences and familiar topics and issues from their own lives (1987, p. 70). In addition, the current English Extension 2 course requires students to maintain a journal for the "recording of research and analysis, as well as critical, imaginative and speculative reflections" (New South Wales Education Standards Authority, n.d.), and the 2012 NSW English syllabus requires students to "recognise, reflect on, interpret and explain the connections between their experiences and the world of texts" (Board of Studies, 2012, p. 32), signalling the legacy of the 1911 syllabus and the personal growth model.

While I do not wish to belabour the point, I do want to be clear: with this student-centred century-old theoretical and pedagogical tradition, I argue that the proposal to include multiple-choice questions in the English examination was dismissive of how English had been constructed and assessed for 100 years.[8] The proposal contravened the tradition in which my curriculum officer and I were immersed. We knew that, to various degrees, our fellow English teachers were also 'preachers of culture' and would have been horrified at the prospect of multiple-choice questions as part of the leaving examinations.

The adoption of such a proposal would have shifted English teaching away from these rich traditions into the mind-numbingly sterile domain of multiple-choice instruction and computer-generated marking, as indicated by my interview with the ten-year-old student. While I am aware that tradition can be "static, and it can be fluid; it can whirl in place, revolving through kaleidoscopic transformations, or it can strike helical, progressive, or retrograde tracks through time" (Glassie, 1994, p. 249), I was pleased that the multiple-choice proposal was consigned to the digital desktop dustbin.

Do you want to lose your f****** jobs?

First, a point about authority. It is no surprise that a senior officer in a highly bureaucratic and hierarchical organisation has – and uses – authority to direct and instruct officers at a lower level, because as Ball (1990) points out, "[P]ower is arguably the single most important organising concept in social and political theory" (p. 14). However, leadership also involves "willingness to accept the risk and advocate and reward innovative behaviour" (Wipulanusat et al., 2019, p. 17). While I am not arguing that the meeting with ACARA officers constituted a 'moment of innovation', it did constitute a 'moment of collaboration'. The meeting reinforced the idea that collaboration involves shared activities, where contributions might include resources, including "intellectual property, knowledge, money, personnel or equipment, to address a shared objective, with a view to obtaining a mutual benefit" (Cankar & Petkovsek, 2013, p. 1602).

The meeting also reflects the findings of Savage (2016) that the development of the Australian curriculum necessitated an unprecedented level of cooperation across the Australian jurisdictions, enabling "new national policy networks and forms of inter-agency collaboration" (p. 842). Savage documents the response of a policymaker from Queensland who argued that ACARA had created a "new language about curriculum" (p. 842) and also cites an NSW policymaker who described ACARA as the impetus for a "network with all other states" (p. 842). The meeting between BIs and ACARA officers confirmed this line of thinking. However, as Savage indicates, the formation of a national curriculum across a range of jurisdictions is a complex and contested task, and my point here is not to understate the enormity and complexity of this task.

The behaviour of the senior officer is worth considering. I write that my inspector colleagues lost respect for this senior officer, which may be an overreaction to the situation because all workplaces have their tensions and dramas. Additionally, one could argue that because no one was injured, no lives were at risk – perhaps just some egos were a little damaged – the incident was of little consequence. However, interactions between workplace colleagues and associated notions of authority, leadership and discipline have long been at the heart of organisational theory (Oyibo & Gabriel, 2020), and recounting this interaction reminded us that numerous theorists have speculated on the origins and exercise of power and authority in organisations. We briefly explore a sample of these theories below to try to make sense of the outburst of the senior officer.

In an earlier chapter, Weber's typologies of power, the traditional (kings, queens, monarchs), the charismatic (the attractive, charismatic leader) and the legal-rational (legally enacted rules and authority) were briefly explored. These typologies provide a partial explanation for the senior manager's behaviour: his outburst was most likely generated by the authority invested in his government-sponsored position within the hierarchy, providing him (in his mind) with a 'licence' to speak in the way he did. The legal-rational typology anchored in the power of office promotes a kind of domination with "the probability that a command with a given specific content will be obeyed by a given group of persons" (Weber, 1978, p. 53) and becomes normative and routine. While this senior manager had not issued a command as such, his displeasure at the inspectors' cooperation with ACARA officers conveyed a clear message about future collaborations.[9]

Other typologies of power provide a quick method to evaluate the applicability of the typology. For example, the Canadian economist John Kenneth Galbraith (1908–2006) offers the three Cs approach: "Condign (punishment), Compensatory (reward), and Conditioned (persuasive or manipulative)" (1983, pp. 95–96). However, this three-C approach has limited application because no punishment was imposed on the BIs, and there was certainly no reward, nor was any persuasion apparent.[10] And rather than observable manipulation, a degree of petulance from the senior officer was on display. In other power typologies, Wrong (2017), for example, suggests force, manipulation, persuasion and authority as the drivers in organisational relationships, while Bachrach and Baratz (1963, 1970) offer a slight variation by dividing "Persuasion" into "Influence and Coercion" (p. 96).

However, another alliterative typology of power which is more useful is offered by Nyberg (1981), who argues that workplace interactions within hierarchical structures use four forms of power: "F's – Force, Finance, Fiction, and Fealty" (1981, p. 2). The first of these, "force", is characterised as primitive, erratic, potentially costly to those wielding power because the use or the threat of force requires ongoing vigilance and maintenance and can generate resentment and rebellion. The second form of power is "fiction", which denotes the power of the storyteller who wields power through the use of words and images to persuade others to act in a way that supports and advances the agenda of the storyteller but may not be in the best interests of others. The third form of power is "finance" (p. 4), where the acquisition of money, opportunity, position or consent is sought, sometimes accompanied by the positive endorsement of others where the consent offered appears to be voluntary, knowledgeable and cognisant.

Nyberg's fourth form of power is labelled "fealty". The most acceptable form of power according to Nyberg is "fealty", which requires trust, loyalty, faithfulness and a shared common goal, where those who possess fealty do not need to enforce their power because consent from all parties arrives in the shape of mutually agreed common goals. Fealty is a manifestation of power, based on mutual and consensual commitment and commonality and is apparent in professional associations, clubs or groups charged with specific tasks and goals (p. 96). As a manifestation of power, fealty is steady, reasonably noncoercive and generally effective; however, it does not ensure the path to individual happiness or wellbeing[11] (p. 6).

This particular typology of power is useful due to the 'fiction' component, which was evident in the 'story' promoted to BIs. This story promoted the idea that working closely with ACARA would be a worthwhile and valuable exercise for not only the development of the national curriculum but also in building relationships with ACARA staff in a kind of 'trans-agency' collaboration. The 'fiction' here was splintered by the BOS' senior officer's outburst, which had exposed a lack of forward planning on his part, in that there was no 'game plan' for the meeting with set goals towards which we would all work.[12] Consequently, there was no 'fealty' between this officer and the inspectors where common aims and an ensuing mutuality would have directed the meeting in a way that was acceptable to this officer.

While I may appear to be making much of this incident, it does point to the importance of a manager being cognisant of Nyberg's typology and attending to one or more of the '*F*s' in accordance with the outcomes desired by the actors involved. Finance is obviously important in any organisation, and the capacity for generating support through persuasive storytelling is an essential element in co-opting the allegiance of colleagues. While Nyberg's term 'fiction' implies storytelling which deals with untruths and also suggests the use of manipulation, it is a useful 'lens', in that the inspectors had been encouraged to involve themselves with ACARA drafts of the national curriculum for a couple of years prior to this event. Prior to the meeting, the 'story' was that cooperation and collaboration was important, and in the promotion of this 'story', the senior officer was able to build a consistent theme in his storytelling. This subsequently helps to build fealty with colleagues and enlist their services and, in turn, negates the need for the fourth '*F*' – force. And while this senior officer did not use force, the authority attached to his state-sponsored senior role constituted a type of force that did not require any exercise of overt force or coercion.

"I'm scared of NAPLAN"

These words constitute the other face of education – the child. As outlined in the previous chapter, these words were spoken by a ten-year-old girl during a research project in southwestern Sydney. And as I wrote, I felt for this girl and other students who felt this way. This is not to say that efforts to improve student literacy and numeracy should be abandoned or the NAPLAN tests jettisoned. Government policy, quite rightly, seeks to improve the rates of student literacy and numeracy. No one could argue that a highly literate and numerate, well-informed and articulate population is not a priority or unimportant for a healthy and smoothly functioning democracy.

But the statement from this young girl reminded us that a 'gulf' exists between the 'big picture' aims of education and what actually happens at the local level. The broad mission statements of education, which set out the aims and goals about what we want education to be and do for our children, are found in documents issued by governments and school system authorities. The current 'big picture' statement in Australia is the *Alice Springs (Mparntwe) Education Declaration* (2019), which sets out the national vision for education, signed by the Australian ministers for education across all states and territories. In these educational documents, it is usual to read statements about the transformative nature of education and its importance to individuals and communities in developing skills and knowledge for the workplace and life in general. You will find statements committing to the fair and equitable provision of education for all children regardless of background and economic circumstance.

The *Alice Springs (Mparntwe) Education Declaration* (2019) includes such statements, as did its precursor, the *Melbourne Declaration on Educational Goals for Young Australians* (2008). These two documents form part of a sequence of 'big picture' statements issued by successive Australian governments from 1989, with the *Hobart Declaration on Schooling* and the *Adelaide Declaration on National Goals for Schooling in the Twenty-First Century* (1999). These four documents emphasise the importance of childhood and the importance of developing social, emotional and cognitive skills as well as confidence and motivation. These documents identify childhood as the site to "grow peer relationships and have a growing understanding of their place in the world" (Education Council, 2019, p. 13). And education is the vehicle that will enable these transformations to occur.

However, the sometimes bold and expansive rhetoric of such documents do not reflect the reality for many teachers and students. Research has revealed the negative side to mass standardised testing, both in Australia and internationally (Jones, 2007; Thompson & Harbaugh, 2013). This follows an ongoing preoccupation with standardised testing by successive Australian governments and reflects similar priorities in other developed Western nations, including the United States, the United Kingdom, as well as Singapore and China, where a "strengthening commitment to . . . standardised testing" reveals an "insatiable appetite for data" (Wyatt-Smith & Jackson, 2016, p. 233). In an era dominated by educational accountability (Biesta, 2017; Lindgard et al., 2016), standardised testing is now the main apparatus for "educational reform" (Au, 2011, p. 29). In many countries, including Australia, standardised testing renders the classroom vulnerable to external scrutiny and judgement, making teachers "accountable to and for student performance data" (Lindgard et al., 2016, p. 1).

Standardised testing, however, in the form of system-wide formal examinations and mass literacy and numeracy tests, remains controversial within both the educational realm and the wider community. Critics point to the decontextualised use of statistics in education (Enslin & Tjiattas, 2017; Ozoliņš, 2017; Stolz, 2017), the implementation of mass testing as diverting attention from the important aims of education (Biesta, 2017; Ozoliņš, 2017), the identification of a series of unintended negative outcomes of mass testing (Jones, 2007; Thompson & Harbaugh, 2013) and also point to standardised testing as an expression of neoliberal discourses (Biesta, 2017; Jones, 2007; Prøitz et al., 2017; Werler & Klepstad Faerevaag, 2017).

Evidence exposing the damage that NAPLAN is visiting upon Australian education is mounting, including negative impacts on learning and student wellbeing and significant levels of stress and anxiety for students (Carter et al., 2018; Cumming et al., 2016; Jones, 2007); increased pressure on teachers to improve student test results (Davies, 2008; Goldstein & Beutel, 2009); an increase in teacher-centred instructional approaches, at the expense of other strategies (Au, 2011); and diminished student motivation (Au, 2011; Jones, 2007; Thompson & Harbaugh, 2013).

In 2018, the then–NSW education minister Rob Stokes spoke of being

anaesthetised by the data around us – and hypnotised by the neo-liberal fixation with quantification – we place inordinate emphasis on tests such as PISA and NAPLAN that reduce a student's educational journey to a number and a school system to a line in a league table.

(Stokes, 2018)

This statement is significant, in that it constitutes an unusual deviation from the conventional 'script' used by political leaders that typically uses terms such as 'rigour', 'standards', 'benchmarks' and 'student performance'.[13]

Childhood and the importance of education

For many nations, education is an ongoing programme to increase productivity and promote social equity, regardless of gender, ethnic and religious background or social and economic status. The role and purposes of education have been conceived and promoted variously as the development of moral judiciousness (Dewey, 1964), the transmission of "something worthwhile . . . in a morally acceptable manner" (Raulo, 2002, p. 507), moral and intellectual development (Kohlberg, 1963), skill development for employment (Mourshed et al., 2012), for democratic principles (Laclau, 2007; Mannion et al., 2011), to name just a few.

The notion of education for children is integrally connected to notions of childhood. And the idea that childhood is a special and precious time of life is not new. Prior to the end of the eighteenth century, children were considered as lacking in knowledge, authority and power and were afforded a subordinate social status (Cassidy & Mohr Lone, 2020). However, from the Enlightenment onwards, childhood was increasingly considered as a discrete period of life, as distinct from a period of transition (Giesinger, 2017). This eventuated in a view of childhood as a special but limited time of one's life, a period prior to the pressures and vicissitudes of adulthood, with the years between the ages of 2 and 14 generally considered as 'childhood' (p. 6). This view of childhood was largely shaped by Jean-Jacques Rousseau (1712–1778), who promoted childhood as the site of freedom, where a child can learn to respond to unforeseen and unpredictable challenges and situations as a kind of preparation for the challenges of adulthood. Rousseau's conceptualisation of childhood is based on a comparison between the growth of a child and a tree that bears fruit. The child should not be weighed down by adult expectations, and the teacher needs to wait with patience until the child reaches a new stage of development. Rousseau asserted that every phase of human existence has its place and the phase of childhood has its unique place and that "we must regard the man (sic) as a man and the child as a child" (Rousseau, 2004, p. 126).

A different view came from the English philosopher John Locke (1632–1704), who argued that at birth, the infant's intellect was tabula rasa, an 'empty mind', a metaphorical blank slate, ready for inscription by experience, sensations and reflections. Locke considered education a "hegemonic instrument to stabilize the common good" (Houswitschka, 2006, p. 84) by those who control the education system.

By the early nineteenth century, the focus on childhood also saw the emergence of paediatrics and an increase in the number of childcare manuals (Müller, 2006, p. 6) in a context where parents increasingly considered the lives of their children as precious, not only in economic terms but also in emotional terms (p. 6). The family unit, which afforded an identity to the group, was replaced by "age-specific cohorts" (Long, 2013, p. 4), in association with a shift in emphasis from a child's competence to a child's age. This view of education was adopted by many of the Romantics such as William Wordsworth, whose ideas have long influenced school-based curriculum and higher education.[14]

These notions of childhood remain powerful presences in the contemporary curriculum (Carter, 2012; Reid, 2004). Their presence, however, is constantly challenged by standardised testing agendas and the priorities to improve student literacy and numeracy, often at the expense of other areas in the curriculum. In my view, the classroom teacher is constantly challenged by the "intersection of official goals, teacher lesson plans, student biographies and the contingencies of daily classroom life" (Priestley et al., 2021, p. 22) and the time pressures associated with these competing challenges. These competing tensions inevitably give rise to the question, what are the purposes of education? Do schools exist mainly to provide students with the skills for the workplace?

I believe that a public debate and a reexamination of the purposes of education is required. Previously, I have written about the importance of identifying the purposes of education (Carter, 2019), and the distinguished education researcher, teacher and scholar Emeritus Professor Alan Reid makes a strong call for this in his excellent book *Changing Australian education: How policy is taking us backwards and what can be done about it* (2019). In this book, Reid argues that in the absence of clearly articulated purposes underpinning education, particular ideologies and interests that are contradictory to "broadly accepted notions", for example, "access to quality education is the right of all children and young people" (p. 168) are potentially undermined. We witness such distortions when blanket media coverage of test results dominates the news cycle and leads us to think that the key purpose of education is to improve test results rather than seeing these results as one component of a child's progress.

My contention is that education for children is too important a period of life to leave to chance. The development of well-rounded individuals, who are highly literate and numerate, who have an innate capacity for learning and are able to work collaboratively, needs to be at the top of the list of education authorities and governments. And while I do not oppose NAPLAN as a 'snapshot' of student capabilities in literacy and numeracy at the time students sit for the tests, I am concerned that the importance of NAPLAN continues to be exaggerated, particularly in the media, and the test results have been afforded a broader and more significant role than was originally intended by ACARA.

Conclusion

In this analytical contemplation, I have sought to present two faces of education: the prospect of multiple-choice questions in the HSC and the hardnosed approach of a senior manager, working within a large and at times impersonal bureaucracy, and the reaction of a ten-year-old girl who has sat through NAPLAN literacy and numeracy tests. While many 'big picture' documents set out a vision for education, highlighting the importance of childhood, the reality is that for many students, their school lives are increasingly interrupted by assessment and performance measures. And while we can trace notions of childhood as a precious time of life to Rousseau and Romantics like William Wordsworth and identify these notions in educational thinking throughout the twentieth century, childhood is increasingly viewed as the 'site' for demonstrating the acquisition of skills through performativity mechanisms such as the NAPLAN tests. And perhaps for this generation of students, their memories of school will be largely shaped by the 'routinisation' of tests and assessments they undertook throughout their 13 years of education rather than by other experiences from their schooldays.

Notes

1 A. Flew (1979) *A Dictionary of Philosophy*, p. 101.
2 See Manuel and Carter (2020) *The English Teacher's Handbook A-Z*, pp. 199–200.
3 For a comprehensive account, see Selleck's (1968) *The New Education. The English Background 1870–1914.*
4 See Barcan, 2009; Campbell and Proctor, 2014; Crane and Walker, 1957; Meadmore, 2003.
5 The organisation of primary schools remained largely unchanged.
6 It should be noted that educational change was underway before Board's appointment, with commissioners Knibbs and Turner releasing a comprehensive report on education following a tour of several countries in 1902.
7 The inquiry was led by Sir Henry Newbolt (1862–1938), an English poet, historian and novelist.
8 I am not suggesting that there have been no other influences on how English should be taught in schools over the past century. Various approaches such as the genre approach, critical literacy and functional grammar (and more) have all influenced English teaching to varying degrees. I am, however, pointing out that the epistemological and curricular traditions were ignored by the senior manager or, at the very least, that person had no idea or understanding of these traditions.
9 We do not believe the other type of power – charismatic power – is applicable in this incident because it is defined as "the attractiveness and magnetism that certain personalities seem to be graced with – to ineffable personal qualities which a few possess in contrast to the many, attracting not just attention, but also fascination and devotion to their persons" (T. Magalhães, 2022, p. 70).
10 One might argue that volunteer groups can be satisfying. But perhaps that says as much about the individual as the group – if it were not satisfying, one would cease to volunteer. Presumably, the nature of the task holds some sort of 'charisma' or some other worth in the eye of the participants too.
11 In retrospect, I also feel that this senor officer felt inadequate in these discussions because they were about specific and in-depth syllabus content, components and structures.
12 It is interesting for me to reflect on my 'journey' in education. As a teacher, the finances 'just had to be found', whereas I came to see that it was a more complex issue when I moved into other more senior roles.
13 Adrian discusses the 'datafication' of education in his interview for the UTS *Talking Teachers* podcast: "Power and education" with Professor Adrian Piccoli – Impact Studios. Talking Teachers | University of Technology Sydney (uts.edu.au).
14 See Carter, D. (2012). *The influence of romanticism on the NSW stage 6 English Syllabus: interwoven storylines and the search for a unifying narrative,* for an account of the influence of Wordsworth on school-based English curriculum (reference list). See Reid (2004) *Wordsworth and the formation of English studies* for an account of the influence of Wordsworth in university courses (reference list).

Conclusion

Adrian Piccoli

Being an education minister is a critical leadership position in education and an incredible privilege. That's why education ministers have no time to waste understanding the power and authority that comes with the role. Having spent six years as the NSW minister for education, I learnt a great deal. I hope the stories in this book and the lessons learnt, including those listed below, can help future ministers, and those who deal with ministers, to better understand the powers they have and what to do with those powers. The true, genuine and enduring power in education is the power to influence, the power to cajole, the power to motivate, the power to inspire others to follow. In education, the most important area of public policy, it is the power to change children's lives.

Constantly build, and renew your authority – talk to everyone

- Gain a deep knowledge and understanding of the stakeholders in education. Beyond the ideology, what drives them, what is important to them?
- Communicating vertically through the organisation is just as important as communicating horizontally, across stakeholders.
- Loyalty is the reward for communicating effectively.
- Everyone in an organisation wants to be part of something bigger than themselves.
- Lying is very hard and very dangerous, so don't do it.
- Consulting people doesn't mean you will agree with them and do what they say. Don't let people tell you otherwise.
- Listen to your adversaries. They usually have some of the best ideas.
- Have a deep, genuine respect for experts, particularly classroom teachers, and their essential contribution to policy and implementation.

Relationships, relationships, relationships

- Keep bringing people back to you, and be kind, especially to your enemies.
- Don't burn bridges until you have no choice.

DOI: 10.4324/9781003312451-19

- To make change, you have to upset your enemies and your friends. Just don't upset them all at the same time.
- Remember your friends when you had no power.
- Triangulate advice. No one knows everything.
- Trust, but verify.

Exercise power for the right reasons

- Be humble. Ego will ruin your crucial relationships as a leader.
- Leadership isn't effective without personal integrity. There are lines that you personally cannot cross.
- Don't sell out your integrity to get ahead.
- Be loyal. Loyalty is such a rare commodity in politics that people don't recognise it when they see it.

Use your power to do the right work

- Do the boring but essential work.
- Use evidence as both a sword and a shield to guide how you use your power.
- Always be happy to replace a good idea with a better one.
- Use fairness as a guiding principle – the public do understand fairness . . . eventually.

Don't let the political cycle run policy reform: avoid populist but superficial reforms in education

- Stay out of the weeds. Don't get distracted by the day-to-day issues that arise.
- What you don't do as a minister is just as important as what you do.
- Don't make stuff up.
- If reforms are right and supported by the profession, then they will survive ministers, and they will survive governments.

Keep your eyes on the horizon

- Play the long game. Set a course, and stick to it.
- Change takes time. Don't go for the quick fix; go for the right fix.
- Ignore demands for immediate results.
- Avoid the superficial, shiny balls thrown your way by people who have an eye for media, not education.
- Don't hold grudges.
- Don't get distracted from leadership – don't worry, people want you to be!
- Leadership is about taking criticism but proceeding anyway.

Impact! Play for impact; otherwise, the cost of leadership is not worth it

- If it doesn't work in schools, then it doesn't work.
- Make unpopular, but right decisions. Leadership is not management.
- Drift is the biggest danger to reform. Stay on top of it and, preferably, in front of it. Reform is not a firework; it's a multistage rocket, with each stage propelling the next.

Renew your power by continually putting students at the centre of your decision-making and thus continually cultivating your support base

- Ensure the best interests of children come before the interests of adults in education.
- By trusting the profession.
- By being unconventional.
- By standing up for clearly articulated principles.
- By doing the 'right little things', not just the 'high-profile big things'.
- By doing the 'boring' important work in education.
- By listening to the criticism when it is warranted and changing what you are doing.

Afterword

Don Carter

At the outset of this book, we noted the confused and contested definitions of power and authority, the overlaps, conflations and contradictions. In this final chapter, I draw together some of the insights gleaned from compiling and reflecting on our experiences in education. My aim is not to attempt a definitive statement about power and authority in education but to document some thoughts that may provoke discussion and further research into this area. And, in doing so, I also hope to illuminate aspects of power and authority to enable the reader to identify the features of both and, where possible, use these insights in their own interactions with individuals and groups.

One key understanding is that the exercise of power and authority does not occur in a vacuum. Both are always contextually constrained and historically dependent, with local and broader contexts impacting on how, when and with whom power and authority are exercised. As noted in earlier chapters, contexts are imbued with discourses which influence, guide and constrain (and perhaps liberate) the behaviours, attitudes and expectations of actors. And the historical constraints in which we operate as individuals and collectives include the influences of tradition, which affect the content that is selected for study in schools and how schools are organised (see analytical contemplation for chapter 10).

Fields of agency and power resources

For an individual or group to exercise power and authority, a commitment to engage in social relations activities must occur. To capture the fluid and multilayered interactions and hierarchies of the social relations domain, I have coined the term 'fields of agency', which denotes the production of the linguistic and paralinguistic conditions that enable the deployment of power resources within the flexible and recursive interactions between individuals, as well as within and across groups.

Inherently dynamic, fields of agency are the sites for the cultivation, allocation and reallocation of specific power resources such as persuasion, credibility, trust, familiarity and strategic narrative, social and cultural capital, all of which depend on the acumen, verve and expertise of participants. Individuals in these continually altering and organic contexts accumulate (or surrender) resources in the pursuit of both specific and general agendas, with the practised actor able to both cultivate and accumulate these resources over the course of multiple interactions. The accumulation and skilful deployment of power resources strengthens the attractiveness of the actor (or group) to others, in turn strengthening their power and authority.

Of course, the accumulation and use of power resources can also include the use of Nyberg's typology of force, finance, fiction and fealty. As indicated in the analytical contemplation in chapter 10, these resources draw on the soft power approach of narrative and can be combined with force, a hard power resource, available to the individual or group. What is essential in the deployment of power resources in any situation is not only commitment and linguistic dexterity but also the individual's agility in managing the shifting lexical and paralinguistic conditions and strategies of participants.

The activation of fields of agency also creates the potential for the emergence of dominant coalitions (see analytical contemplation for chapter 10). This is heightened with the alignment of similarly practised individuals who share a vision or specific agenda and can result in previously antagonistic groups working together (see chapter 10). However, the formation of dominant coalitions is also contingent on the capacity of actors to meld, manipulate and maintain power resources in irresistible ways that attract other actors to their programme within and beyond their respective coalitions. Dominant coalitions often enjoy the innate status of direct access to other coalitions or influential individuals in government and other significant organisations without the need for mediation to do so.

Fields of agency, authority and legitimacy

The deployment of power resources can include the deployment of Bourdieu's four types of capital: economic, cultural, social and symbolic power (see analytical contemplation for chapter 8). Authority can be established and strengthened by symbolic power (see the analytical contemplation for chapter 8). Here, power is embedded in the things we take for granted, such as the powers afforded to government ministers, law enforcement agencies and other groups that represent the interests of collectives of individuals. And a raft of 'taken for granted' procedures, such as the issuing of birth certificates for newborns, underpin the symbolic power of the state and strengthen the exercise of authority. Symbolic power permeates economic, political, legal and military functions and, in doing so, enhances the legitimacy of socially sanctioned roles and institutions representing the state or its agencies.

In addition, economic capital and symbolic power are usually embedded in socially sanctioned roles which are, in turn, complemented by the availability of socially sanctioned resources, usually strengthened by the legitimisation of the state. A state-sanctioned role permits its holder to implement certain state-sanctioned rules and regulations, supported by the resources of the state and, as noted in chapter 4, is called 'possessive authority'. Should the holder of a state-sanctioned role be sufficiently expert in the use of power resources such as credibility and persuasion, they have the opportunity to employ 'associative authority' (see the analytical contemplation for chapter 4), where they enlist the support of another actor (or actors) who hold similarly socially sanctioned roles. This, in turn, strengthens state-sanctioned legitimacy, as in the minister who holds a position in government. However, both authority and legitimacy can be diminished if the actor appears to forfeit these to another actor or group.

Developing credibility and trust through recursion

The repeated cultivation of power resources over a series of interactions can strengthen the expertise of actors in their deployment of resources. For example, the actor who uses strategic narrative to elicit allegiance might cultivate their use of this resource over repeated interactions with others, with both successes and failures informing them on how the resource might be used more effectively on the next occasion. The recruitment of others to a particular point of view through the adept use of strategic narrative can also develop a sense of collaboration, credibility and trust. And with that trust, a sense of familiarity and stability, which assists the promotion of that actor's agenda, is also established.

Summary

The activation of fields of agency will draw on the power resources necessary for the actor/s to work towards achieving their goals. The resources might include accessing and using a combination of soft and hard power resources based on the social status of the actor and the availability of resources, including economic capital and possessive authority. The utilisation of such resources can occur between individuals, within groups and across groups. The acquisition, retention and accumulation of power resources depends on the actor's capacity to navigate and adapt to various scenarios in fluid social relations and cultivate and strengthen their use of resources according to these shifting conditions. And, finally, perhaps the last word should belong to Foucault, who argues that power reflects the "redistributions, realignments, homogenisations, serial arrangements, and convergences" of relationships (1990, p. 94), all of which are constantly in a state of flux, reflecting the complexities, richness and challenges of human beings.

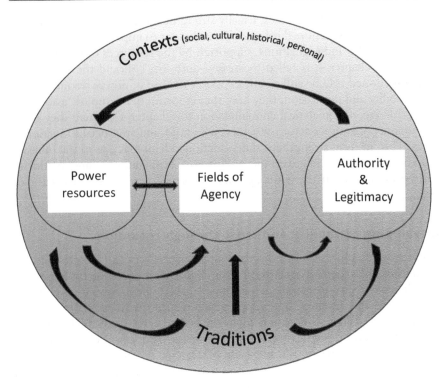

Figure 12.1 The interrelationships between power resources, fields of agency and authority and legitimacy, within contexts and subject to the influence of traditions.

References

Aghion, P., & Tirole, J. (1997). Formal and real authority in organisations. *Journal of Political Economy, 105*(1), 1–29.

Alansari, R. (2018). Strategic contemplation as one Saudi mother 's way of reflecting on her children's learning only English in the United States: An autoethnography and multiple case study of multilingual writers at the college level. In *Eastern Washington University EWU digital commons*. Washington University.

Allen, A. (2014). *Benign violence: Education in and beyond the age of reason*. Palgrave Macmillan.

Althusser, L. (1971). *Lenin, philosophy and other essays*. Monthly Review Press.

Anderson, L. (2006). Analytic autoethnography. *Journal of Contemporary Ethnography, 35*(4), 373–395.

Apple, M. (1997). What postmodernists forget: Cultural capital and official knowledge. In A. Halsey, H. Lauder, P. Brown, & A. Stuart Wells (Eds.), *Education: Culture, economy, society*. Oxford University Press.

Apple, M. (2005). Education, markets and an audit culture. *Critical Quarterly, 47*(1–2), 11–29.

Apple, M. (2006). Producing inequalities: Neoliberalism, neo-conservatism, and the politics of educational reform. In H. Lauder, P. Brown, J.-A. Dillabough, & A. Halsey (Eds.), *Education, globalization and social change*. Oxford University Press.

Apple, M. A. (2012). *Education and power*. Routledge.

Arendt, H. (1958). What was authority? *NOMOS: American Society for Political and Legal Philosophy, 1*, 81.

Arendt, H. (1972). *Crises of the republic*. Harcourt Brace Jovanovich.

Aristotle. (1962). *The politics* (T. A. Sinclair, Trans.). Penguin.

Arquilla, J. & Ronfeldt, D. (2001). *Networks and Netwars*. Rand.

Au, W. (2011). Teaching under the new Taylorism: Highstakes testing and the standardization of the 21st century curriculum. *Journal of Curriculum Studies, 43*(1), 25–45. https://doi.org/10.1080/00220272.2010.521261

Audi, R. (2008). Intellectual virtue and epistemic power. In J. Greco (Ed.), *Ernest Sosa and his critics* (pp. 3–16). John Wiley & Son.

Austin, A. G., & Selleck, R. J. W. (1975). *The Australian Government School 1830–1914: Select documents with commentary*. Pitman Publishing.

Australian Curriculum Assessment and Reporting Authority. (n.d.). *My School*. Accessed 27 February 2024: https://www.myschool.edu.au/

Avelino, F. (2021). Theories of power and social change. Power contestations and their implications for research on social change and innovation. *Journal of Political Power, 14*(3), 425–448.

Bacalja, A., & Bliss, L. (2019). *A report on trends on senior English text-lists.* Victorian Association for the Teaching of English.

Bachrach, P., & Baratz, M. (1970). *Power and poverty: Theory and practice.* Oxford University Press.

Ball, S. J. (1990). *Politics and policy making in education. Explorations in policy sociology.* Routledge.

Ball, S. J. (2006). Competition and conflict in the teaching of English: A socio-historical analysis. *Journal of Curriculum Studies, 14*(1), 1–28.

Ball, S. J. (2013). *Foucault, power, and education.* Routledge.

Ball, S. J., & Olmedo, A. (2013). Care of the self, resistance and subjectivity under neoliberal governmentalities. *Critical Studies in Education, 54*(1), 85–96. https://doi.org/10.1080/17508487.2013.740678

Barcan, A. (2009). Three pathways to change New South Wales education, 1937–1952. *Education Research and Perspectives, 36*(2), 45–80.

Barends, E., Rousseau, D. M., & Brinds, R. B. (2011). Becoming an evidence-based HR-practitioner. *Human Resource Management Journal, 21*(3), 221–235.

Barley, S. R. (1996). Technicians in the workplace: Ethnographic evidence for bringing work into organizational studies. *Administrative Science Quarterly, 41*(3), 404–441.

Barnard, C. (1938). *The functions of the executive.* Harvard University Press.

Barnes, S. T. (1990). Ritual, power, and outside knowledge. *Journal of Religion in Africa,* 248–268.

Barnett, M., & Duvall, R. (2005). Power in international politics. *International Organization, 59*(1), 39–75.

Barthwal-Datta, M. (2015). Strategic narratives and non-state actors. *Critical Studies on Security, 3*(3), 328–330. http://dx.doi.org/10.1080/21624887.2015.1103014©

Beavis, C. (1996). Changing constructions: Literature, 'text' and English teaching 1 in Victoria. In *Teaching the English subjects: Essays on English curriculum and history in Australian schooling* (pp. 15–39). Deakin University.

Bell, D. (1974). *The coming of post-industrial society.* Basic Books.

Bell, E. C. (2022). Understanding soft power discourse in the National Library of Australia. *Journal of Documentation, 78*(6), 1457–1475. https://doi.org/10.1108/JD-11-2021-0231

Bencherki, N., Matte, F., & Cooren, F. (Eds.). (2019). *Authority and power in social interaction: Methods and analysis.* Routledge.

Bendix, R. (1956). *Work and authority in industry ideologies of management in the course of industrialization.* Wiley.

Bennis, W. G. (1959). *Leadership theory and administrative behavior: The problem of authority.* 4, Ardent Media.

Berger, B. K. (2005). Power over, power with, and power to relations: Critical reflections on public relations, the dominant coalition, and activism. *Journal of Public Relations Research, 17*(1), 5–28.

Bernstein, B. (2000). *Pedagogy, symbolic control, and identity: Theory, research, and critique.* Taylor & Francis.

Bidwell, C. (1970). Students and schools: Some observations on client trust in client-serving organizations. In W. R. Rosengren & M. Lefton (Eds.), *Organizations and clients: Essays in the sociology of service* (pp. 37–70). Charles E. Merrill.

Biesta, G. (2007). Why "what works" won't work: Evidence-based practice and the democratic deficit in educational research. *Educational Theory, 57*(1), 1–22.

Biesta, G. J. J. (2013). *The beautiful risk of education.* Paradigm Publishers.

Biesta, G. J. J. (2017). Education, measurement and the professions: Reclaiming a space for democratic professionality in education. *Educational Philosophy and Theory, 49*(4), 315–331.

Blau, P. (1974). *On the nature of organizations.* John Wiley.

Bliss, L., & Bacalja, A. (2021). What counts? Inclusion and diversity in the senior English curriculum. *The Australian Educational Researcher, 48,* 165–182 https://doi.org/10.1007/s13384-020-00384-x

Blum-Ross, A., & Livingstone, S. (2017). Sharenting, parent blogging, and the boundaries of the digital self. *Popular Communication, 15*(2), 110–125.

Board of Studies. (2012). *English years 7–10 syllabus.* Board of Studies NSW.

Boaz, A., Ashby, D., & Young, K. (2002). *Systematic reviews: What have they got to offer evidence based policy and practice?* ESRC UK Centre for Evidence Based Policy and Practice.

Bolton, G. (2007). A history of drama education: A search for substance. In *International handbook of research in arts education* (pp. 45–66). Springer.

Bourdieu, P. (1990). *The logic of practice.* Polity Press.

Bourdieu, P. (1997). The forms of capital. In A. H. Halsey, H. Lauder, P. Brown, & A. Stuart Wells (Eds.), *Education, culture, economy, society* (pp. 46–59). Oxford University Press.

Bourdieu, P. (2000). *Pascalian meditations* (R. Nice, Trans.). Polity Press.

Bourdieu, P., & Wacquant, L. J. D. (1992). *An invitation to reflexive sociology.* University of Chicago Press.

Bourke, T., & Lidstone, J. (2015). What is Plan B? Using Foucault's archaeology to enhance policy analysis. *Discourse: Studies in the Cultural Politics of Education, 36*(6), 833–853. https://doi.org/10.1080/01596306.2014.903611

Brennan, M. (2011). National curriculum: A political-educational tangle (Special issue on national curriculum, edited by Parlo Singh and Bill Atweh). *Australian Journal of Education, 55*(3), 259–280.

Bridges, D., Smeyers, P., & Smith, R. (Eds.). (2009). *Evidence-based education policy: What evidence? What basis? Whose policy?* Wiley-Blackwell.

Bruns, G. L. (1991). What is tradition? *New Literary History. Institutions of Interpretation, 2*(2), 1–21.

Buber, M. (2008). *Distance and relationship. Contributions to a flosophic anthropology.* Dualis.

Bulger, M. (2016). Personalized learning: The conversations we're not having. *Data and Society, 22*(1), 1–29.

Burawoy, M. (1979). *Manufacturing consent: Changes in the labor process under monopoly capitalism.* University of Chicago Press.

Busemeyer, M. R. (2015). *Skills and inequality: The political economy of education and training reforms in Western Welfare States.* Cambridge University Press.

Busemeyer, M. R., Garritzmann, J. L., & Neimanns, E. (2020). *A loud but noisy signal? Public opinion and education reform in Western Europe.* Cambridge University Press.

Buzan, B., & Lawson, G. (2013). The global transformation: The nineteenth century and the making of modern international relations. *International Studies Quarterly, 59*(1), 1–39.

Campbell, C., & Proctor, H. (2014). *A history of Australian schooling*. Allen & Unwin.

Cankar, S. S., & Petkovsek, V. (2013). Private and public sector innovation and the importance of cross-sector collaboration. *Journal of Applied Business Research (JABR)*, *29*(6), 1597–1606.

Carter, B., Stevenson, H., & Passy, P. (2010). *Industrial relations in education: Transforming the school workforce*. Routledge.

Carter, D. (2012). *The influence of romanticism on the NSW stage 6 English Syllabus: Interwoven storylines and the search for a unifying narrative* (Unpublished PhD thesis). University of Sydney.

Carter, D. (2016). Retrieving the forgotten influence of Herbart on subject English. *English Teaching: Practice & Critique*, *15*(1), 40–54.

Carter, D. (2019). Restoring purpose: Applying Biesta's three functions to the Melbourne Declaration. *Curriculum Perspectives*, *39*, 125–134.

Carter, D., Manuel, J., & Dutton, J. (2018). How do secondary school English teachers score NAPLAN?: A snapshot of English teachers' views. *Australian Journal of Language and Literacy*, *41*(3), 144–154.

Carter, D., & Yoo, J. (2022). Developing teachers' writing lives: A case study of English teacher professional learning. In *International perspectives on English teacher development* (pp. 215–225). Routledge.

Cartwright, N. (2013). Knowing what we are talking about: Why evidence doesn't always travel. *Evidence & Policy*, *9*(1), 97–112.

Cash, D. W., & Belloy, P. G. (2020). Salience, credibility and legitimacy in a rapidly shifting world of knowledge and action. *Sustainability*, *12*, 1–15. https://doi.org/10.3390/su12187376

Cassidy, C., & Mohr Lone, J. (2020). Thinking about childhood: Being and becoming in the world. *Analytic Teaching and Philosophical Praxis*, *40*(1), 16–26.

Chaban, N., Miskimmon, A., & O'Loughlin, B. (2019). Understanding EU crisis diplomacy in the European neighbourhood: Strategic narratives and perceptions of the EU in Ukraine, Israel and Palestine. *European Security*, *28*(3), 235–250. https://doi.org/10.1080/09662839.2019.1648251

Chong, D., & Druckman, J. N. (2007). Framing theory. *Annual Review of Political Science*, *10*, 103–126. https://doi.org/10.1146/annurev.polisci.10.072805.103054

Christie, F., Martin, J., & Rothery, J. (1989). Genres make meaning: Another reply to Sawyer and Watson. *English in Australia*, *90*, 43–59. https://search.informit.org/doi/10.3316/ielapa.535957229496462

Clegg, S. (1989). *Frameworks of Power*. Sage.

Clegg, S. R. (2019). Radical revisions: Power, discipline and organizations. In *Postmodern management theory* (pp. 73–91). Routledge.

Clegg, S. R., & Haugaard, M. (Eds.). (2009). *The SAGE handbook of power*. SAGE.

Clifford, J., & Marcus, G. E. (Eds.). (1986). *Writing culture: The Poetics and politics of ethnography*. SAGE.

Cohen, L., Manion, L., & Morrison, K. (2011). *Research methods in education* (6th ed.). Routledge.

Collins, J. (2009). Social reproduction in classrooms and schools. *Annual Review of Anthropology*, *38*(1), 33–48. https://doi.org/10.1146/annurev.anthro.37.081407.085242

Coloma, R. (2011). Who's afraid of Foucault? History, theory, and becoming subjects. *History of Education Quarterly, 51*(2), 184–210. https://doi.org/10.1111/j.1748-5959.2011.00329

Connolly, P., Keenan, C., & Urbanska, K. (2018). The trials of evidence-based practice in education: A systematic review of randomised controlled trials in education research 1980–2016. *Educational Research, 60*(3), 276–291.

Cook, C. (1917). *The play way: An essay in educational method.* Frederick A. Stokes Company.

Courpasson, D., & Dany, F. (2009). Cultures of resistance in the workplace. In S. R. Clegg & M. Haugaard (Eds.), *The SAGE handbook of power* (pp. 323–347). SAGE.

Cox, B. (1991). *Cox on Cox. An English curriculum for the 1990s.* Hodder & Stoughton.

Crafts, N. (1996). "Post-neoclassical endogenous growth theory": What are its policy implications? *Oxford Review of Economic Policy, 12*(2), 30–47. https://doi.org/10.1093/oxrep/12.2.30

Crane, A. R., & Walker, W. G. (1957). *Peter Board: His contribution to the development of education in New South Wales.* ACER.

Crossley, N. (2012). Social class. In M. Grenfell (Ed.), *Pierre Bourdieu. Key concepts* (pp. 85–97). Routledge.

Crozier, M. (1964). *The bureaucratic phenomenon.* University of Chicago Press.

Cull, N. J. (2022). Rethinking public diplomacy and cultural diplomacy for a dangerous age. In *The Routledge handbook of diplomacy and statecraft.* Routledge.

Cumming, J. J., Wyatt-Smith, C., & Colbert, P. (2016). Students at risk and NAPLAN: The collateral damage. In *National testing in schools* (pp. 126–138). Routledge.

Cunningham, K. S. (1972). Ideas, theories, and assumptions in Australian education. In *Australian education in the twentieth century, studies in the development of state education* (pp. 99–124). Longman Australia.

Cyert, R. M., & March, J. G. (1963). *A summary of basic concepts in the behavioral theory of the firm.* M. Wiener.

Dahl, R. A. (1957). The concept of power. *Behavioural Science, 2*, 201–205.

Daliri-Ngametua, R., & Hardy, I. (2022). The devalued, demoralized and disappearing teacher: The nature and effects of datafication and performativity in schools. *Education Policy Analysis Archives, 30*, 102.

Daliri-Ngametua, R., Hardy, I., & Creagh, S. (2022). Data, performativity and the erosion of trust in teachers. *Cambridge Journal of Education, 52*(3), 391–407.

Danzon-Chambaud, S., & Cornia, A. (2023). Changing or reinforcing the "rules of the game": A field theory perspective on the impacts of automated journalism on media practitioners. *Journalism Practice, 17*(2), 174–188. https://doi.org/10.1080/17512786.2021.1919179

Darlington, R. (2014). *The role of trade unions in building resistance: Theoretical, historical and comparative perspectives.* Palgrave Macmillan.

Davies, C. A. (2012). *Reflexive ethnography: A guide to researching selves and others.* Routledge.

Davies, R. S. (2008). AYP accountability and assessment theory conflicts. *Mid-Western Educational Researcher, (21)*, 2–8.

Davis, C., & Breede, D. C. (2015). Holistic ethnography: Embodiment, emotion, contemplation, and dialogue in ethnographic fieldwork. *The Journal of Contemplative*

Inquiry, *2*(1), 77–99. http://journal.contemplativeinquiry.org/index.php/joci/article/view/34

De Jouvenel, B. (2009). *On power. The natural history of its growth*. Liberty Fund.

Dekker, I., & Meeter, M. (2022). Evidence-based education: Objections and future directions. *Frontiers in Education, 7*, 1–9.

Depaepe, M., & Hulstaert, K. (2015). Demythologising the educational past: An attempt to assess the "power of education" in the Congo (DRC) with a nod to the history of interwar pedagogy in Catholic Flanders. *Paedagogica Historica, 51*(1–2), 11–29. https://doi.org/10.1080/00309230.2014.987790

Department of Education (DfE). (2016). *Educational excellence everywhere*. Author.

Dewey, J. (1899). *The school and society*. University of Chicago Press.

Dewey, J. (1916). *Democracy and education*. Macmillan.

Dewey, J. (1938). *Experience and education*. Macmillan.

Dewey, J. (1964). *John Dewey on education: Selected writings*. Modern Library.

Di Maggio, P. (1979). On Pierre Bourdieu. *American Journal of Sociology, 84*(6), 1460–1474.

Dolin, T., Jones, J., & Dowsett, P. (2017). Conditional assent: Literary value and the value of English as a subject. In T. Dolin, J. Jones, & P. Dowsett (Eds.), *Required reading. Literature in Australian Schools since 1945* (pp. 1–18). Monash University Publishing.

Donnelly, K. (2010). The Ideology of the National English Curriculum. *Quadrant*. Accessed 27 February 2024: https://quadrant.org.au/magazine/2010/05/the-ideology-of-the-national-english-curriculum/

Donnelly, K. (2019). *How political correctness is destroying education and your child's future*. Wilkinson Publishing.

Drucker, P. F. (1993). *Post-capitalist society*. Butterworth-Heinemann.

Dubin, R. (1957). Power and union-management relations. *Administrative Science Quarterly*, 60–81.

Dubinski, Y. (2019). From soft power to sports diplomacy: A theoretical and conceptual discussion. *Place Branding and Public Diplomacy, 15*, 156–164.

Duhigg, C. (2012). How companies learn your secrets. *The New York Times*. http:nytimes.com

Dunne, J. (1993). *Back to the rough ground: 'Phronesis' and 'Techne' in modern philosophy and in Aristotle*. University of Notre Dame Press.

Durrani, S. (2023). What happens when a country bleeds soft power? Conceptualising 'negative watch': Towards an epistemology for negative and adversarial place branding. *Place Branding and Public Diplomacy*, 1–20. https://doi.org/10.1057/s41254-023-00302-9

Eacott, S. (2017). School leadership and the cult of the guru: The neo-Taylorism of Hattie. *School Leadership & Management, 37*(4), 413–426. https://doi.org/10.1080/13632434.2017.1327428

Education Council. (2019). *The Alice Springs (Mparntwe) education declaration*. Australian Government. Department of Education, Skills and Employment. www.dese.gov.au/alice-springs-mparntwe-education-declaration

Edwards, L. (2009). Symbolic power and public relations practice: Locating individual practitioners in their social context. *Journal of Public Relations Research, 21*(3), 251–272. https://doi.org/10.1080/10627260802640674

Edwards, M. (2000). *NGO rights and responsibilities: A new deal for global governance.* The Foreign Policy Centre.

Elliott, J. (2004). Making evidence-based practice educational. In G. Thomas & R. Pring (Eds.), *Evidence-based practice in education.* Open University Press.

Endrawes, M., Leong, S., & Matawie, K. M. (2023). The moderating effect of culture on the relationship between accountability and professional scepticism. *Meditari Accountancy Research, 31*(2), 381–399.

Enloe, C. (1996). Margins, silences, and bottom rungs: How to overcome the underestimation of power in the study if international relations. In S. Smith, K. Booth, & M. Zalewski (Eds.), *International theory: Positivism and beyond* (pp. 186–202). Cambridge University Press.

Enslin, P., & Tjiattas, M. (2017). Getting the measure of measurement: Global educational opportunity. *Educational Philosophy and Theory, 49*(4), 347–361.

Erickson, F. (1987). Transformation and school success: The politics and culture of educational achievement. *Anthropology & Education Quarterly, 18,* 335–355.

Fantasia, R. (1988). *Cultures of solidarity: Consciousness, action, and contemporary American workers.* University of California Press.

Farhan, R. (2019). Understanding postmodernism: Philosophy and culture of postmodern. *International Journal Social Sciences and Education, 2*(4), 22–31.

Fayol, H. (1949). *General and industrial management.* Pitman.

Fischer, C., Pardos, Z. A., Baker, R. S., Williams, J. J., Smyth, P., Yu, R., & Warschauer, M. (2020). Mining big data in education: Affordances and challenges. *Review of Research in Education, 44*(1), 130–160.

Fleming, M. (2017). *Starting drama teaching.* Taylor & Francis.

Follett, M. P. (1940). The psychological foundations: The giving of orders. In H. C. Metcalf (Ed.), *Scientific foundations of business administration* (pp. 132–149). The Williams & Wilkins Company.

Foucault, M. (1981). *Power/knowledge.* Pantheon.

Foucault, M. (1990). *A history of sexuality. Volume 1.* Penguin Books.

Fowers, B. J., Novak, L. F., Calder, A. J., & Sommer, R. K. (2021). Courage, justice, and practical wisdom as key virtues in the era of COVID-19. *Frontiers in Psychology, 12,* 647912.

Frank, A. W. (2012). The feel for power games: Everyday phronesis and social theory. *Real Social Science: Applied Phronesis,* 48–65.

French, J. R., Raven, B., & Cartwright, D. (1959). *Studies in social power.* Ann Arbor, MI: Institute for Social Research.

Furlong, J., & Whitty, G. (2017). Knowledge traditions in the study of education. In G. Whitty & J. Furlong (Eds.), *Knowledge and the study of education: An international exploration* (pp. 13–57). Symposium.

Galbraith, J. K. (1983). The anatomy of power. *Challenge, 26*(3), 26–33.

Garcia, D. M., Gee, S. S., & Orazietti, K. (2011). The merit of meritocracy. *Journal of Personality and Social Psychology, 101*(3), 433–450.

Garner, J. K., & Kaplan, A. (2021). A complex dynamic systems approach to the design and evaluation of teacher professional development. *Professional Development in Education, 47*(2–3), 289–314. https://doi.org/10.1080/19415257.2021.1879231

Gaventa, J. (1982). *Power and powerlessness: Quiescence and rebellion in an Appalachian Valley.* University of Illinois Press.

Gaventa, J. (2003). *Power after Lukes: An overview of theories of power since Lukes and their application to development*. Participation Group, Institute of Development Studies.

Gavin, M. (2019). Working industrially or professionally? What strategies should teacher unions use to improve teacher salaries in neoliberal times?. *Labour & Industry: A Journal of the Social and Economic Relations of Work, 29*(1), 19–33.

Gavin, M., & McGrath-Champ, S. (2017). Devolving authority: The impact of giving public schools power to hire staff. *Asia-Pacific Journal of Human Resources, 55*(2), 255–274. doi:10.1111/1744- 7941.12110

George, M. A., Shoffner, M., & Scherff, L. (2022). The complex enterprise of US secondary English teacher education. *International Perspectives on English Teacher Development: From Initial Teacher Education to Highly Accomplished Professional*. Routledge.

Gerarrd, J., & Holloway, J. (2023). *Expertise*. Bloomsbury Academic.

Giddens, A. (1984). *The constitution of society: Outline of the theory of structuration*. Polity Press.

Giddens, A. (2015). *Studies in social and political theory*. Routledge.

Giesinger, J. (2017). The special goods of childhood: Lessons from social constructionism. *Ethics and Education, 12*(2), 201–217. https://doi.org/10.1080/17449 642.2017.1314168

Giroux, H. A. (2020). Thinking dangerously: The role of higher education in Authoritarian Times. *Chowanna, 1*(54), 1–12.

Giroux, H. A. (2023). Trumpism and the challenge of critical education. *Educational Philosophy and Theory, 55*(6), 658–673.

Glassie, H. (1994). Values in clay. *The Studio Potter, 22*(2), 2–7.

Göhler, G. (2009). 'Power to' and 'power over'. In *The SAGE handbook of power* (pp. 27–39). SAGE.

Goldstein, R. A., & Beutel, A. R. (2009). 'Soldier of democracy' or 'enemy of the state'? The rhetorical construction of teacher through no child left behind. *Journal for Critical Education Policy Studies, 7*, 276–300.

Goodwyn, A. (2001). Second-tier professionals: English teachers in England. *L1: Educational Studies in Language and Literature, 1*(2), 149–161.

Goodwyn, A. (2020). The origins and adaptations of English as a school subject. In *Ontologies of English reconceptualising the language for learning, teaching, and assessment* (pp. 101–122). Cambridge University Press.

Gordon, R. (2009). Power and legitimacy: From Weber to contemporary theory. In S. R. Clegg & M. Haugaard (Eds.), *The SAGE handbook of power* (pp. 256–273). SAGE.

Gouldner, A. W. (1971). *The coming crisis of western sociology, and the two marxisms: Contradictions and anomalies in the development of theory*. Avon Books.

Grant, G. (1988). *The world we created at Hamilton high*. Harvard University Press.

Gratton, M. & Rood, D. (2006). PM attacks 'dumb' English. *The Age*. Accessed: 27 February 2024, https://www.theage.com.au/national/pm-attacks-dumb-english-20060421-ge2633.html

Green, B., & Cormack, P. (2008). Curriculum history, 'English' and the new education; or, installing the empire of English? *Pedagogy, Culture and Society, 16*(3), 253–267.

Green, B., & Hodgens, J. (1996). Manners, morals, meanings: English teaching, language education and the subject of 'grammar'. In *Teaching the English subjects: Essays on English curriculum and history in Australian schooling* (pp. 204–228). Deakin University Press.

Greenwell, T., & Bonnor, C. (2022). *Waiting for Gonski: How Australia failed its schools.* NewSouth Publishing.

Grek, S. (2009). Governing by numbers: The PISA effect in Europe. *Journal of Education Policy, 24*(1), 23–37.

Grek, S. (2015). Seeing from the top of the tower: PISA and the new governing panoramas in Europe. *Compare – A Journal of Comparative and International Education, 45*(3), 479–481.

Grenfell, M. (2012). Methodology. In M. Grenfell (Ed.)., *Pierre Bourdieu. Key concepts* (pp. 213–228). Routledge.

Grossmann, I., Weststrate, N. M., Ardelt, M., Brienza, J. P., Dong, M., Ferrari, M., et al. (2020). The science of wisdom in a polarized world: Knowns and unknowns. *Psychological Inquiry, 31,* 103–133. https://doi.org/10.1080/1047840X.2020.1750917

Grunig, J. E. (Ed.). (1992). *Excellence in public relations and communications management.* Lawrence Erlbaum Associates.

Guba, E. G., & Lincoln, Y. S. (1994). Competing paradigms in qualitative research. *Handbook of Qualitative Research, 2,* 163–194.

Guzmán, S. G. (2015). Substantive-rational authority: The missing fourth pure type in Weber's typology of legitimate domination. *Journal of Classical Sociology, 15*(1), 73–95.

Habermas, J. (1990). Discourse ethics: Notes on a program of philosophical justification. In *Moral consciousness and communicative action* (pp. 43–115). MIT Press.

Haddon, M. (2003). *The curious incident of the dog in the night-time.* Jonathan Cape.

Hage, J. (1980). *Theories of organizations: Form, process, and transformation.* Wiley.

Halpin, D., Moore, A., Edwards, G., George, R., & Jones, C. (2000). Maintaining, reconstructing and creating tradition in education. *Oxford Review of Education, 26*(2), 133–144.

Hammersley, M. (2007). *Educational research and evidence-based practice.* SAGE.

Hanushek, E. A., & Woessmann, L. (2012). Do schools lead to more growth? Cognitive skills, economic outcomes, and causation. *Journal of Economic Growth, 17,* 267–321.

Hardy, B. (1968). Towards a poetics of fiction: 3) An approach through narrative. *NOVEL: A Forum on Fiction, 2*(1), 5–14.

Hardy, C., & Clegg, S. R. (1999). Some dare call it power. In S. R. Clegg & C. Hardy (Eds.), *Studying organization: Theory & method* (pp. 754–773). SAGE.

Haugaard, M. (1997). *The constitution of power: A theoretical analysis of power, knowledge and structure.* Manchester University Press.

Haugaard, M., & Lentner, H. H. (Eds.). (2006). *Hegemony and power: Consensus and coercion in contemporary politics.* Lexington Books.

Henson, D. (2017). Fragments and fictions: An autoethnography of past and possibility. *Qualitative Inquiry, 23*(3), 222–224.

Hickson, D. J., Hinings, C. R., Lee, C. A., Schneck, R. E., & Pennings, J. M. (1971). A strategic contingencies' theory of intraorganizational power. *Administrative science quarterly,* 216–229.

Hobsbawm, E. (1983). Inventing traditions. In P. Heelas, S. Lash, & P. Moros (Eds.), *The invention of tradition* (pp. 1–14). Cambridge University Press.

Hodgson, J. (2019). Newbolt revisited: The teaching of English in England. *National Association for the Teaching of English*, *21*, 82–83.

Hodkinson, P., & Smith, J. (2004). The relationship between research, policy and practice. In G. Thomas & R. Pring (Eds.), *Evidence-based practice in education*. Open University Press.

Holloway, J., & Brass, J. (2018). Making accountable teachers: The terrors and pleasures of performativity. *Journal of Education Policy*, *33*(3), 361–382. https://doi.org/10.1080/02680939.2017.1372636

Höpfl, H. M. (1999). Power, authority and legitimacy. *Human Resources Development International*, *2*(3), 217–234.

Hordern, J., Muller, J., & Deng, Z. (2021). Towards powerful knowledge? Addressing the challenges facing educational foundations, curriculum theory and *Didaktik*. *Journal of Curriculum Studies*, *53*(2), 143–152.

Houghton, J. D. (2010). Does Max Weber's notion of authority still hold in the twenty-first century? *Journal of Management History*, *16*(4), 449–453.

Houswitschka, C. (2006). Locke's education or Rousseau's freedom alternative socializations in modern societies. In A. Muller (Ed.), *Fashioning childhood in the eighteenth century. Age and identity* (pp. 81–90). Ashgate.

Howlett, J. (2019). Henry Caldwell Cook (1886–1939): Play, performance and the perse. In *Unfolding creativity: British pioneers in arts education from 1890 to 1950* (pp. 147–166). Emerald.

Hughes, J. (2019). The antecedents of the New South Wales curriculum review: An introduction to the New South Wales curriculum style. *Curriculum Perspectives*, *39*, 147–157.

Hunter, I. (1987). Culture, education and English: Building 'the principal scene of the real life of children'. *Economy and Society*, *16*(4), 568–588.

Hurn, C. (1985). Changes in authority relationships in schools: 1960–1980. *Research in Sociology of Education and Socialization*, *5*, 31–57.

Independent Education Union. (n.d.). *How does the IEU represent me?* Retrieved November 24, 2023, from www.ieu.asn.au/

Jacobsen, I. D. (2002). *What, how and why? – On the choice of method in business administration and other social science subjects*. Studentlitteratur.

Jarke, J., & Breiter, A. (2019). Editorial: The datafication of education. *Learning, Media and Technology*, *44*(1), 1–6. https://doi.org/10.1080/17439884.2019.1573833

Jessop, B. (2009). The state and power. In S. R. Clegg & M. Haugaard (Eds.), *The SAGE handbook of power* (pp. 367–382). SAGE.

Jones, B. (2007). The unintended outcomes of high-Stakes testing. *Journal of Applied School Psychology*, *23*(2), 65–86. https://doi.org/10.1300/J370v23n02_05

Joullié, J. E., Gould, A. M., Spillane, R., & Luc, S. (2021). The language of power and authority in leadership. *The Leadership Quarterly*, *32*(4), 1–12.

Jover, P. B. (2019). *The datafication of education in Australia: Exploring teachers' use of digital data* (Doctoral dissertation, Master's thesis). Universitetet I Oslo. www.duo.uio.no/handle/10852/70939.

Kampmark, B. (2020). Looking back on Alan Jones. *Eureka Street.com.au*, *30*(9), 3–5.

Kelly, L. (2021). Melbourne to ease world's longest COVID-19 lockdowns as vaccinations rise. *Reuters*. Accessed 27 February 2024: https://www.reuters.com/world/asia-pacific/melbourne-ease-worlds-longest-covid-19-lockdowns-vaccinations-rise-2021-10-17/

Kestere, I., Rubene, Z., & Stonkuviene, I. (2015). Introduction: Power – invisible architecture of education. *Paedagogica Historica*, *51*(1–2), 5–10.

Kirsch, G. E., & Royster, J. J. (2010). Feminist rhetorical practices: In search of excellence. *College Composition and Communication*, *61*(4), 640–672.

Kohl, H. (1967). *36 children*. Signet.

Kohlberg, L. (1963). The development of children's orientation towards moral order: Sequence in the development of moral thought. *Vita Humana*, *6*, 11–13.

Koopman, C. (2019). *How we became our data. A genealogy of the informational person*. The University of Chicago Press.

Kristjánsson, K., Fowers, B., Darnell, C., & Pollard, D. (2021). Phronesis (practical wisdom) as a type of contextual integrative thinking. *Review of General Psychology*, *25*(3), 239–257.

Laclau, E. (2007). *On populist reason*. Verso.

Lang, C., Siemens, G., Wise, A., & Gasevic, D. (Eds.). (2017). *Handbook of learning analytics* (1st ed.). Society of Learning Analytics Research.

Langlois, R. N. (1998). Rule-following, expertise, and rationality: A new behavioral economics? In *Rationality in economics: Alternative perspectives* (pp. 55–78). Springer Netherlands.

Lasswell, H. D., & Kaplan, A. (2014). *Power and society. A framework for political inquiry*. Transaction Publishers.

Lawn, M. (2013). A systemless system: Designing the disarticulation of English state education. *European Educational Research Journal*, *12*(2), 231–241. https://doi.org/10.2304/eerj.2013.12.2.231

Lee, J.-S., & Stacey, M. (2023). Fairness perceptions of educational inequality: The effects of self-interest and neoliberal orientations. *The Australian Educational Researcher*. https://doi.org/10.1007/s13384-023-00636-6

Lester, L. (2010). Big tree, small news: Media access, symbolic power and strategic intervention. *Journalism*, *11*(5), 589–606.

Lingard, B., Thompson, G., & Sellar, S. (2016). *National testing in schools. An Australian assessment*. Routledge.

Lisett, S. M., Trow, M., & Coleman, J. S. (1956). *Union democracy: The internal politics of the international typographical union*. Free Press.

Livingstone, S., Atabey, A., & Pothong, K. (2021). *Addressing the problems and realising the benefits of processing children's education data: Report on an expert roundtable*. Rights Foundation.

Locke, J. (1990). *Second treatise on civil government* (C. B. MacPherson, Ed.). Hackett.

Long, F. (2013). *Educating the postmodern child. The struggle for learning in a world of virtual realities*. Bloomsbury.

Longhurst, B., & Savage, M. (1997). Social class, consumption and the influence of Bourdieu: Some critical issues. *The Sociological Review*, *44*(1_suppl), 274–301. https://doi.org/10.1111/j.1467-954X.1996.tb03445.x

Luhrmann, N. (1979). *Trust and power*. Wiley.

Luke, A. (1991). Literacies as social practices. *English Education*, *23*(3), 131–147.

Lukes, S. (2005). *Power: A radical view* (2nd ed.). Palgrave.

Ma, Y. (2021). Evidence-based Education: Why it is a problematic platform for educational research to participate in education policymaking. *Advances in Social Science, Education and Humanities*, *615*, 2103–2107.

MacIntyre, A. (1988). *Whose justice? Which rationality?* University of Notre Dame Press.

Magalhães, P. (2022). Charisma and democracy: Max Weber on the riddle of political change in modern societies. *Topoi, 41*(1), 69–78.

Malsch, B., Gendron, Y., & Grazzini, F. (2011). Investigating interdisciplinary translations: The influence of Pierre Bourdieu on accounting literature. *Accounting, Auditing & Accountability Journal, 24*(2), 194–228. https://doi.org/10.1108/09513571111100681

Mann, M. (1986). *The sources of social power, 1.* Cambridge University Press.

Mannion, G., Biesta, G., Priestley, M., & Ross, H. (2011). The global dimension in education and education for global citizenship: Genealogy and critique. *Globalisation, Societies and Education, 9,* 443–456.

Manuel, J., & Carter, D. (2017). Inscribing culture: The history of prescribed text lists in senior secondary English in NSW, 1945–1964. In T. Dolin, J. Jones, & P. Dowsett (Eds.), *Required reading. Literature in Australian schools since 1945* (pp. 78–105). Monash University Publishing.

Manuel, J., & Carter, D. (2019). Resonant continuities: The influence of the Newbolt Report on the formation of English curriculum in New South Wales, Australia. *English in Education, 53*(3), 223–239. https://doi.org/10.1080/04250494.2019.1625709

Manuel, J. & Carter, D. (2020). *The English Teacher's Handbook A-Z.* Five Senses Press.

Marquis, C., & Lounsbury, M. (2007). Vive la resistance: Competing logics and the consolidation of US community banking. *Academy of Management Journal, 50*(4), 799–821.

Marshall, B. (2014). *English teachers – the unofficial guide. Researching the philosophies of English teachers.* Routledge.

Marshall, B. (2023). *Comparative study of literature in English curricula across jurisdictions.* NCCA.

Matheson, C. (1987). Weber and the classification of forms of legitimacy. *British Journal of Sociology,* 199–215.

Mathieson, M. (1975). *The preachers of culture: A study of English and its teachers.* George Allen and Unwin.

Mattern, J. B. (2005). Why 'soft power' isn't so soft: Representational force and the sociolinguistic construction of attraction in world politics. *Millennium – Journal of International Studies, 33,* 583–612.

Mayer-Schoenberger, V., & Cukier, K. (2013). *Big Data.* John Murray.

McClory, J. (2015). *The Soft Power 30 report: A global ranking of soft power, 8.* Retrieved June 24, 2023, from https://The-Soft-Power-30-Report-2019–1.pdf (softpower30.com)

McDermott, R. P. (1974). Achieving school failure: An anthropological approach to illiteracy and social stratification. In G. D. Spindler (Ed.), *Education and cultural process: Toward an anthropology of education* (pp. 82–118). Holt, Rinehart & Winston.

McGaw, K. (2005). HSC English in the media: The reporting of conventions and controversies. *English in Australia, 143,* 27–35.

McIlveen, P. (2008). Autoethnography as a method for reflexive research and practice in vocational psychology. *Australian Journal of Career Development, 17*(2), 13–20.

Meadmore, P. (2003). The introduction of the 'new education' in Queensland, Australia. *History of Education Quarterly, 43*(3), 372–392.

Mechanic, D. (1964). Sources of power of lower participants. *New Perspectives in Organization Research.* Wiley.

Merriam, S. B. (1998). *Qualitative research and case study application in education.* Jossey-Bass.

Metz, M. H. (2003). *Different by design: The context and character of three magnet schools* (Reiss. ed.). Teachers College Press.

Ministerial Council on Education, Employment, Training and Youth Affairs. (1989). *The Hobart declaration on schooling.* MCEETYA.

Ministerial Council on Education, Employment, Training and Youth Affairs. (1999). *The Adelaide declaration on national goals for schooling in the twenty-first century. National Goals.* MCEETYA.

Ministerial Council on Education, Employment, Training and Youth Affairs. (2008). *Melbourne declaration on educational goals for young Australians.* MCEETYA.

Miskimmon, A., O'Loughlin, B., & Roselle, L. (2013). *Strategic Narratives: Communication Power and the New World Order.* Routledge.

Mitchell, T. (1990). Everyday metaphors of power. *Theory and Society, 19*(5), 545–77.

Mitchell, T. (2013). *Carbon democracy: Political power in the age of oil* (2nd rev. ed.). Verso.

Moore, R. (2012). Capital. In M. Grenfell (Ed.), *Pierre Bourdieu. Key concepts* (pp. 98–113). Routledge.

Morgner, C., & King, M. (2022). *The making of meaning from the individual to social order: Selections from Niklas Luhmann's works on semantics and social structure.* Oxford University Press.

Morrison, K. (2001). Randomised controlled trials for evidence-based education: Some problems in judging 'what works'. *Evaluation & Research in Education, 15,* 69–83.

Mouffe, C. (1979). *Gramsci and Marxist theory.* Routledge.

Mourshed, M., Farrell, D., & Barton, D. (2012). *Education to employment: Designing a system that works.* McKinsey Center for Government. Retrieved August 31, 2023, http://mckinseyonsociety.com/downloads/reports/Education/Education-to-Employment_FINAL.pdf

Müller, A. (2006). Fashioning age and identity: Childhood and the stages of life in eighteenth-century English periodicals. In A. Muller (Ed.), *Fashioning childhood in the eighteenth century. Age and identity* (pp. 91–100). Ashgate.

Muller, J., & Young, M. (2019). Knowledge, power and powerful knowledge re-visited. *The Curriculum Journal, 30*(2), 196–214.

Nelson, R., & Winter, S. (1982). *An evolutionary theory of economic change.* Harvard University Press.

Neri, R. C., Lozano, M., & Gomez, L. M. (2019). (Re) framing resistance to culturally relevant education as a multilevel learning problem. *Review of Research in Education, 43*(1), 197–226.

New South Wales Education Standards Authority. (n.d.). Accessed 27 February 2024: http//https://educationstandards.nsw.edu.au/wps/portal/nesa/home

New South Wales Department of Education. Centre for Education Statistics and Evaluation. n.d. Accessed 27 February: //http:https://education.nsw.gov.au/about-us/education-data-and-research/cese

New South Wales Department of Education. (1987). *Writing K-12.* Department of Education.

New South Wales Department of Public Instruction. (1905). *Course of instruction primary schools.* NSW Department of Education.

New South Wales Department of Public Instruction. (1911). *Courses of study for high schools*. NSW Department of Education.

New South Wales Education Standards Authority. (n.d.). Accessed 27 February 2024 http: https://educationstandards.nsw.edu.au/wps/portal/nesa/home

New South Wales Primary Principals Association. (n.d.). Retrieved November 24, 2023, from www.nswppa.org.au/

New South Wales Secondary Principals Association. (n.d.). Retrieved November 24, 2023, from https://www.nswspc.org.au/

New South Wales Teachers Federation. (n.d.). *Our vision*. Retrieved November 24, 2023, from www.nswtf.org.au/about-us/who-we-are/

Nolder, C. J., & Kadous, K. (2018). Grounding the professional skepticism construct in mindset and attitude theory: A way forward. *Accounting, Organizations and Society, 67*(1), 1–14.

Nyberg, D. (1981). A concept of power for education. *Teachers College Record, 82*(4), 1–15. https://doi.org/10.1177/016146818108200405

Nye, J. S. (1990). *Bound to lead: The changing nature of American power*. Basic Books.

Nye J. S. Jr. (2006). Transformational leadership and US grand strategy. *Foreign Affairs. 85*, 139.

Nye, J. S. (2008). Public diplomacy and soft power. *The ANNALS of the American Academy of Political and Social Science, 616*(1), 95.

Nye, J. S. (2009). Smart power. *New Perspectives Quarterly, 26*(2), 7–9.

Nye, J. S. (2011). *The future of power*. Public Affairs.

Nye, J. S. (2021). Soft power: The evolution of a concept. *Journal of Political Power, 14*(1), 196–208. https://doi.org/10.1080/2158379X.2021.1879572

Oliver, P. (2010). *Foucault – the key ideas*. Hodder Education.

Organisation for Economic Co-operation and Development. (2010). *The state's legitimacy in fragile situations: Unpacking complexity*. The State's Legitimacy in Fragile Situations. oecd.org

Orland, M. (2009). Separate orbits: The distinctive worlds of educational research and policymaking. In G. Sykes, B. Scheider, D. Plank, & T. Ford (Eds.), *Handbook of education policy research* (pp. 113–128). Routledge.

Orlikowski, W. J., & Baroudi, J. J. (1991). Studying information technology in organizations: Research approaches and assumptions. *Information Systems Research, 2*(1), 1–28.

Osterman, P. (2006). Overcoming oligarchy: Culture and agency in social change-oriented organizations. *Administrative Science Quarterly, 51*(4), 622–649.

Oyibo, C. O., & Gabriel, J. M. (2020). Evolution of organization theory: A snapshot. *International Journal of Innovation and Economic Development, 6*(3), 46–56.

Ozga, J. (2009). Governing education through data in England: From regulation to self-evaluation. *Journal of Education Policy, 24*(2), 149–162.

Ozoliņš, J. (2017). Creating the civil society East and West. Relationality, responsibility and the education of the humane person. *Educational Philosophy and Theory, 49*(4), 362–378.

Pace, J. L. (2003). Managing the dilemmas of professional and bureaucratic authority in a high school English class. *Sociology of Education, 76*, 37–52.

Pangrazio, L., & Selwyn, N. (2021). Towards a school-based 'critical data education'. *Pedagogy, Culture & Society, 29*(3), 431–448.

Pardo, I. (2000). *Introduction – morals of legitimacy: Between agency and system*. Berghahn.

Pardo, I., & Prato, G. B. (2019). Ethnographies of legitimacy: Methodological and theoretical insights. In I. Pardo & G. B. Prato (Eds.), *Legitimacy. Ethnographic and theoretical insights*. Palgrave Macmillan.

Parise, S. (2016). Big data: A revolution that will transform how we live, work, and think, by Viktor Mayer-Schonberger and Kenneth Cukier. *Journal of Information Technology Case and Application Research, 18*(3), 186–190. https://doi.org/10.10 80/15228053.2016.1220197

Parsons, T. (1947). Introduction. In M. Weber (Ed.), *The theory of social and economic organization* (A. M. Henderson & T. Parsons, Trans., pp. 3–86). Free Press.

Parsons, T. (1963). On the concept of political power. In S. Lukes (Ed.), *Power*. New York University Press.

Parsons, T. (2010). *Essays in sociological theory*. The Free Press.

Peterson, C., & Seligman, M. E. P. (2004). *Character strengths and virtues: A handbook and classification*. Oxford University Press.

Pettigrew, A. M. (1973). *The politics of organizational decision-making*. Tavistock.

Piety, P. J., Hickey, D. T., & Bishop, M. J. (2014). *Educational data sciences – framing emergent practices for analytics of learning, organizations and systems*. LAK '14, March 24–28, Indianapolis.

Pitkin, H. F. (1993). *Wittgenstein and justice: On the significance of Ludwig Wittgenstein for social and political thought*. University of California Press.

Poulson, L. (1998). *English curriculum in schools*. A&C Black.

Prato, G. B. (2000). The cherries of the mayor. Morals of Legitimacy. Berghahn Books, 57–82.

Price, J. (2019). *Destroying the joint: A case study of feminist digital activism in Australia and its account of fatal violence against women* (Unpublished thesis submitted to fulfil requirements for the degree of Doctor of Philosophy). University of Sydney.

Priestley, M. (2011). Whatever happened to curriculum theory? Critical realism and curriculum change. *Pedagogy, Culture and Society, 19*(2), 221–237.

Priestley, M., Philippou, S., Alvunger, D., & Soini, T. (2021). *Curriculum making: A conceptual framing. In Curriculum making in Europe: Policy and practice within and across diverse contexts* (pp. 1–28). Emerald Publishing Limited.

Prior, N. (2011). Critique and renewal in the sociology of music: Bourdieu and beyond. *Cultural Sociology, 5*(1), 121–138.

Prøitz, T. S., Mausethagen, S., & Skedsmo, G. (2017). Data use in education: Alluring attributes and productive processes. *Nordic Journal of Studies in Educational Policy, 3*(1), 1–5. https://doi.org/10.1080/20020317.2017.1328873.

Raimzhanova, A. (2015). Power in IR: Hard, soft, and smart. *Institute for Cultural Diplomacy and the University of Bucharest, 20*, 1–20.

Rancière, J. (1990). *The ignorant schoolmaster. Five lessons in intellectual emancipation*. Stanford University Press.

Rathbun, B. C. (2007). Uncertain about uncertainty: Understanding the multiple meanings of a crucial concept in international relations theory. *International Studies Quarterly, 51*(3), 533–57.

Raulo, M. (2002). Moral education and development. *Journal of Social Philosophy, 31*, 507–51.

Reid, A. (2019). *Changing Australian education: How policy is taking us backwards and what can be done about it*. Allen & Unwin.

Reid, I. (2004). *Wordsworth and the formation of English studies*. Ashgate Publishing Limited.

Ribot, J. C., & Peluso, N. L. (2003). A theory of access. *Rural Sociology, 68*(2), 153–181.

Rogers, E. M. (2003). *Diffusion of innovations* (5th ed.). Free Press.

Roselle, L., Miskimmon, A., & O'Loughlin, B. (2014). Strategic narrative: A new means to understand soft power. *Media, War & Conflict, 7*(1), 70–84.

Rousseau, J. J. (2004). *Emile of Jean Jacques Rousseau* (B. Foxley, Trans.). Project Gutenberg.

Sadan, E. (1997). Empowerment and Community Planning. Accessed 27 february 2024: http://www.mpow.org/elisheva_sadan_empowerment.pdf, p. 35–40.

Salancik, G. R., & Pfeffer, J. (1974). The bases and use of power in organizational decision making: The case of a university. *Administrative science quarterly, 453*–473.

Savage, G. (2016). Who's steering the ship? National curriculum reform and the re-shaping of Australian federalism. *Journal of Education Policy, 31*(6), 833–850.

Sawyer, W. (2009). Language, literature and lost opportunities: 'Growth' as a defining episode in the history of English. In J. Manuel, P. Brock, D. Carter, & W. Sawyer (Eds.), *Imagination, innovation, creativity: Re-visioning English in education* (pp. 71–86). Phoenix Education.

Schildkamp, K. (2019). Data-based decision-making for school improvement: Research insights and gaps. *Educational Research, 61*(3), 257–273.

Schmitt, O. (2018). When are strategic narratives effective? The shaping of political discourse through the interaction between political myths and strategic narratives. *Contemporary Security Policy, 39*(4), 487–511. https://doi.org/10.1080/135232 60.2018.1448925

Scott, J. C. (1990). *Domination and the arts of resistance: Hidden transcripts*. Yale University Press.

Self, C. C., & Roberts, C. (2019). Credibility. In D. W. Stacks, M. B. Salwen, & K. C. Eichhorn (Eds.), *An integrated approach to communication theory and research* (3rd ed., pp. 435–446). Routledge.

Sellars, M., & Imig, D. (2021). Pestalozzi and pedagogies of love: Pathways to educational reform. *Early Child Development and Care, 191*(7–8), 1152–1163.

Selleck, R. J. W. (1968). *The new education. The English background 1870–1914*. Sir Isaac Pitman and Sons.

Shils, E. (1971). *Tradition*. Faber & Faber.

Silberman, C. (1970). *Crisis in the classroom: The remaking of American education*. Random House.

Simionescu, C., Danubianu, M., & Turcu, C. O. (2021). *Data mining in educational data – useful tool for sustainable learning development. Contemporary scientific and technological aspects towards an entrepreneurial approach*. The 16th Edition of the International Conference European Integration Realities and Perspectives, pp. 349–353.

Simon, H. A. (1997). *Administrative behavior: A study of decision-making processes in administrative organizations* (4th ed.). Free Press.

Solga, H. (2014). Education, economic inequality and the promises of the social investment state. *Socio-Economic Review, 12*(2), 269–297.

Spady, W. (1974). The authority system of the school and student unrest: A theoretical explanation. In C. W. Gordon (Ed.), *Uses of the sociology of education: Seventy third year book of the National Society for the Study of Education* (Part II, pp. 36–77). University of Chicago Press.

Special Broadcasting Service (2011–2015). *Go back to where you came from.* Retrieved Go Back to Where You Came From (TV Series 2011–2015) – IMDb.

Stake, R. E. (1995). Case studies. In N. K. Denzin & Y. Lincoln (Eds.). *Handbook of qualitative research* (pp. 236–247). Sage Publications.

Steiner-Khamsi, G. (2003). The politics of league tables. *Journal of Social Science Education.* Retrieved from ojs,+Zeitschriftenverwalter_in,+khamsi-tables-1–2003.pdf

Stevenson, H. (2017). The "datafication" of teaching: Can teachers speak back to the numbers? *Peabody Journal of Education, 92*(4), 537–557. https://doi.org/10.1080/0161956X.2017.1349492

Stichter, M. (2018). *The skillfulness of virtue: Improving our moral and epistemic lives.* Cambridge University Press.

Stinebrickner, B. (2015). Robert A. Dahl and the essentials of modern political analysis: Politics, influence, power, and polyarchy. *Journal of Political Power, 8*(2), 189–207. https://doi.org/10.1080/2158379X.2015.1054579

Stokes, R. (2018, December 14). Let's end our neo-liberal school testing fixation. *Sydney Morning Herald.* Retrieved December 6, 2019, from www.smh.com.au/education/let-s-end-our-neo-liberal-school-testing-fixation-20181213-p50m3q.html

Stolz, S. A. (2017). Can educationally significant learning be assessed? *Educational Philosophy and Theory, 49*(4), 379–390.

Taubman, P. M. (2010). *Teaching by numbers: Deconstructing the discourse of standards and accountability in education.* Routledge. https://doi.org/10.4324/978020387951

Teles Fazendeiro, B. (2021). Keeping a promise: Roles, audiences and credibility in international relations. *International Relations, 35*(2), 299–319.

Tello-Rozas, S., Pozzebon, M., & Mailhot, C. (2015). Uncovering micro-practices and pathways of engagement that scale up social-driven collaborations: A practice view of power. *Journal of Management Studies, 52*(8), 1064–1096.

Thomas, G., & Pring, R. (Eds.). (2004). *Evidence-based practice in education.* Open University Press.

Thompson, G., & Harbaugh, A. G. (2013). A preliminary analysis of teacher perceptions of the effects of NAPLAN on pedagogy and curriculum. *The Australian Educational Researcher, 40,* 299–314.

Thompson, G., Hogan, A., & Rahimi, M. (2019). Private funding in Australian public schools: A problem of equity. *Australian Educational Researcher. 46,* 893–910. https://doi.org/10.1007/s13384-019-00319-1

Tilly, C. (1992). *The formation of national states in Western Europe.* Princeton University Press.

Torfing, J. (2009). Power and discourse: Towards an anti-foundationalist concept of power. In *The Sage handbook of power* (pp. 108–124). SAGE.

Uphoff, N. (1989). Distinguishing power, authority & legitimacy: Taking Max Weber at his word by using resources-exchange analysis. *Polity, XXII*(2), 295–322.

Vallas, S. P. (2006). Empowerment redux: Structure, agency, and the remaking of managerial authority. *American Journal of Sociology, 111*(96), 1677–1717.

Vuving, A. L. (2009, September 3). *How Soft Power Works.* Paper presented at the panel "Soft Power and Smart Power," American Political Science Association annual meeting, Toronto.

Weaver, D. K. (2001). Dressing for battle in the new global economy: Putting power, identity, and discourse into public relations theory. *Management Communication Quarterly, 15*, 279–288.

Weber, M. (1978). *Economy and society*. University of California Press. (Original work published 1922)

Webster, R. S. (2017). Valuing and desiring purposes of education to transcend miseducative measurement practices. *Educational Philosophy and Theory, 49*(4), 331–346.

Werler, T., & Klepstad Faerevaag, M. (2017). National testing data in Norwegian classrooms: A tool to improve pupil performance? *Nordic Journal of Studies in Educational Policy, 3*(1), 67–81. https://doi.org/0.1080/20020317.1320188

Werthman, C. (1963). Delinquents in schools: A test for the legitimacy of authority. *Berkeley Journal of Sociology, 8*(1), 39–60.

West, P. (1983). Australia and the United States: Some differences. *Comparative Education Review, 27*(3), 414–416.

Whitty, G. (2008). Twenty years of progress?: English education policy 1988 to the present. *Educational Management Administration & Leadership, 36*(2), 165–184. doi:10.1177/17411432 07087771

Williams, R. (1976). *Keywords*. Fontana.

Wilson, E. J. (2008). Hard power, soft power, smart power. *Annals, American Academy of Political and Social Science, 616*, 110–124.

Winch, C. (1996). The aims of education revisited. *The Journal of the Philosophy of Education, 30*(1), 33–44.

Wipulanusat, W., Panuwatwanich, P., Stewart, R. A., & Sunkpho, J. (2019). Drivers and barriers to innovation in the Australian public service: A qualitative thematic analysis. *Engineering Management in Production Services, 11*(1), 7–22.

Wrong, D. (2017). *Power: Its forms, bases and uses*. Routledge.

Wyatt-Smith, C., & Jackson, C. (2016). NAPLAN data on writing: A picture of accelerating negative change. *Australian Journal of Language and Literacy, 39*(3), 233–234.

Yadgar, Y. (2013). Tradition. *Human Studies, 36*, 451–470.

Yoo, J., & Carter, D. (2017). Teacher emotions and learning as praxis: Professional development that matters. *Australian Journal of Teacher Education, 42*, 38–52. https://doi.org/10.14221/ajte.2017v42n3.3

Young, M. (2013). Overcoming the crisis in curriculum theory: A knowledge-based approach. *Journal of Curriculum Studies, 45*(2), 101–118. https://doi.org/10.108 0/00220272.2013.764505.

Zhou, Y., & Chen, Y. (2020). Practice of educational drama in primary and secondary education: Review and prospect. *Frontiers in Educational Research, 3*(12).

Zwitter, A., & Hazenberg, J. (2020). Decentralized network governance: Blockchain technology and the future of regulation. *Hypothesis and Theory, 3*(12), 1–12.

Index

Note: Page numbers in *italic* indicate a figure on the corresponding page.

For Product Safety Concerns and Information please contact our EU
representative GPSR@taylorandfrancis.com Taylor & Francis Verlag GmbH,
Kaufingerstraße 24, 80331 München, Germany

Printed and bound by CPI Group (UK) Ltd, Croydon, CR0 4YY

08/06/2025

01897006-0009